"DRACULA" A Universal Production MADE IN U.S.A.

MagicImage Filmbooks Presents

DRACULA

(The Original 1931 Shooting Script)

Production Background
by
Philip J. Riley

Special Introduction by Bela Lugosi

Foreword by Ivan Butler

Preface by Carla Laemmle

Additional Production Background by George Turner

Atlantic City · Hollywood

**UNIVERSAL FILMSCRIPTS SERIES
CLASSIC HORROR FILMS - VOLUME 13**

DRACULA

(The Original 1931 Shooting Script)

FIRST EDITION

Published by MagicImage Filmbooks, 740 S. 6th Avenue, Absecon, NJ 08201

Copyright © 1990, MagicImage Productions, Inc. All rights reserved.
Reproduction in whole or in part is prohibited without the written permission of the copyright holder.

Photographs, filmscript and other production materials used with the permission of and by special arrangement with Universal Studios.

The opinions expressed in this book are those of the individual authors and not the publisher.

The film DRACULA Copyright 1931 by Universal Pictures Company, Inc., Renewed 1958.

This book includes the original script by Tod Browning and Garrett Fort, adapted by Dudley Murphy; & treatments by Fritz Stephani and Louis Bromfield.

The Library of Congress Cataloging in Publication Data:

MagicImage Filmbooks presents Dracula : the 1931 shooting script / production background by Philip J. Riley ; foreword by Ivan Butler ; preface by Carla Laemmle ; special introduction by Bela Lugosi ; additional production background by George Turner. -- 1st ed.
   p. cm. -- (Universal filmscripts series. Classic horror films ; v. 13)
  ISBN 1-882127-09-9 : $19.95
  1. Dracula, Count (Fictitious character)--Drama. 2. Dracula (Motion picture : 1931) I. Riley, Philip J., 1948-
II. MagicImage Filmbooks (Firm) III. Dracula (Motion picture : 1931) IV. Title: Dracula. V. Series.
PN1997.D73 1990
791.43'72--dc20   90-61035
                                                                      CIP

10 9 8 7 6 5 4 3 2 1

    The purpose of this series is the preservation of the art of writing for the screen. Rare books have long been a source of enjoyment and an investment for the serious collector, and even in limited printings there usually were a few thousand produced. Scripts however, numbered only 50 at the most, and we are proud to present them in their original form. Some will be final shooting scripts and some earlier drafts, so that students, libraries, archives and film-lovers might, for the first time, study them in their original form. In producing these volumes, we hope that the unique art of screenplay writing will be preserved for future generations.

"DRACULA" A Universal Production MADE IN U.S.A.

CREDITS AND ACKNOWLEDGMENTS

A Michael D. Stein Production

Editor, Philip J. Riley

Art Director, Marisa Donato-Riley

Artists, Robert Semler, A.S.I.
       Marisa Donato-Riley

Creative Consultant, Andrew Lee, Head of Research, Universal Studios (retired)

Editorial Assistant, Janet Stein

Cover Poster and Pressbook - courtesy The Ronald V. Borst Collection, Hollywood Movie Posters

Pages of Bram Stoker's working manuscript - courtesy The Book Sail, Orange, California, John McLaughlin

English Playbill for *Dracula*, pictures from the stage production, portraits of Hamilton Deane courtesy John Burton, for the Deane Estate, England

The author wishes to thank the following individuals and institutions for their generous assistance:

Ronald V. Borst
Edward G. Brady III
James Cerone
Ned Comstock
Nancy Cushing-Jones
Sue Dwiggins
Rita Duenas
Donald Fowle
Robert Furmanek
Maria Jochsberger
Yvon Kartak

Urbano Lemus
Linda Mehr
John Poorman
Anne Schlosser
Michael Sington
David Skal
Viviana Strahl
Ron Stransky
Dorothy Swerdlove
Wallace Worsley

THE BILLY ROSE THEATER COLLECTION, New York Public Library, Lincoln Ctr., New York City
THE MARGARET HERRICK LIBRARY, Academy of Motion Picture Arts and Sciences
USC ARCHIVES OF PERFORMING ARTS SPECIAL COLLECTIONS

The author gratefully acknowledges permission to reprint excerpts from the following:
Music for the Monsters, Universal Pictures Horror Film Scores of the Thirties by William H. Rosar: Fall, 1983 issue of The Quarterly Journal of the Library of Congress

A Biography of Dracula, The Life Story of Bram Stoker by Harry Ludlam, The Fireside Press, W. Foulsham & Co., London, England, 1962

The Bela Lugosi Scrapbooks, courtesy Forrest J Ackerman Fantasy Film Collection

Tod Browning: Child of the Night by Elias Savada
Art Deco borders by Tom Menton, Dover Pub.

Manufactured in the United States of America

Typesetting by Computer House, Absecon, New Jersey

Printed and bound by
McNaughton & Gunn Lithographers

MAGICIMAGE PUBLICATIONS

THE ACKERMAN ARCHIVES SERIES
(Restoring Lost Films)
By Philip J. Riley
Volume 1 - LONDON AFTER MIDNIGHT
Volume 2 - A BLIND BARGAIN
Volume 3 - THE HUNCHBACK OF NOTRE DAME
Volume 4 - THE DIVINE WOMAN
Volume 5 - THE ROGUE SONG

• •

UNIVERSAL FILMSCRIPTS SERIES
Classic Horror Series
Volume 1 - FRANKENSTEIN
Volume 2 - THE BRIDE OF FRANKENSTEIN
Volume 3 - SON OF FRANKENSTEIN
Volume 4 - THE GHOST OF FRANKENSTEIN
Volume 5 - FRANKENSTEIN MEETS THE WOLF MAN
Volume 6 - HOUSE OF FRANKENSTEIN
Volume 7 - THE MUMMY
Volume 13- DRACULA
Classic Comedy Series
Volume 1 - ABBOTT AND COSTELLO MEET FRANKENSTEIN
Volume 2 - ONE NIGHT IN THE TROPICS
Volume 3 - BUCK PRIVATES
Volume 4 - HOLD THAT GHOST
Science Fiction Series
Volume 1 - THIS ISLAND EARTH
Academy Award Series
Volume 1 - ALL QUIET ON THE WESTERN FRONT
Classic Silents Series
Volume 1 - THE PHANTOM OF THE OPERA (1925)
Alfred Hitchcock Series
Volume 1 - PSYCHO

IN PRODUCTION

§ **AUTOBIOGRAPHY** §
The Wizard of MGM- 42 Years of Special Effects
- By A. Arnold Gillespie
(Introduction by Katharine Hepburn and Spencer Tracy)

Mr. Technicolor - By Dr. Herbert Kalmus

"DRACULA" *A Universal Production* MADE IN U.S.A.

Dedicated to
Tod Browning & Bela Lugosi
and
The Cast & Crew of *Dracula*

and to:
Armando Ponce
(Here's to the Official Universal Archives!)

In Memory of Wendy

Bela Lugosi visited the original Ackerman Museum in 1955 - seated to the right are Wendy and Forrest J Ackerman.

"DRACULA" A Universal Production MADE IN U.S.A.

Special Introduction
By
Bela Lugosi

On March 27, 1931, Bela Lugosi was to give a speech on radio station KFI Los Angeles to promote the opening of the film DRACULA. Reproduced now from our archives, is the text from a typewritten sheet of paper glued to his personal scrapbooks that was composed and typed by him for this broadcast. The text is reproduced exactly as it appears, in his own spelling, grammar and punctuation. - Ed

I read the book, "DRACULA," written by Bram Stoker, eighteen year ago, and I always dreamed to create and to play the part of "DRACULA". Finally the opportunity came. Horace Liveright, stage producer of New York, acquired the stage rights of the novel and he chose me for the part. I have played the role of "DRACULA" about a thousand times on the stage, and people often ask me if I still retain my interest in the character. I do - intensely. Because many people regard the story of "DRACULA" simply as a glorified superstition, the actor who plays the role is constantly engaged in the battle of wits with the audience, in a sense, since he is constantly striving to make the character so real that the audience will believe in it.

Now that I have appeared in the screen version of the story which Universal has just completed, I am of course not under this daily strain in the depiction of the character. My work in this direction was finished with the completion of the picture, but while it was being made I was working more intensely to this end than I ever did on the stage.

Although "DRACULA" is a fanciful tale of a fictional character, it is actually a story which has many essential elements of truth. I was born and reared in almost the exact location of the story, and I came to know that what is looked upon merely as a superstition of ignorant people, is really based on facts which are literally hair-raising in their strangeness - but which are *true*. Many people will leave the theatre with a sniff at the fantastic character of the story, but many others who think just as deeply will gain an insight into one of the most remarkable facts of human existence.

"DRACULA" is a story which has always had a powerful effect on the emotions of an audience, and I think that the picture will be no less effective than the stage play. In fact, the motion picture should even prove more remarkable in this direction, since many things which could only be talked about on the stage are shown on the screen in all their uncanny detail.

I am sure you will enjoy "DRACULA". I am sure you will be mightily affected by its strange story, and I hope that it will make you *think* - about the weirdest, most remarkable condition that ever affected mankind.

    I Thank You.

"DRACULA" A Universal Production MADE IN U.S.A.

Foreword
By
Ivan Butler

In the late summer of 1927 I was a young actor with one performance to my credit - in a week's run of John Drinkwater's "Abraham Lincoln" at the London suburban theatre. Playing Lincoln himself was a gaunt, striking-looking man named W.E. Holloway, who had taken the play all over the world. A few weeks later I was summoned to meet a Mr. Hamilton Deane; also in the agent's office was W.E. Holloway, who had been engaged to play Dracula in a tour of Deane's version. I also was selected (for the minuscule part of Lord Godalming) and thus made the acquaintance of the character who was to stay fairly close by my side for many years - the Vampire Count.

Bram Stoker, his creator, was born in Dublin in 1847, and was so sickly a child that he seldom left his bed for seven years. Later, after an almost miraculous recovery, he became a notable athlete at Dublin University, and after a period of less than stimulating office jobs joined Henry Irving as business manager. During his twenty-seven years with the great actor he wrote - among other tales of horror and the macabre - his undoubted masterpiece, Dracula, published in 1897. In this book, described as "the last great gothic novel," he managed with consummate skill to interweave the ancient superstition of the Undead (Nosferatu) with the historical Rumanian Prince the Voivode Drakul, or Dracula, known because of his ruthlessness as Vlad the Impaler.

Despite the fact that publication of the book caused a certain sensation, Stoker would surely have been totally disbelieving had he been informed of what was to happen (and is still happening after more than ninety years) to his creation. During his lifetime only one stage performance, for copyright purposes, was given. The full cast list, which included Ellen Terry's daughter, Edith Craig, can be found in Harry Ludlam's excellent study, A Biography of Dracula, The Life Story of Bram Stoker.

It is strange to recollect, incidentally, that the Count originally sported a long white moustache - long since shorn from his impressive features; it surely must have slightly impeded his most noted activity.

Although a Hungarian film has been noted in 1921, the first generally accepted cinematic production was F.W. Murnau's striking *Nosferatu*, a freely adapted version which, despite a change

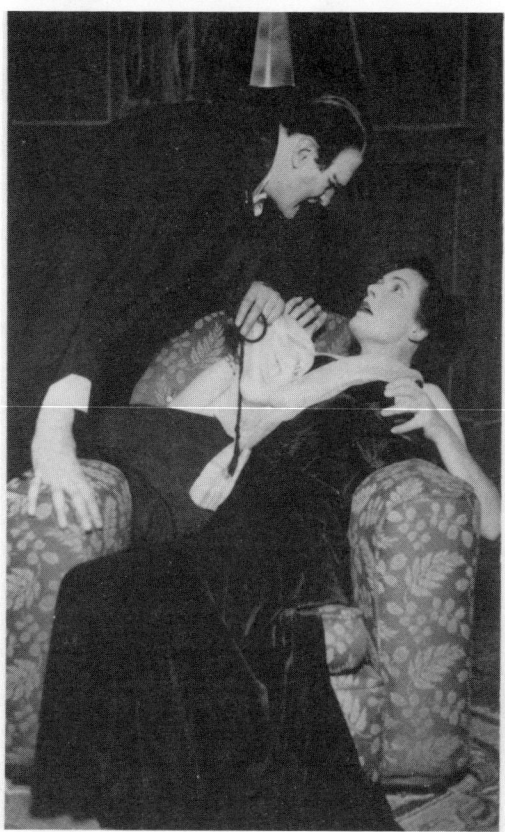

Ivan Butler in a scene from a touring stage revival

This rare edition of Dracula's Guest contained a paper bat with hinged springs. When the patrons of the 250th performance opened the book, the theatre was filled with bats popping all about.

of title, ran into copyright difficulties. (*Nosferatu* has been restored from 35mm negatives and the original score and tints preserved by the Berlin Archives. There is no knowledge, as of the date of this publication, as to its availabity to the American audience, either in the theater or on home video - Ed.)

Hamilton Deane's original stage version was first produced at the Grand Theatre, Derby, in 1924, with Deane as Van Helsing and the young Raymond Huntley as Dracula. It made its London debut at the Little Theatre (noted home of Grand Guignol) on February 14, 1927. In spite of receiving a generally less than enthusiastic critical reception (to put it mildly) the play almost instantly caught alight, and later in the same year - leaving the London productions still happily running - Deane sent out three simultaneous tours, himself appearing again as Van Helsing, with W.E. Holloway as Dracula, in the Number One company. I remember to this day the extraordinary scenes night after night as we travelled all over the country, from the Opera House, Manchester to the Cosy Cinema, Porthcawl, Wales, playing to packed and exciting audiences.

People seemed to come and see the play again and again. There was a famous curtain speech at the end of the play, when the actor playing Van Helsing, bidding the audience goodnight and telling them not to be afraid when they went to bed, suddenly changed his manner, reverted to the accent and character of the play and finished, 'Just one word of warning, ladies and gentlemen...THERE ARE such things!' More than once we found the audience knowing the play so well that there was a mighty yell of 'There are such things!' before Deane could get the words out himself.

Disturbances in the circle or stalls as people felt faint and had to be taken out were not uncommon - and were perfectly genuine, not a publicity stunt. Strangely enough, they were generally men. There were some rather chilling effects. Renfield's blood-curdling howls (off-stage) were accomplished by the actor simply howling through cupped hands or a megaphone. For Dracula's weird 'wail' call we used either a violin or a swannee whistle. The bat which tried to fly in through the windows was an ingenious affair of black cloth and wire about 18 inches across with the wings spread, its glowing red eyes lit up by a torch battery fixed to the body. It was operated by the assistant stage manager, who used to stand on a chair outside the windows using a sort of fishing rod to swing the bat around. On one famous occasion when the string broke, the bat sailed in through the window and landed in the footlights, where it stayed glaring unwinkingly out at the audience. As it was supposed to be Dracula in one of his guises, it tended to make his eventual entry a little difficult.

Two smoke bombs were used for the mist to herald the Count's appearance at the big climax in the second act. This, together with the various revolver shots, used to make the stage look like a pea-souper. We also used flash-boxes for Dracula's entrance and exits - both for the thrill and to blind the audience while he slipped through his secret panels.

Hamilton Deane was a gentle man, but his anger when these failed to go off (as inevitably happened at times) was awe-inspiring!

During the four years I was with him, Deane produced and discarded many plays in his travelling repertory company, but Dracula remained faithfully among them throughout.

By skillful compression, Deane contrived to fit the entire

action of the book (which is written in a series of journals, diaries and letters and ranges widely from Rumania to Whitby to the outskirts of London) into two rooms in Jonathan Harker's house and a brief finale in the Carfax cellar where the Count is resting in his coffined bed. This first version, by Deane alone and based largely on Stoker's sometimes over-literary dialogue, is little known today. When an offer came from the American producer, Horace Liveright, Deane collaborated with John L. Balderston in a somewhat tightened and modernised version, and it is this from which the Lugosi film - and all that flooded from it - was derived. The original Deane version was placed in the contemporary period - i.e., the 1920's. I produced it (and played Dracula) a few years after the war, when it showed - through the reactions of the audience - that it had lost none of its power to grip and startle.

                Ivan Butler
                Middlesex, England
                      October 31, 1989

Hamilton Deane

Ivan Butler in the role of Dracula in the play's later revival.

(Above) Carla Laemmle poses on the piano with George Gershwin and Billy Rose, THE KING OF JAZZ, 1930.

(Below) The opening scene in DRACULA in which Carla played the secretary of the sour-faced English lady. In Dudley Murphy's script the part was strictly comedy relief. The group arrives at the Inn, the Englishwoman gets out of the coach, and Sara (Carla) follows her around reading about the local superstitions - becoming more frightened as she reads. The lady calls for her Golf chair but keeps changing her mind as to where to sit. They hear a wolf and Sara is near hysterics. The lady finally decides on a spot to sit and snaps a command. By now the howling has Carla so scared that she sets the Golf chair upside down - sharp point up. The result is obvious as the lady, quite disgusted with the superstitions, plants herself on the pointed stake! Passengers are (Left to right) Dwight Frye, Carla Laemmle, on his lap, Nicholas Bela, Donald Murphy and Daisy Belmore.

Preface
By
Carla Laemmle

1927 - Carl Laemmle is greeted at the train by Director & Mrs. Edward Laemmle (far right), and Carla. (Next to Carl Laemmle are Mrs. Julius Mayer and Manny Lowenstein, Universal Executives.)

Universal Studios had already been operating for six years when my uncle Carl finally succeeded in persuading his brother, Joseph Laemmle, to leave the harsh winters of Chicago and move his family out to California.

Joseph, my father, Carrie Belle Laemmle, my mother, my dear grandmother, Mrs. Imogene Norton, and I, arrived at our new home-to-be in Universal City, California in 1921.

Universal Studios was actually a 230 acre city; It had a mayor, post office, police and fire departments, a school and a hospital with a resident doctor and nurse.

Our bungalow lay some distance away from the road, separated from the sidewalk by a fenced-in, golf course size lawn that stretched all the way to a row of tall, pungent, pepper trees which marked the main entrance to the Studio.

A lush growth of sweet-smelling petunias and other flowering plants bordered the fence and extended the full length of the lawn. Around dusk, some of the largest and most beautiful, velvety-winged moths that I had ever seen congregated there, attracted by the fragrance and nectar. I loved going out there at sundown; it was a very enchanting time of day for me.

Across the road from our house, situated on what used to be El Camino Real, was Campo de Cahuenga, the most historic landmark in California. There, on January 13, 1847, U.S. Army General John Fremont and General Andree Pico of Mexico signed the treaty ceding California to the U.S.

Behind our bungalow was a set that they named "Old New York Street." It was a perfect replica - down to the smallest detail. I could almost smell the spicy aroma of corned beef and pickles coming from the corner delicatessen.

To the north of the New York set lay an uncultivated area with a rather deep overgrown ravine. During the rainy season a goodly amount of water flowed through it. A quaint, rustic, wooden bridge spanned the two sides of the gully. This site was used in film after film for the early Lon Chaney and Warren Kerrigan melodramas, romantic love scenes and westerns.

Imagine the wonderful opportunity that we had as children. Tarzan's Jungle, romantic Monte Carlo, the old Paris of *The Hunchback of Notre Dame*, Western Towns, and the New York City streets - a fantasy world for me and my playmates.

The area on the opposite side of the ravine was used primarily for horticultural purposes. A Norwegian gardener and his wife lived in a small house on the premises. He worked as a caretaker of the greenhouses and gardens and also looked after an aviary.

About a mile or so east of the main Studio office buildings and stages lay an extensive area known as the "Back-lot." A Studio shuttle bus would transport tourists, actors and crews down and back.

It was here on the back lot that the great sets for *The Hunchback Of Notre Dame* were being built. The elaborate sets for Eric Von Stroheim's *Foolish Wives* had already been erected here. I vividly remember the excitement that I felt in watching the spectacular fire sequence in the picture. It was shot at night, during which a tall hotel structure was to be totally destroyed by the fire. Everybody in Hollywood was there to watch the filming. It was a very tense moment, for they had to get it right on the first take as they wouldn't get a second chance. They did it. It was a print!

The back lot was home for a large chicken farm, scores of horses, sheep, goats, and other animals. But the most interesting attraction for me on the back lot was the Zoo. Among the animals it housed were lions, tigers, a giraffe, a couple of elephants,

Joseph Laemmle (far left 3rd row), Mrs. Joseph Laemmle (seated without hat, center), Carla's adored grandmother Mrs. Imogene Norton (the little old lady in black hat, seated far left), and Carla on ground with Betty Egan, entertain guests on the set of Von Stroheim's FOOLISH WIVES.

monkeys, a chimpanzee, a variety of exotic birds and a camel appropriately named Houdini. I was to find out why, later.

It seemed that no matter how well the trainers were to tether Houdini he would get loose and make the mile-long trek from the back lot to our front lawn.

I have no idea what sixth or seventh, sense led that camel to the grass in the first place, but once he found it he never forgot. Many a morning I would awaken to find the creature out there happily grazing away.

I soon learned I could tempt Houdini with a bowl of oatmeal, then surreptitiously lure him into one of the garages. He always fell for that ruse. My next move was to phone the zookeeper and tell him that I had Houdini and ask him to please come up and take him back home.

Carla and the camel: JOSEPH AND HIS BRETHREN at the Hollywood Bowl

Most of the low-lying hills around Universal City were still more or less on the wild side and sparsely built up with houses. Orange groves covered much of the countryside. Having come to California from the cement jungle of Chicago, it took me a while to become accustomed to the barking of the coyotes at night, or, when the wind was right, the roaring of the lions from the back lot Zoo early in the morning at feeding time.

Other kinds of wildlife frequented the grounds around our bungalow. There were possums, gophers, squirrels, owls, sometimes bats, lizards, snakes (mostly harmless garter) and skunks -- especially skunks. I had a beautiful Collie dog that got into an unfortunate confrontation with a skunk and never smelled the same again.

Universal was known for its famous westerns. I became acquainted with a real, leather-neck cowboy with the rather distinguished name of Raleigh J. Malco. I never knew what the "J" stood for. Uneducated in the formal sense, he had a quick, native intelligence and he was as honest as they come. He worked at Universal as a stuntman along with his trained horse, Trixie.

Trixie was a very smart horse and she would perform on command any one of her repertoire of tricks....sit on her haunches, play dead, roll over, whinny a horse laugh, shake hands, rear up and paw the air, or count out a number by pawing the ground. She could also sashay around and dance a little jig.

I had never ridden a horse before, but Mr. Malco taught me how to ride Trixie bareback and to perform tricks with her. One day he told me that an uncle in Kansas had died and left him a small inheritance. He had to go back there, he said, but didn't have the money. Would my mother loan him $100.00 on trust? Yes, she said she would. But there was still the matter of Trixie. Someone would have to feed and look after her while he was gone. Would I do it? Yes, I said I would. I became a horse-sitter for the next three months.

Trixie, the Laughing Horse and Carla, SHOWBOAT 1929.

The Halloween party -- (?), Betty Egan, later Mrs. Ernie Westmore, Carla and Dorothy Weigal (The girl who fainted).

Until Mr. Malco returned, Trixie lived in one of our garages, and I saw that she had plenty of water and bought her hay at a nearby feed store. For exercise I rode her around Universal and the nearby hills. We both enjoyed it.

He not only paid mother back, but also for the hay!

Of all the pleasant memories I have of living and growing up at Universal Studios, my annual birthday-costume parties rank among the happiest.

Since the date of my birth was October 20, it was decided one year to combine my birthday with a Halloween party. I had been taking dancing lessons from the Ernest Belcher School of the Dance for several years by then, and each year, I invited my young classmates to my party.

My guests began to arrive on the big day, in mid-afternoon, but the main Halloween fun wasn't scheduled to begin until after dark and was to take place outside on the ground. The area chosen was a long, winding, tree-bordered trail known as "lover's lane," not very far from our bungalow.

I had discovered that fringe benefits came naturally with the territory of being Uncle Carl's niece. I had no problem in calling upon the pros from the Studio Property Department to set up some real professional scary Halloween stuff for the party. And they did. Even in the Silent days Universal was famous for its gothic and mystery movies, so the crew rigged the narrow, tree-lined lane with a variety of weird and spooky gimmicks and created a special effects masterpiece, complete with eerie lighting and sound effects.

It proved all too much for one of my young classmates. When a life-sized, bone-rattling skeleton suddenly jumped out at her from behind a tree, she gave a piercing scream and fainted dead away. A whiff of smelling salts revived her, the only casualty of the evening.

Around 1924, Universal began production on *The Phantom of the Opera*. My ballet master, Ernest Belcher, was signed to do the choreography for the elaborate ballet sequence in the film. I was both proud and thrilled, of course, to have been chosen as Prima Ballerina. Uncle Carl had an elaborate new stage built especially for this film, duplicating the Paris Opera House. And they filmed our scenes in color! People tell you about how they were (and still are) terrified by Lon Chaney's living death-mask in *The Phantom*. But to actually see *that face* walking about on a body dressed in black, standing next to you? Mary Philbin and I have been friends since our early Chicago days and even today I still do not know how she managed to be so close to Mr. Chaney. It was truly horrible, beyond words - much more so than on the screen.

(Center) Carla and Mary Philbin (left) Mary's mother (right) J. Laemmle and Mr. Philbin, Paul Kohner in military costume.

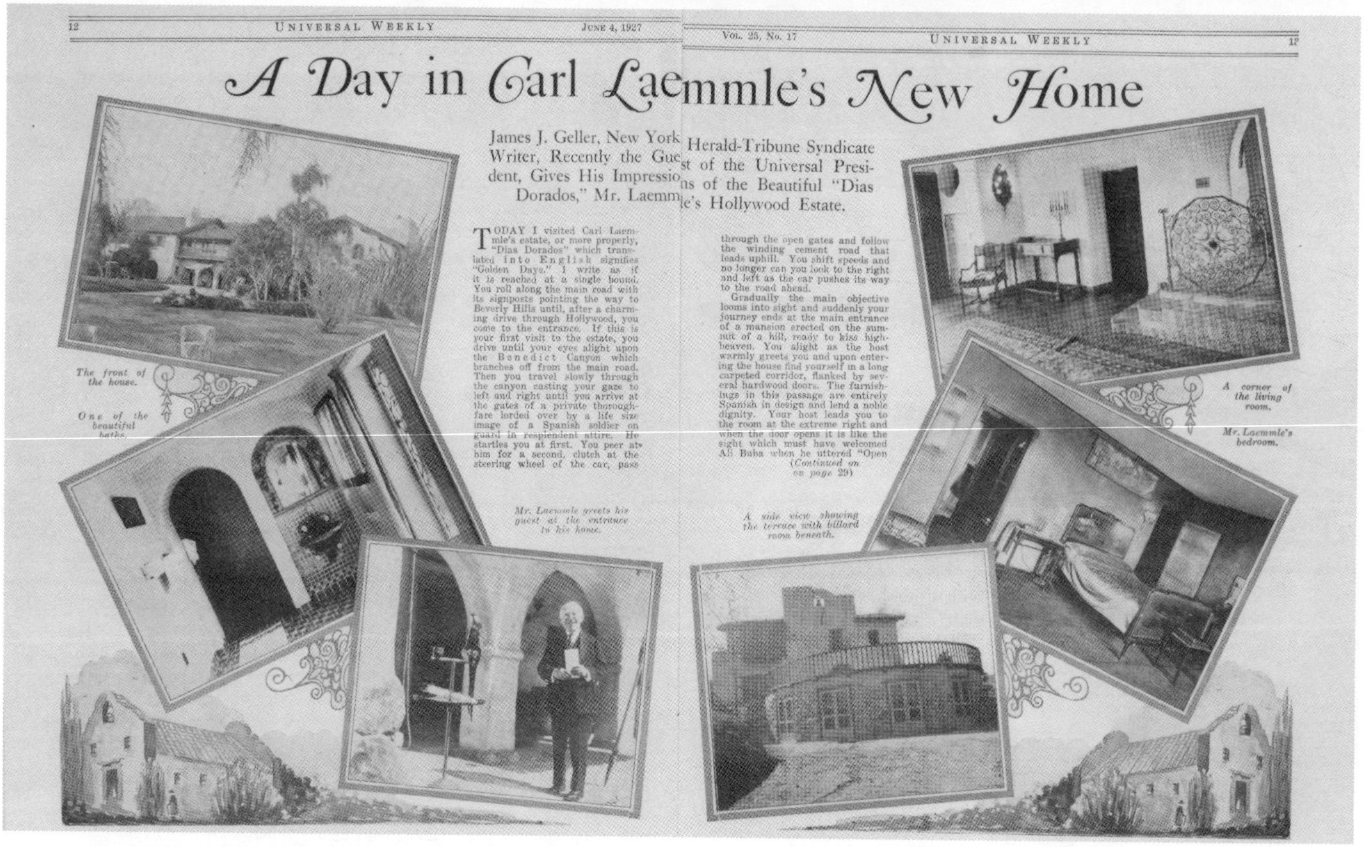

A Day in Carl Laemmle's New Home

James J. Geller, New York Herald-Tribune Syndicate Writer, Recently the Guest of the Universal President, Gives His Impressions of the Beautiful "Dias Dorados," Mr. Laemmle's Hollywood Estate.

TODAY I visited Carl Laemmle's estate, or more properly, "Dias Dorados" which translated into English signifies "Golden Days." I write as if it is reached at a single bound. You roll along the main road with its signposts pointing the way to Beverly Hills until, after a charming drive through Hollywood, you come to the entrance. If this is your first visit to the estate, you drive until your eyes alight upon the Benedict Canyon which branches off from the main road. Then you travel slowly through the canyon casting your gaze to left and right until you arrive at the gates of a private thoroughfare lorded over by a life size image of a Spanish soldier on guard in resplendent attire. He startles you at first. You peer at him for a second, clutch at the steering wheel of the car, pass through the open gates and follow the winding cement road that leads uphill. You shift speeds and no longer can you look to the right and left as the car pushes its way to the road ahead.

Gradually the main objective looms into sight and suddenly your journey ends at the main entrance of a mansion erected on the summit of a hill, ready to kiss high-heaven. You alight as the host warmly greets you and upon entering the house find yourself in a long carpeted corridor, flanked by several hardwood doors. The furnishings in this passage are entirely Spanish in design and lend a noble dignity. Your host leads you to the room at the extreme right and when the door opens it is like the sight which must have welcomed Ali Baba when he uttered "Open

(Continued on on page 29)

The front of the house.

One of the beautiful baths.

Mr. Laemmle greets his guest at the entrance to his home.

A side view showing the terrace with billard room beneath.

A corner of the living room.

Mr. Laemmle's bedroom.

In 1927, *Dracula* was a big stage hit in England and was about to open on Broadway with a new Count portrayed by a man with the strange name of Bela Lugosi. Today, with the instant images transmitted by television, it is hard to imagine how far away New York City was in perspective. We had to wait a full year before Mr. Lugosi came to California with the play, so we had a full year to read the magazine and press to keep us West Coast residents trying to outdo each other with scary tales about the play. All the studios, including Universal, considered the story too horrible to film.

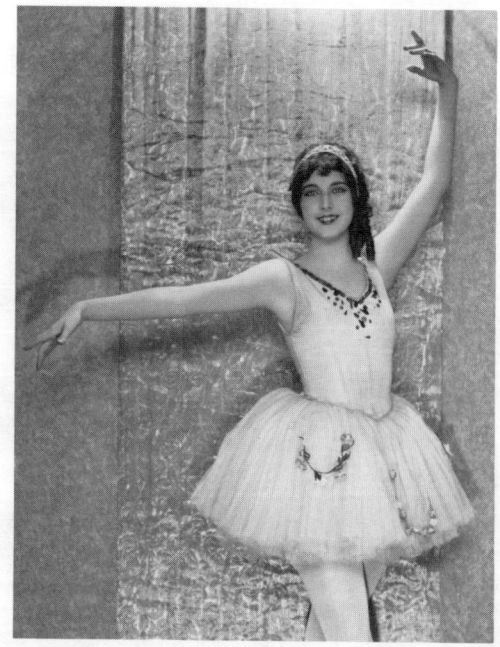

Carla as Prima Ballerina in the original THE PHANTOMOF THE OPERA.

It was also in 1927 that Uncle Carl bought the magnificent Tom Ince mansion from Mr. Ince's widow. It was to become the traditional Sunday dinner site for many years to come.

In January of 1928, I signed up with the Shrine Light Opera Co. as Prima Ballerina and actress for a 10-week Light Opera season at the Shrine Auditorium in Los Angeles. Uncle Carl seemed impressed with my performance and arranged for me to have a screen test made at Universal. The scene chosen for me was from *The Merry Widow* (made at MGM in 1925). The director was the great Erich Von Stroheim. Can you imagine that! Anyway, I guess Uncle Carl thought I had some potential as an actress, as soon after that I signed a contract with Unversal.

About that time, Universal began production on their great musical extravaganza *The King of Jazz,* starring Paul Whiteman. I was given the rather challenging assignment in the "Rhapsody in Blue" sequence, of performing a ballet routine, specifically a toe dance, on top of the keys of a giant piano. Happily I managed to do it without breaking my neck.

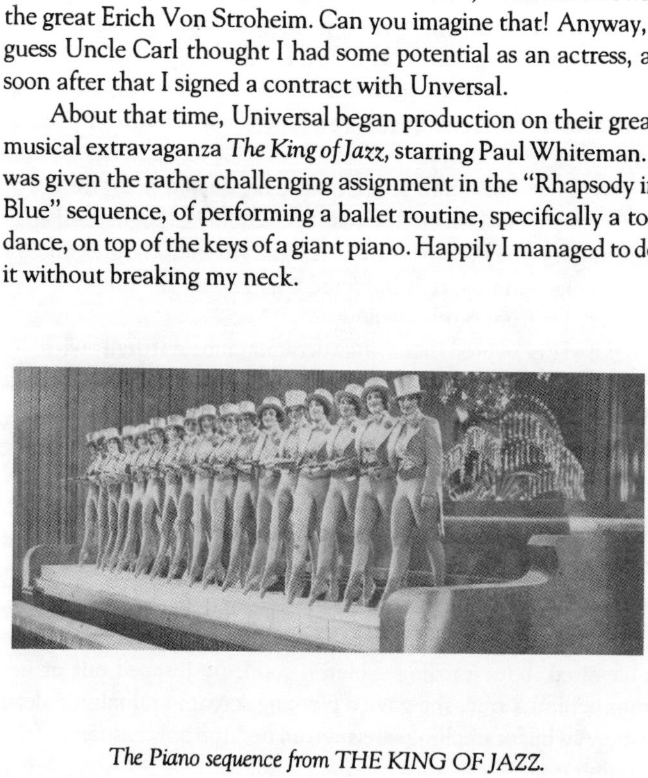

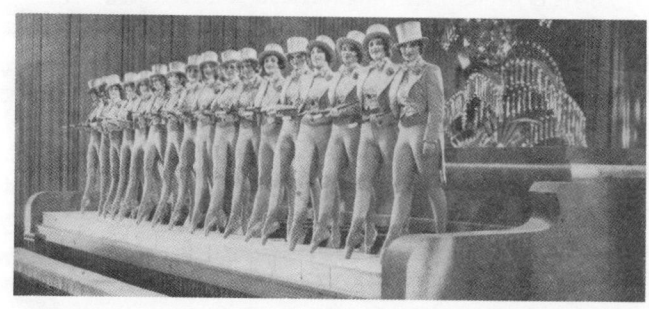

The Piano sequence from THE KING OF JAZZ.

In 1929 my father passed away, but my mother and grandmother and I continued to live on at Universal until my uncle sold the Studio in 1936. It had been a happy, eventful and wonderful time of my life.

Carl Laemmle did not just come by the moniker "Uncle Carl" for no good reason. The fact was, he gave jobs to so many of his relatives at Universal Studios that it got to be kind of a joke. Some called it nepotism.

Here are some members of the Laemmle clan who worked at Universal at one time or another:

Edward Laemmle, son of Joseph Laemmle, my half-brother, was a film director at Universal. He married Peppi, the younger sister of Frieda Laemmle, my uncle Louis' wife.

My two cousins, Walter and Ernst Laemmle, sons of Carl's brother Siegfried, both worked at Universal as assistant directors. Ernst later became a director. Ernst's wife, Nina Laemmle, later won acclaim as the producer of the highly successful TV series "Marcus Welby." She was also a screen writer. Walter's wife, Connie, was not connected with the film industry.

My cousin, Richard Laemmle, son of Carl's brother Louis Laemmle, was also employed for a time at Universal. Richard was undeniably the eccentric of the Laemmle family. Well educated and articulate, he chose early on to drop out of the mainstream establishment; to live the unfettered life of a vagabond of sorts, living, sleeping and travelling around the countryside in his old Cadillac with his six to ten dogs as companions. He was a world class character, without a doubt, but for all his quirkiness he had dignity and integrity and a love for the natural world around us.

My cousin, William Wyler, was brought over to this country by Carl Laemmle. He got his start at Universal, working first as an assistant director, then as a director. Later, Willie was to be recognized as one of Hollywood's greatest directors. He was the

recipient of the Motion Picture Academy's Highest Achievement Award and nominated to the Hall of Fame.

Robert Wyler, Willie's younger brother, also worked at Universal as an assistant director.

Julius Bernheim was the son of Carl Laemmle's sister, and worked as General Manager of Universal in 1924.

Stanley Bergerman is Carl Laemmle's son-in-law. He was married to Carl's only daughter, Rosebelle. She was a lovely person and always the perfect hostess at all festivities. Stanley was a film producer at Universal from 1930 to 1936 with many of their better pictures under his control.

Paul Kohner, while not a relative, was brought to America by Carl Laemmle, who was so impressed with his salesmanship ability that he gave him a job at Universal as a sales representative. Later, Paul was to become a top hollywood agent and open his own very successful Actors' Agency.

A garden party at Uncle Carl's estate Carl Jr. is seated on ground (right). Behind him, seated, is Ernst Laemmle. Standing with Lupita Tovar (in black scarf hat) is Paul Kohner. Seated far left, cousin Willie Wyler. In swing, Robert Wyler and (behind him) Isadore Bernstein, Carla, & Julius Bernheim.

Victor Noerdlinger was another young man, not a relative, given the nod by Carl Laemmle. He came over to this country from Europe to work at Universal. He started as an assistant director then became a casting director.

I have intentionally left my cousin Carl Laemmle Jr's name for last. While he did hold the office of General Manager of Universal Studios for a time, it is his accomplishment as a film producer that is most relevant here.

In spite of his detractors who say he had no talent, Carl, Jr. was no dummy. He was receptive to new ideas and not afraid of a challenge. He had insight and certain gut instincts about the films he was involved in and perhaps most importantly, he had the gift of choosing the right people for the right job, and he made the most of it.

Carl Junior's outstanding achievement as a film producer, of course, was the great anti-war epic, *All Quiet on the Western Front*.

But the going had not been easy. Everyone in the front office had turned thumbs down on Junior's proposal to make Erich Maria Remarque's celebrated war novel into a motion picture. Too costly and ill-advised, they said.

Carl Laemmle, however, overruled them and made the decision to back Junior in his ambitious project.

All Quiet on the Western Front was made, and so was motion picture history. Not only did the film win the Academy Award for best picture of 1930, but it is still considered by many to be the greatest war film ever made.

The same thing happened with *Dracula* the very next year. Uncle Carl's advisors in the front office said no, but Junior won; and the result of his talents led Universal into a series of classic films full of Monsters that are remembered today as the greatest in the genre. And his final film, *Show Boat*, directed by James Whale in 1936, is still considered the best of the three versions. Musicals, monster films and war films, Westerns and comedies -- of all the films produced by Universal during the 30's, Carl Junior's films are the ones that are the most popular today and are still contributing to Universal Pictures alongside of their present day hit movies.

It was a sorry fate indeed that due to developing health problems, Junior was forced into early retirement. He died on September 24, 1979, forty years to the day after the death of his father, Carl Sr., in 1939.

It is fitting that MagicImage Filmbooks is paying tribute to Carl Laemmle Jr. on the 75th Anniversary of Universal by the publication of Philip J. Riley's books on two of Carl's greatest accomplishments, *All Quiet on the Western Front* and this book, *Dracula* (along with their volumes on *Frankenstein* and other classic horror films).

I didn't realize that, other than David Manners, I am the only one left from the cast! The author, Mr. Riley, had asked me to relate my family memories rather than concentrate on the film-related stories, to honor the 75th Anniversary of Universal's West Coast studio. Today there are once again (and finally!) men of vision and courage in charge again, Mr. Wasserman and Mr. Sheinberg. Uncle Carl would have liked them. Their television shows have replaced Uncle Carl's weekly serials and shorts, they make several big hits a year, and they expanded his original tour idea into such a fantastic attraction for tourists and film lovers around the world.

So, in closing this preface to *Dracula* I would like to say a few words in tribute to that great little man who started this whole business - **Carl Laemmle Sr.** He was small in stature, yes, but, oh so big in **vision, courage,** and **determination.** His motto was:
"It can be done!"
and by God he did it. He dreamed the Impossible and made it into a reality. He built his own City and created an Entertainment Empire.

I wish you could see it now, Uncle Carl!

I Love You,

Carla.

Today Carla Laemmle is still strikingly beautiful and has retained her youthful dancer's figure. Her eyes sparkled as she remembered the early days of her family's studio (of the original family only Carla and Walter are left - Ed), and of her career as a dancer. Her film credits: PHANTOM OF THE OPERA, LA BOHEME, DON JUAN, TOPSY AND EVA, GEORGE WHITE'S SCANDALS, THE GATE CRASHER, ON YOUR TOES, THE CHOCOLATE SOLDIER, BROADWAY MELODY, NIGHT AND DAY, THE KING OF JAZZ, DRACULA, WATERLOO BRIDGE and THE ADVENTURES OF FRANK MERRIWELL. Aside from her strenuous ballet seasons she also appeared in popular plays such as "No, No Nanette," "Sally," "Jigsaw Revue," "Tsk Tsk Paree," "The Great Waltz," "Her Majesty the Prince" by Ray Cannon and "Bittersweet".

She can look back with great pride at the history of Universal Studios and of all the Laemmle relatives who contributed so much to our entertainment. As Ogden Nash put it:

"Uncle Carl Laemmle has a very big faemmle."

§

Production Background
By
Philip J. Riley and George Turner

Universal Studios, 1932. 1) Remains of the old mill from FRANKENSTEIN; 2) Path and Inn from DRACULA; 3) Notre Dame Cathedral & the European village; 4) The Phantom stage; 5) Jack Pierce & Lon Chaney's makeup studio; 6) Billboards announce MURDERS IN THE RUE MORGUE.

Around February 14, 1931, New York impresario S.L. Rothafel delivered an unusual Valentine to the patrons of his Roxy Theater. Advertised as "...*the story of the strangest passion the world has ever known,*" *Dracula* corralled the customers in droves. Of greater importance, ultimately, is its trailblazing position as the forerunner of a genre which has ebbed and flowed as a film perennial ever since: the supernatural horror "talkie."

It's true that a number of sound pictures of the spine-chilling variety had preceded Dracula, including such popular numbers as *The Terror, Stark Mad, The Cat Creeps, The Bat Whispers,* and *The Gorilla.* (*The Terror* is considered a lost film. In it, the early motion picture term of "all talking" was taken literally, for the actors, producers, and technicians actually appeared on screen in place of the main titles and introduced themselves to the theater audience before the picture itself began.) Most of these were adapted from Broadway plays in which the scary stuff was intermingled with comedy and anything that appeared paranormal was always revealed as the machinations of malevolent human beings. What had made *Dracula* different was that the audience was expected to accept the villain as a *genuine* vampire and not another crook in disguise. There was a strong feeling in the industry that the producers were insane to ask moviegoers, who had just emerged from the Roaring Twenties and stumbled into the morass of the Great Depression, to suspend disbelief in a Medieval superstition.

Actually, *Dracula* proved that hard times enhanced the charm of such a picture. The movie companies found in short order that realistic stories which tried to come to grips with the realitites already bedevilling the public were not generally popular. After all, the idea of a 500-year old Carpathian nobleman surviving on the blood of lovely young English ladies was only slightly more fantastic than such popular fare as Westerns, murder mysteries, musical comedies, the Marx Brothers, and Hollywood's notions of romance among the millionaires. The allegorical aspects of a tale in which an evil outside force intrudes upon the lives of ordinary people who manage to overcome the menace may have triggered subconscious responses from a populace beleaguered by destructive forces against which it was helpless. The grimness of the theme was alleviated by its abnormality -- viewers could forget for a time the realities of the Depression and share vicariously in problems that they knew would never touch their own lives.

It is difficult today to understand why *Dracula* was considered such a gamble in its day, and why, in light of the truly gruesome films that have come in its wake, it was repugnant to many who saw it. Whatever its faults, the picture is done in admirable taste. The only show of blood is a single drop on a man's finger following an accident with a paper clip; even those telltale "two little marks" that are discovered on the necks of the vampire's victims are kept discreetly out of sight of the camera -- and there is only one instance of on-screen violence. Yet this picture, now more admired for its atmosphere and the commanding presence of Bela Lugosi than for any ability to horrify, stirred controversy when it first appeared.

it was a power that ceased, as did all evil things, at sunrise. He could not eat ordinary food, cast no reflection in mirrors and even in the light of the full moon had no shadow. Count Dracula became the essence of evil, living only by drinking the blood of living beings. The victim of the vampire would eventually die, but if they died by night they would become a vampire themselves.

Stoker's favorite story was that the idea came from a dream, as had Mary Shelley's <u>Frankenstein</u> and Robert Lewis Stevenson's <u>Dr. Jekyll and Mr. Hyde</u>. However, if you take note of the pages of Stoker's original manuscript as presented on the following pages, there is indication that the final result came about not from the dream caused by "an undercooked dinner of cracked crab," but from extensive research. He was one of the first popular authors to use the typewriter, which gave him the convenience of cutting and pasting entire sections of text while tying them together with his annotations.

The first English Edition of <u>Dracula</u> - 1897

The first edition of <u>Dracula</u>, published by (Westminster) Constable and Sons, appeared in a very small pressrun in May of 1897. Its blood-red lettering on yellow background drew such excited press that a second issue of the edition, containing advertisements for other books, was added to the end signature, and rushed into production. The added excitement of having the top edge of the pages uncut in its folds allowed the Victorian reader the opportunity to cut his way through the book with a book-knife as the suspense builds.

Here, at last, the supressed Victorian populace of England had a dark hero. Behind the horror of the character was the knowledge that he regarded *human* life as a human regards a chicken, merely a means of sustaining life; the sacrifice of a lower lifeform for a higher lifeform's benefit and nourishment.

The reviews were mostly favorable.

<u>The Daily Mail</u>: *In seeking a parallel to this weird, powerful and horrible story our minds revert to such tales as 'The Mysteries of Udolpho', 'Frankenstein', 'Wuthering Heights',' The Fall of the House of Usher', and 'Majaery of Quelher'. But Dracula is even more appalling in its gloomy fascination than any one of these!*

Bram Stoker 1847 -1912

Bram Stoker's book published in England in 1897 was suggested by Central European vampire legends, which for many years had been utilized by authors of Gothic novels, and the historical accounts of a Wallachian war lord whose cruelty during his reign from 1455-62 had earned him a reputation of being in league with Satan. From these sources emerged a remarkable work in which the vampire, instead of being a crawling graveyard creature, is a Transylvanian *voyevoda* possessing fantastic strength and the magical ability to transform himself into a wolf, or a bat; he could dematerialize into the form of mist or travel on moonlight rays as dust. He had the ability to command the elements, the storms, lightning, winds, fog and thunder. Creatures associated with the evils brought to natural waking by the setting sun such as rats, owls, bats, moths and wolves were all under his powers - but

Bram Stoker's original manuscript

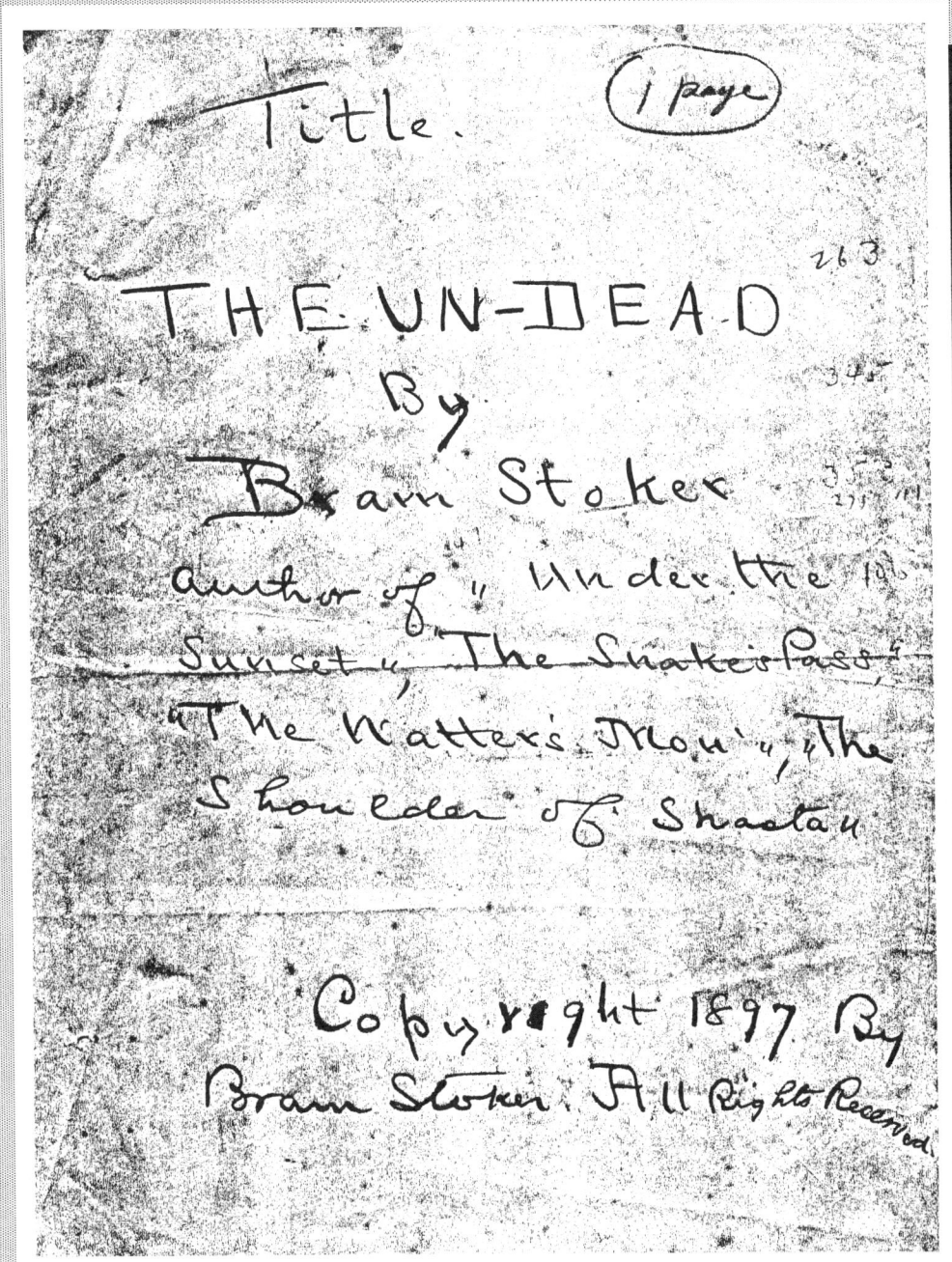

The original title of Dracula

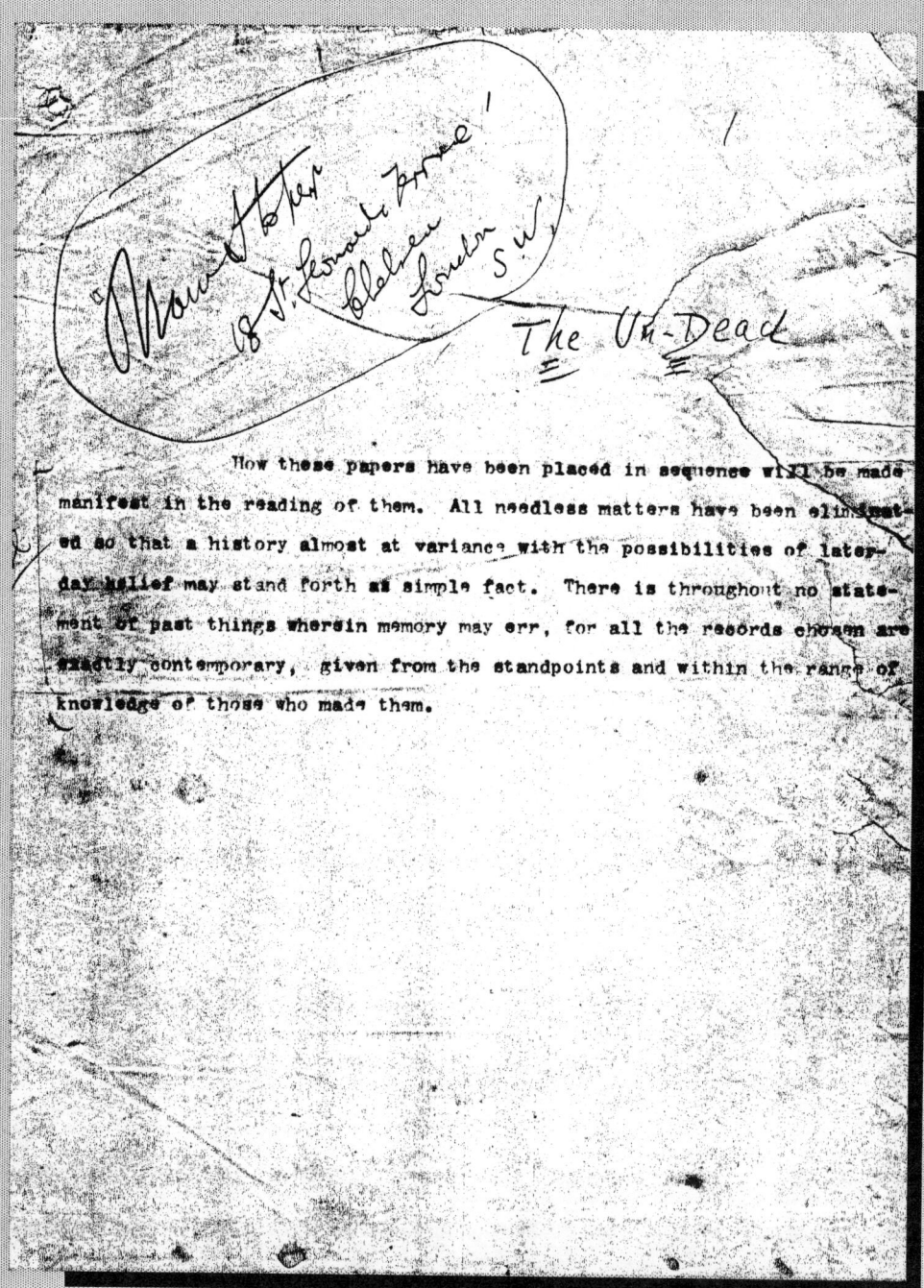

Stoker's preface: note his signature and address in his own hand

Jonathan Harker's first diary entry in Transylvania

(1891)

We left pretty well in time, and came after nightfall to Klausenburgh. Here I stopped for the night at the hotel Royale. I had, for dinner, or rather supper, a chicken done up some way with red pepper which was very good but thirsty (Mem. get receipt for Mina) I asked the waiter and he said it was called Paprika hendl, and that as it was a national dish I should be able to get it anywhere along the Carpathians. I found my smattering of German very useful here; indeed, I don't know how I should be able to get on without it. Having some time at my disposal when in London I visited the British Museum and made search among the books and maps in the library regarding Transylvania - as it struck me that some foreknowledge of the country could hardly fail to have some importance in dealing with a noble of that country. I find that the district he names is in the extreme East of the country just on the borders of three states: Transylvania, Moldavia and Bukovina in the midst of the Carpathian mountains, one of the wildest and least known portions of Europe. I was not able to light on any map or work giving the exact locality of the Castle Dracula, as there are no maps of this country as yet, to compare with our own Ordnance Survey maps; but I find that Bistritz which is the post town named by Count Dracula is a fairly well known place. I shall enter here some of my notes as they may refresh my memory when I talk over my travels with Mina.

In the population of Transylvania there are four distinct nationalities - Saxons in the South and mixed with them the Wallachs who are the descendants of the Dacians - Magyars in the West, and Szekelys in the East and North. I am going among the latter, who claim to be descended from Attila and the Huns. This may be so for when the Magyars conquered the Country in the eleventh Century they found the Huns settled in it. I read that every known superstition in the world is gathered into the horse-shoe of the Carpathians as if it were the centre of some sort of imaginative whirlpool, and if so my stay may be very interesting (Mem. I must ask the Count all about them). I did not sleep well though my bed was comfortable enough, for I had all sorts of queer dreams.

Stoker's original version of the destruction of Dracula - not only Dracula but his castle turned to dust

~~could have~~ imagined could have rested there!

The Castle of Dracula now stood out against the red sun and every stone of its broken battlements was articulated against the light. ~~As we looked there came a terrible convulsion of the earth so that we~~ seemed to rock to and fro and fell to our knees. At the same moment with a roar which seemed to shake the very heavens the whole castle and the rock and even the hill on which it stood seemed to rise into the air and scatter ~~skywards~~ in fragments while a mighty cloud of black and yellow smoke volume on volume in rolling grandeur was shot upwards with inconceivable rapidity. Then there was a stillness in nature as the echoes of that thundrous report seemed to come as with the hollow boom of a thunder clap - the long reverberating roll which seems as though the floors of heaven shook. Then down in a mighty ruin falling whence they rose ~~came~~ the fragments that had been tossed skywards in the cataclysm.

From where we stood it seemed as though the one fierce volcano burst had satisfied the need of nature and that the castle and the structure of the hill had sunk again into the void. We were so appalled with the suddenness and the ~~grandeur that we forgot to think of ourselves.~~ ~~The first to recover were~~ The gypsies, ~~and these probably~~ taking us as in some way the cause of ~~the earthquake as well as of~~ the extraordinary disappearance of the dead man, turned without a word and rode away as if for their lives, those who were unmounted jumping upon the leiter-waggon and ~~whilst they followed the horsemen~~ shouting to them (horsemen) not to desert them, the wolves which had withdrawn to a safe distance followed in their wake, leaving us alone.

~~When we noticed~~ Mr Morris, who had sunk to the ground ~~we saw that he had not risen like the rest of us after he had been thrown down by the shock. He~~ leaned on his

The Pall Mall Gazette: It is horrid and creepy to the last degree. It is also excellent, and one of the best things in the supernatural line that we have been lucky enough to hit upon.

By transporting his evil daeity to the then-modern city of London he gave his readers the added thrill of "possibility" of the impossible. Early adventures of vampires such as Varney the Vampyr, an earlier Penny Dreadful or Le Fanu's Carmilla were set in distant lands. The general attitude of the publishing and theater world was reflected in "The Adventure of the Sussex Vampire" by Arthur Conan Doyle, where Sherlock Holmes dismisses them as "Rubbish."

But Stoker being a man of the theater produced his own theatrical production within weeks of the book's publication in order to protect the dramatic copyright. This production was a "reading" offered in a prologue and five acts. It was the only production during his lifetime.

The stage's first Dracula was "Mr. Jones."

The book was then published in America by Doubleday in 1899 and offered a gold embossed cover with a dramatic castle, full moon and bats. Again it was an instant success.

Stoker continued his writings while serving as manager for the great English actor Henry Irving until his health began to fail. After completing his last novel The Lair of the White Worm, he died at age 64 in April of 1912.

He left a little less than £5000.

Florence Stoker, his wife, continued to promote his works and even published the excized chapter from Dracula, which was titled "Dracula's Guest."

In Germany, the brilliant Friedrich Wilheim Murnau directed a highly effective but unauthorized film version titled *Nosferatu Eine Symphonie des Grauens* (Nosferatu, a Symphony of Horror).

Florence Stoker sued the production company (Prana Film) which caused its bancruptcy, and the plaintiffs had to be content with having prints destroyed. Fortunately, the picture survives as an excellent example of the German Expressionist school. Readily available on home video, the film has been extremely underrated even in its praise, for as Enno Patalas of the Film Museum of Munich (who has restored the film) reports, the recently restored German print of the film shows the brilliance of its director. All current prints showing the Vampire walking about in what appears to be broad daylight, casting reflections in the mirror, and erratic cuts cause the film to be a curiosity. A dated curiosity. However, when viewed with the proper pale blue tints for the night scenes and amber tints for candle light and greens for the underground crypts, and projected at proper projection speed with the original musical score, it becomes truly "A Symphony in Horror" with moments of terror that surpass even today's shock films. The blend of the original music makes for ultimate cinematic art in combining music and visual images with colors.

The rare flyer from Nosferatu, Prana 1922 (Courtesy - Frankfurt Archives, Germany)

An original title courtesy the Deutsches Institut für Filmkunde.

In 1924, after 6 years of trying to find a writer who could adapt Stoker's novel for the theatre, provincial play producer and actor Hamilton Deane, prompted by the urging of his wife, wrote an authorized stage production which proved so popular that he soon had two touring companies on the road. He didn't muster the courage to present it to a London audience until 1927, when he opened it at the Little Theatre on February 14 with Raymond Huntley as Dracula and himself as the vampire's nemesis, Professor Van Helsing. Despite bad critical response, the play was popular with the London audiences and ran for 391 performances.

Raymond Huntley as Count Dracula in the first stage production.

Portrait of Huntley taken around the same time period.

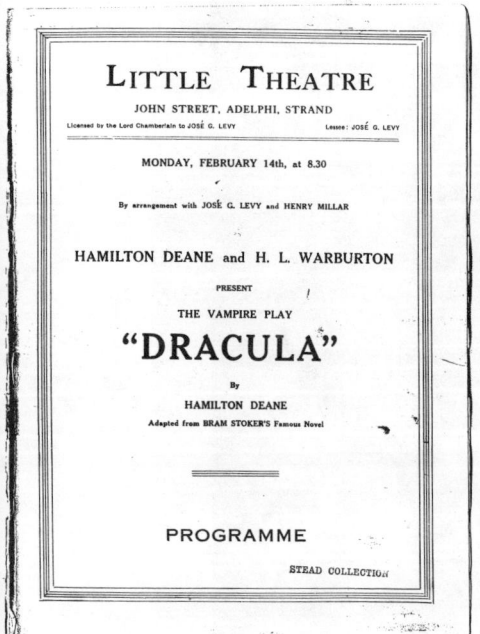

Three pages from the opening night program from the Premiere of "Dracula".

26

An American producer, Horace Liveright, saw it in March, and with very little fanfare and publicity purchased rights to produce the play in the United States.

He imediately hired John L. Balderston, London correspondent for the New York World and a noted playwright, to adapt the show for Broadway premiere.

Balderston's main task was to modernize the settings of the play and update the dialogue for the American audience.

The following pages are from the original Deane version of the play (courtesy of John Burton for the Deane estate).

(Above) Horace Liveright

(Below) John L. Balderston

ACT ONE

The study of JONATHAN HARKER's house on Hampstead Heath. An ordinary enough looking room but furnished with taste, and bearing evidence of a woman's hand in the arrangement of the furniture. There are folding doors centre. The entrance to the dining room is L.U.E. The fireplace is R. and has a broad club fender, and two large armchairs are close by. A full-sized mirror is over mantelpiece. There is another door above fireplace R.U.E. A roomy Chesterfield is set square to and actually touching wall L.

The time is just before dinner.
The season is mid-winter.

The period is today.

As THE CURTAIN RISES, Bus.

    DOCTOR SEWARD ENTERS from R. He comes briskly down stage and consults his watch, he then crosses to fireplace and compares watch with the clock on mantelpiece. He stands for a few seconds drumming impatiently with his fingers on mantelpiece.

    JONATHAN HARKER ENTERS.

SEWARD   Well, how is she now ?

HARKER   No change. Pale and listless, but doing her best to keep up a show of brightness.

SEWARD   Well this thing has beaten me. First of all Lucy and now your wife. In all my experience as a medical man I've never seen anything like it. I've tried everything I know of to get at the cause of it all, and now I'm back to where I started.

HARKER   My God, if only your friend the scientist would come !

SEWARD   I wrote him days ago describing the case fully - had a wire this morning - and I'm expecting him any minute now.

HARKER   You have great confidence in him Seward ? (Sits couch)

I - 2

SEWARD   He's an old friend, and master of mine, Professor Van Helsing of Amsterdam, who knows as much about obscure diseases as anyone in the world. He would, I know, do anything for me, for a personal reason, and we must just accept his wishes. Seemingly he is an arbitrary man. But this is only because he knows what he is talking about. He's a pilosopher and a metaphysician. One of the most advanced scientists of his day, and he has an absolutely open mind.

HARKER   Well, it seems to me that when a man of your experience admits he's up against it - this Van Helsing will have need of all his science to diagnose the case. By the way, Mina wanted to come down to dinner, but I persuaded her to let me send some up to her. She's dreadfully weak - and as Van Helsing is certain to want to see her tonight, she'll have to husband her strength.

SEWARD   Quite right, I'll have to see Van Helsing first - and give him all the details, then afterwards no doubt he'll want to see her - he's not the man to waste a moment.

HARKER   (ringing bell) The gong will be going for dinner in a moment.

    ENTER MAID.

    (to MAID) Professor Van Helsing's room is ready, isn't it ?

MAID   Yes, sir.

HARKER   Well, directly he comes show him in here.

MAID   And shall I call you sir ?

HARKER   No. Doctor Seward will see him first.

MAID   Very good, sir. (EXIT)

SEWARD   Where are the others ?

HARKER   Quincy Morris is upstairs, dressing, and you know Count Dracula never eats a thing after sunset. I left him just now superintending the placing of his extraordinary baggage in the coach house at Carfax.

SEWARD   What baggage ?

From Tod Browning: Child of the Night by Elias Savada

Tod Browning, 1880-1962

Charles Albert (Tod) Browning, born July 12, 1880, was a director generally remembered for his integral role in Hollywood's early cycle of horror films. His obsession with the absurd and the unusual originated during the late 19th Century when the lure of the circus tempted him away from public high school in Louisville, Kentucky, his home town. He quickly made his mark as a clown, acrobat, ringmaster, and contortionist. Over a span of nearly 15 years Browning would become an expert side-show barker, escape artist, and a black face comedian with the *Lizard and Coon Company*. He also portrayed the character "Mutt" in the original sketches of "Mutt and Jeff."

One of his first stunts evolved in association with a celebrated hypnotist amidst a carnival setting. Browning, billed as "The Living Corpse," would pretend to be put into a somnambulistic trance, then lowered several feet into an earthern pit and covered with dirt. A small wooden shaft allowed awestruck crowds to gaze down upon an inert body (and incidentally provide air for Browning to breathe. During slack periods Browning would eat food he had stuffed in his shirt and drink from a water bottle lowered by his partner. He toured extensively in all corners of the world, visiting locations to which he returned when time allowed later in his life.

When he was 30 years old, Browning was discovered as a potential screen slapstick clown by comedian Charles Murray. Murray introduced his new friend to another Louisvillian, D.W. Griffith, who immediately signed him to a contract to appear in several split-reel comedies produced at the Biograph Studio in New York. When Griffith became production chief for the Reliance and Majestic Companies, he made Browning the lead man with the new Komic Company brand, where he appeared opposite Fay Tincher for more than a year in the one-reel comedies that were released weekly.

By March 1915 Browning become a director for Reliance/Majestic. Beginning with *The Lucky Transfer*, Browning was responsible for the direction or writing of 12 one-to-two reelers. After making his first feature film, *Jim Bludso*, in 1917, Browning moved back East to work for Metro, but soon returned to California to film *The Legion of Death*, Metro Special de Luxe's first production to be filmed on the west coast. He married actress Alice Wilson, also known professionally as Alice Rae, at the Salem Baptist Church in New Rochelle, New York, on June 11, 1917.

By mid-1918 Browning was directing program pictures identified as Bluebird Photoplays for Universal. In 1919 he moved to Universal Special Attractions with his first release of that year, *The Wicked Darling*, significant for his initial collaboration with two other members of his profession - Waldemar Young and Lon Chaney Sr. Young, one of the most colorful and successful scenarists of his day, was admired for his ability to embellish his work with lyrical moods. Later, he would be the person responsible for the large doses of romance, murder, and suspense in most of the pictures Browning directed at MGM in the twenties. The relationship Browning developed with Lon Chaney became legendary -- one of the most renowned horror and melodrama combinations in motion picture history.

Browning's contract with Universal ended in December of 1923, his tenth anniversary in the business. His break coincided with Irving Thalberg's move to Metro.

With the release of *The Unholy Three* (MGM, 1925), he was not only listed as one of "top ten best directors in Hollywood," but his films carried the legend "A Tod Browning Production" before the main title. He continued at MGM until 1929, where he made his first talking picture, *The Thirteenth Chair*, with Bela Lugosi in a character part.

In 1932, after completing a three-picture deal with Universal, he returned to MGM where his next project, *Freaks* (1932), was considered so horrible that it was withdrawn from the theaters in just two months. He made only five more films. On January 3, 1942, he retired to his Malibu beach home with his wife, who quietly passed away on May 12, 1944.

Browning's early circus habits as a night person never changed. Often he'd be up all night talking with his bachelor brother Avery, a business executive from Pittsburgh, Pennsylvania. He lived well, having wisely invested his earnings in a Northern California grape vineyard. In his final years, he and fellow directors Allan Dwan and Victor Schertzinger were still friends. In the summer of 1962 he was diagnosed and treated for cancer of the larynx. On October 6, 1962 he suffered a fatal stroke.

Edgar Ulmer, another director generally associated with the horror genre, wrote of Browning in 1965:

"We know very little about his private life; he was reticent and introverted. At night, after work, Browning got into his car and disappeared...He was a strange man. He had a funny habit; when he was shooting a film, between takes he would get the actors and crew together and tell them the most extraordinary stories...I don't know any other director who would do such a thing so passionately. His films were very popular. The tradition he established at Universal took root, and no year went by without its quota of horror films. And then James Whale was hired. You must realize that during the silent period visual effects were all-important, more so than the relative realism of sound pictures. Until the end of his career, Browning tried to use as little dialogue as possible; he wanted visual effects. I'm pretty sure that the final shooting script for all his films was Browning's own, no matter who got credit for the scenario. I think so because, even though a number of different script writers are credited with working on his films, the final result was always representative of Browning's own personal style."

Browning, Chaney and Young on the set of THE BIG CITY, 1928

1927 - Browning, now one of MGM's top directors, had attempted to gain the rights to <u>Dracula</u> from Florence Stoker. Browning was aware of the potential of "sound movies." He was closely monitoring Douglas Shearer's experiments with a radio broadcast replacing Vitaphone's record method of sound. However, neither he nor Shearer could convince Irving Thalberg (Shearer's brother-in-law) of its practicality. Thalberg argued in a memo to Shearer that it would be difficult to have a multi-theater engagement of the films, for it would be impossible to coordinate the exact timing of each performance with the broadcast of the sound. But Browning persisted in the attempt to get Thalberg to purchase the rights for him.

There have been many speculative stories that Lon Chaney was to make *Dracula* as his first sound film. In 1927 he had no intention of making a talkie until he was sure that they were perfected. However, among Chaney's personal effects was a copy of the English version of Deane's play dated 1927 and also a later edition of the American reprint of the novel with the play advertisement on the back cover.

The American version of *Dracula* had been in preproduction in August of 1927 when Browning began filming *London After Midnight*. It is interesting to note the description of Count Dracula in the English version as presented here from Lon Chaney's personal copy of the script.

P R O L O G U E

```
   As the CURTAIN RISES it discloses the courtyard of a
vast ruined castle, from whose tall, black windows comes no
ray of light, and whose broken battlements show a jagged
line against a moon-light sky. Fifteen seconds elapse
without sound or movement, and then from the topmost window,
centre stage, leans out the figure of a tall, thin man, with
snow-white hair and long, white moustache. His hands and
feet show "dead white" in the moonlight. Leaning far out
of the window, he slowly emerges, and crawls down the castle
wall face downwards, with his cloak spreading out around
him like great winds. As his whole body emerges from the
window the CURTAIN DROPS.
```

* * * * * *

Note for actor playing DRACULA

```
   Trousers must be strapped under feet - one foot to be
secured inside window to solid rostrum. The Inverness Cape
which he wears must be heavily wired, so that when face
downwards, it assumes the shape of a Bat's Wings.
```

* * * * * *

Page from the original English version of the play

The plot of the film and the book are too close to be coincidence. The settings are two large estates, one long abandoned, filled with bats, spider webs and decay, inhabited by "vampires." There are feminine characters named Lucy with suitors named Arthur. The characters of a maid and groom walk in and out of the plot. The hero of the story is a wise older professor who has knowledge of the occult and ways of the vampire. Chaney is seen turning into mist and materializing before the bedchamber door of the heroine; and walking down a long cobweb-filled stairway holding a lantern in a black Inverness coat which concealed large bat-like wings when the hands were spread above the head. The old professor filled the house with garlic wreaths to protect Lucy. The hero, when finally convinced that "there are such things" as vampires, carves a wooden stake and sets out to destroy it in its lair. However, in the end it all turns out to be a hoax in which the old professor is actually a Scotland Yard detective portraying a vampire to expose a murderer. The story was copyrighted just a few days before the American version of the play and it was released on December 6th, 1927. *Dracula* starring Bela Lugosi opened October 5, 1927 and, significant to the chain of events, *The Jazz Singer* premiered on October 6, 1927.

The question in Hollywood was - Would Chaney play Count Dracula as his first talkie?

§

Universal's interest in Dracula had also begun in the spring of 1927. Carl Laemmle had ordered several studio readers to review the novel and play which was now quite successful in London. Here are some of the readers' response cards submitted to the Story Department in 1927:

Synopsis on
DRACULA. Novel Synopsis.   STEVE MIRANDA
By Byram Stoker   June 15, 1927

TO: DON COBB?

While this may have a fantastic opening and be very engrossing for those who like the wierd, I cannot possibly see how it is going to make a motion picture. It is blood--blood--blood---kill and everything that would cause any average human being to revolt or seek a convenient "railing". Sorry but I cannot see where there is anything in this--unless it is a desire to transpose people who are seeking to be entertained into something that is the direct antithesis of what they seek. Besides the story is anything but convincing.

Miranda.

INTER-OFFICE COMMUNICATION

To Don Cobb   June 15, 19 27
                        From Lucile de Meyers

" DRACULA "
by
Bram Stoker

COMMENT--

This is, without doubt one of the most horribly grewsome stories that has ever been written on the subject of the Vampire and his ways and methods. For a picture it is out of the question because of the censorship. The first part of the story could be shown, but from the moment you take up the part of Lucy, you run into all sorts of difficulties. You cannot cut this and hold the story - nor could you put on the screen, without much explanation the use of the Host and the garlic wreathes - the audience would never understand. This sort of thing can be gotten over on the stage - as it is at the present time - by lines, spoken to get over the horror of the thing and the mental and physical reactions of the characters - but for pictures, it must be worked out in actual picturization, action, background etc - it would the public like it, denuded as it would have to be of most of the real action and import? I doubt it! For years the picture people have been trying to find a way of doing this thing on the screen and so far they have analized what they can and cannot put of it on the screen; or in the story adaptation. It might be a novelty - but would it pay in the end? The story is fascinating to read and in this it tricks you, for you are help by the horrible drama of the thing. When I first read it, I'm frank to admit I kept my light burning all night! and then I couldn't get the thing out of my mind. This is all right until you begin to tear it to pieces to rebuild for pictures - and then you face a problem

---

INTER-OFFICE COMMUNICATION

                June 15, 1927 19
To Mr. Cobb   From Miss Hall

RE: DRACULA

Beautiful women with voluptuous mouths dripping with blood - huge bats with flapping wings - wolves with hungry mouths - vaults, dark and ominous - dusty chapels hung with cobwebs - graves - ships steered by dead men - a man with sharp, white teeth and eyes as red as fire - a vampire feeding on the blood of innocent girls and children in order to perpetuate himself and his kind - a lunatic eating flies, spiders sparrows in order to have devoured as may lives as possible all this and much, much more is contained in DRACULA.

For mystery and blood-curdling horror, I have never read its equal. For sets, impressionistic and weird, it cannot be surpassed. This story contains everything necessary for a wierd, unnatural, mysterious picture.

I understand it is now being played in London and is achieving tremendous success. It is usually the case that if a story can be played upon the stage a screen version can be written from it as well. It will be a difficult task and one will run up against the censor continually, but I think it can be done. It is daring but if done there can be no doubt as to its making money.

READ BY:
George Mitchell, Jr.
June 15, 1927

D R A C U L A   File No. ....
      By   Picture No. ....
BRAM STOKER

COMMENT   Were this story put on the screen, it would be an insult to every one of its audience. We all like to see ugly things...we are all attracted to a certain extent, to that which is hideous. (For instance....the big appeal in the Phantom of the Opera) But when it passes a certain point, the attraction dies and we suffer a feeling of repulsion and nausea. This story certainly passes beyond the point of what the average person can stand or cares to stand. In the first, you use your imagination; in the second, there is nothing left to the imagination.
In the second place, it would take a thousand titles to tell the people what it was all about.....and then they wouldn't know!

NOVEL   REVA WEIL
                                 JUNE 16, 1927

D R A C U L A
by
Bram Stoker

OPINION: ABSOLUTELY NO!! In the first place, it would be impossible to transcribe this novel of horrors to the screen. And, if it were possible, who would want to sit through an evening of unpleasantness such as a picture of this type would afford?

Pictures, after all, are made for entertainment. Mystery stories, and even thrillers, can be had without delving into the unnatural, the unearthly, the ghastly, such as is DRACULA. I am certain that Carl Laemmle, with his mind on the Universal White List, would not care to put his money into a vehicle such as this which I am sure would not be a good box-office bet.

LONDON AFTER MIDNIGHT, MGM 1927

A comparative shot from DRACULA, cut from the film.

Lon Chaney as the vampire in MGM's LONDON AFTER MIDNIGHT (1927).

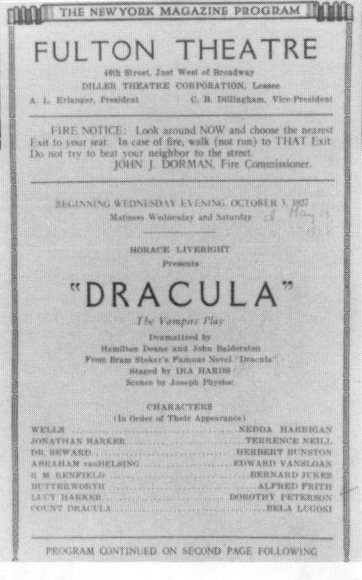

The opening night program, October 5, 1927

Opening night program from the West Coast premiere, 1928

A silent version, in fact any version of *Dracula* was set aside until the following October when the New York play opened to sellout crowds.

Bela Lugosi's dignified but saturnine appearance and heavily accented delivery created a romantic, urbane image far removed from the repulsive ancients envisioned by Stoker and Murnau. The play ran for 261 performances in New York. In Harry Ludlam's work <u>A Biography of Dracula</u>, published by The Fireside Press, W. Foulsham & Co. Ltd, 1962 he states:

"The play ran on Broadway for forty-one weeks. Deane made a bet at the start that it would earn a million dollars in twelve months; in fact it passed that figure in nine months and went on to make a fortune for Horace Liveright."

After its long season in New York, "Dracula" went on tour in the States. Raymond Huntley was invited over to take the lead with the full Broadway company, and the play opened another enormously successful run at Atlantic City. During eighteen months on the road it was retained in Chicago for five months; it broke all records for any modern play on tour in America; and in Philadelphia the takings doubled those of "Journey's End," another British record breaker...In three seasons, played by several companies throughout the United States and Canada, "Dracula" had taken more than two and a half million dollars. It eventually had the <u>New York Sunday Times</u> declaring, "'Dracula', which somebody will have to club to death if it's ever to stop, is still profitably a-tour. It will presently play Brooklyn for the fourth or fifth time."

Newspaper ad for the Atlantic City opening, 1928
(Note that Lugosi was so popular that his image was retained as Dracula.)

Edward van Sloan, Terrence Neill, Bela Lugosi, Bernard Jukes and Herbert Bunston in the original Broadway production.

Bela Lugosi went on tour with the West Coast company and opened at the Biltmore Theater in Los Angeles in 1928.

He remained in Hollywood when the company returned to the east, and appeared in several smaller parts in films for Fox, Universal and First National in 1929-30.

Bela Lugosi's casting composite - between the play and film version of *Dracula* (1929-30).

In 1929 Universal got a new chief studio executive: Carl Laemmle Jr. Eccentric and high strung, the 21-year-old son of the company's president had some ideas that ran contrary to those of many of the studio old-timers. One of them was to put *Dracula* into production on a grand scale. Despite the opposition of his advisors, Laemmle Sr. okayed the project. By 1930, his son would prove his genius as a filmmaker with the Academy Award winning *All Quiet On The Western Front*. Also, he had two fellow countrymen under contract, Paul Leni to direct and Conrad Veidt to star as the Count. Jr. wanted Browning and Chaney.

However, on September 11, 1929 Leni died unexpectedly of blood poisoning and Veidt, without Leni who had guided him through his first American talkie *The Last Warning* (1929), returned to Germany. This did not stop Jr. and even though the studio did not have the rights he proceeded with the production.

In June of 1930 Fritz Stephani submitted the following 32 page treatment to Laemmle Jr.

"DRACULA"
(A Treatment)
By
Fritz Stephani.

FADE IN on an official document held in the hand of a girl. At the top of the page is engraved in bold script "BY THE GRACE OF HIS MAJESTY, THE KING".... a girl's slender finger runs down the page, and we hear her voice reading brief excerpts to the effect that the holder of this document is qualified to act as solicitor and barrister in the doman(sic) of His Majesty, the King.

The finger finally rests on the name JOHN HARKER, and the voice ends with a note of pleasure and triumph.

The camera moves back and we see Mina Seward and John Harker seated on a divan in the library of Dr. Seward's home and sanitorium. The document is still held in the hands of Mina - John's arm is about her waist. Mina looks up at John lovingly. John tells her that now there is no reason for postponing their marriage, and asks her if she will become his wife upon his return from Hungary, where he has been called upon a matter of business. Mina consents happily and they embrace.

The young lovers are interrupted by the entrance of Dr. Seward and Lucy, a girl-friend and guest of Mina's. They congratulate John on his graduation and Dr. Seward says he has only one regret -- that John, with his analytical mind, has not chosen to serve science instead of the law.

This happy scene is intruded upon by Renfield, one of Dr. Seward's patients, who enters, catching and eating flies. The group stops talking and watch Renfield in distaste.

When Renfield sees them, he stops catching flies and his gaze concentrates upon Lucy. Slowly, with out-stretched arms, he moves toward her. He says - "Oh, the Doctor has gotten me a bride, also. Come to me, Darling." Lucy, frightened to death, hides behind the Doctor, who quiets her and sternly orders the maniac to behave himself. Renfield is disappointed -- complains that all men have women, but he must satisfy himself with spiders and flies. The attendant enters to take Renfield away. Lucy, trembling in terror, breathes relief as they disappear through the door.

Doctor Seward addresses John again and points out how interesting such a case as Renfield's is. He calls it - "Zoophgous." John replies lightly that so far as he's concerned, the Doctor can keep all the lunatics for himself -- that he prefers to deal with sane people.

The dialogue establishes that John has already received an order from his first client which will take him to Hungary, but that he is not at liberty to explain the details of his commission. He gains the Doctor's consent to marry Mina as soon as he returns.

Before John leaves, Mina presents him with a little picture of herself and Lucy, as she has no other available for a keep-sake on the voyage.
FADE OUT

(NOTE: This first sequence in England is independent of the rest of the story and can be eliminated, but I think it has a very definite value. It establishes the romance between the boy and girl; we are given a legitimate excuse for the young barrister's secret trip to Hungary; and we establish the time as modern. We are also introduced to the location where, a little later, so much important action follows in the development of the story, and in this way eliminate much explanatory dialogue, which is always a detriment to a talking picture. Another thing, which is even more important, is that the audience is introduced to our players in a normal atmosphere, which makes the weird developments later on even more striking, and which the audience continues to see and feel through the eyes and the emotions of our principals...and they are forced to believe, along with our players, however improbably, the subsequent events.)

FADE IN as John arrives in a little mountain village in Hungary. (The Swiss Village set can be used for this.) He finds quarters at the village Inn. A letter from Count Dracula is presented to him by the Innkeeper, who speaks broken English. The letter instructs John that the Count awaits him and has made arrangements for his transportation by the night coach, which will arrive about midnight on the Pass, where he will be met by the Count's private coach. John's arrangements for this trip are difficult and tiresome - (played for comedy) - and when he pronounces the name of Count Dracula, there is a sudden tenseness. The natives of the village are terror-stricken at the very name and all cross themselves. Upon learning that John is actually contemplating a visit to the castle of Count Dracula, there is a great commotion, and the fat wife of the Innkeeper, who does not speak a word of English, tries to make him understand. Repeating over and over again the name of "Dracula," she pantomimes the cutting of someone's throat, of something flying in the air - of the howling of wolves. The Innkeeper, evidently frightened, tries to quiet his wife, John, unable to understand all this commotion, which seems to him to be about nothing, insists upon starting in the coach immediately.

The old lady is almost hysterical and before John leaves, she insists opon placing a Rosary around his neck which he tries to remove. With frantic insistence and constant repetition of the words "Dracula - nein! Dracula - nein!," she replaces the Rosary around his neck, and John, to please the old lady, finally consents to wear it, hiding it beneath his shirt.

John leaves the village, a lone passenger in the coach. The postillion seems displeased at having make the trip and shows signs of uneasiness. When the Pass is reached, the postillion dismounts and tells John this is as far as he will take him. He warns John of danger - tries to persuade him to return to the Inn. Upon inquiry from John regarding so much fear and mystery, the postillion will not explain, but with a nervous look about, crosses himself.

Suddenly the howling of wolves is heard. A look of terror comes over the face of the postillion and he hurriedly mounts the box. He asks John once again if he does not wish to return to the little village. John smilingly declines. The coach is driven madly down the incline. John is left alone. The moon is full. In its light we can see the silhouette of the Castle in its grotesque outline of the 15th Century. John looks at his watch - it is 11:58. Two minutes until midnight.

A dead quietness lays over the heavy atmosphere. Only now and then the howl of a wolf is heard. John walks nervously up and down. He tries to light a cigarette and a big bat flies close over his head, extinguishing the flame of the match. John has a feeling of weirdness, but tries to shake it off.

He again checks the time by his watch. The hands point to exactly midnight and he hears in the distance the galloping hoofs of horses, and at the same time, twelve short but gruesome howls of wolves. A coach, pulled by three black horses, rushes up to him as the last howl dies away.

A driver, whose face he cannot see, but only two green points where the eyes should be, bends down toward him but does not leave his seat. He inquires curtly - "Mr. John Harker?" John nods. "The Count Dracula is expecting you." The driver motions to the door of the coach. The steps of the vehicle fall down mechanically, and also the door of the quaint old carriage opens, untouched by human hands.

John hesitates for a moment, then shrugging his shoulders, he enters the carriage. He quiets his feelings of nervousness by assuring himself that this is just an eccentric mechanical device of the Count's.

He leans forward to close the door, but before his hand reaches it, it closes with a sharp click. At the same moment, the coach starts in a mad rush toward the Castle.

It seems to have been a signal for the chorus of wolves. The rapid speed of the coach jostles John, and as he leans out of the carriage window to shout to the driver to "take it easy," he is shocked to see that there is no driver on the seat. The horses seem to be led by unseen hands. A bat is flying ahead of the carriage and he sees that they are approaching the doors of the Castle estate. Again, without visible human assistance, the huge doors which guard the estate open and the carriage enters the forecourt of the Castle. The big doors close with a bang behind him. Nobody receives him, but as he approaches the castle again the doors are opened before him and closed behind him.

He wanders through many queer-looking rooms which are lighted by torches, always guided by this mysterious opening and closing of door. (sic) He does not encounter a human soul, but in every room stands a coffin.

At last he reaches a room where a lamp is burning on a table, and to his surprise he finds his baggage is already there. A note attached to it reads:

My dear Friend:
Pardon me for not receiving you personally.
Please consider this room as your own and refresh yourself from your tiresome journey.
I will be with you within the hour.
Count Dracula.

As John finishes reading the note, he hears the scream of a little child - "Mother, Mother!", and at the same time the wild pounding of fists against the big castle doors, and a woman's voice screaming, "Give me back my child, you fiend! Give her back to me!"

As he looks out of the very tall, narrow window, he sees a woman pounding frantically upon the closed doors. Mingled with her screams is the howling of wolves. A voice, coming from nowhere, shouts the command to quiet her. The howling of the wolves increases as the command is given, but the woman will not be quieted. Again the voice commands quiet and is answered by a terrific howl of many wolves - then dead stillness.. and the screams of the woman are heard no more.

John shudders - braces himself - tries to regain his self-possession. He turns from the window and crosses the room where, in one corner, he finds a wash basin. Opening his luggage, he takes out some necessary articles, together with a mirror which he places on the wall. He is just in the act of shaving when he is suddenly startled by a voice behind him -

"Ah-h, my friend, John Harker, has at last arrived. An honor for me to meet you."

Shocked to death, John turns and looks into the smiling, satirical, mystic face of a tall ma, (sic) who stands close behind him. John can hardly yet believe his eyes, as the room is reflected in the mirror and the Count's figure, standing directly behind him, is not reflected.

John's sudden movement has caused him to cut himself slightly with the razor. Bowing, he addresses the Count - "I presume I have the honor to speak to Count Dracula." But he does not receive any reply. The cut on his face is slowly bleeding; the eyes of the Count start blazing with a sort of maniacal fury and he suddenly grabs John by the throat, but just as suddenly draws away as his hands touch the beads of the Rosary.

Dracula's whole manner changes instantly. The fury passes so suddenly that John is unable to believe that anything unusual had actually occured. The cynical smile reappears on the Count's face - "Forgive me, my friend." He points to the mirror as he speaks - "This wretched thing has done the mischief. It is a foul bauble of man's vanity. Away with it!" His terrible hand reaches out for the mirror and dashes it to the floor, shattering it ino a thousand pieces. John's nerves recover slowly, and in an endeavor to handle the situation lightly, he addresses the Count somewhat ironically - "Forgive me, Count. If I had known that the mirror would have upset you, I would not have brought it."

This irony seems lost on the Count. He bows and asks politely if John will come to the library and relate what he has accomplished toward the fulfillment of the commission given him.

Finishing his toilet hurriedly, John follows the Count to the library - feeling that he has a very eccentric client indeed.

Seated at the table in the library, the Count's manner is that of a perfect, suave gentleman. He first inquires politely of John as to whether or not his journey was a pleasant one. John questions him about the fears of the peasants for the castle, but receives only negative answers from the Count, who tells him that unfortunately his country-people are very superstitious. Then, he cleverly changes the subject and begins to discuss the business matter which has brought John to Hungary.

As John takes out some business papers, the picture of the two girls, which John has received from Mina on his departure, falls on the table. The Count's interest is awakened immediately. He asks for the picture, and seeing the two beautiful girls, he asks who they are. John tells him that one of them is his bride-to-be, and the other is her girl friend - and as it happens, the old house which he has secretly purchased for the Count is situated next to the home of Mina, which will make them neighbors.

The Count asks John if he has followed fully his instructions and completed the purchase secretly and unknown to anyone else, anywehre. (sic) John assures him that no one knows of the purchase and that he has taken special care not to mention the name of his client to anybody. The Count praises him, and expresses his thanks for providing him, at the same time, with such lovely neighbors.

He inquires again carefully if anyone knows his name or where John has journeyed to. John again assures him that the desired secrecy has been preserved, and is known only to himself and the Count.

The Count, ironic and suave, tells John that he has not enough praise for such cleverness -- but, that a secret is only a secret so long as it is in possession of only one person, and regrets that for this reason he finds himself forced to eliminate the other person possessing it.

John does not get the full significance of this at first, but when the Count leaves the room and he tries to follow to ask for an explanation, he finds that the door behind the Count is closed and locked. He is a prisoner. He understands now the terrible meaning of the Count's words.

He rushes to the window to see if there is a chance for escape from there. He finds that the window is at a great height from the ground. Suddenly he sees the Count's head coming through another window, then slowly his whole body emerges. The Count begins to crawl down the castle wall above that dreadful abyss, face down - with his cloak spreading out around him like great wings.

John watches in horror. He tres to cry out but cannot. At last, finding his voice, he calls to the Count. A blood-curdling laugh is the only response he receives. He continues to watch the Count's movements, spellbound.

Reaching the court below, the Count carries seven coffin-like boxes from a hole in the wall of the castle. A short distance away, the immense wings of a big aeroplane can be seen. It looks like a huge bat. The Count loads the big boxes in the plane, then the sound of an engine starting can be heard, and the gigantic plane flies away, accompanied by the chorus of howling wolves.

John, maddened, rushes to the door - tries violently to open it, but the strong construction will not give way under the pressure which he can exert.

He goes frantically over every inch of the walls, but cannot find a weakness in them anywhere. All his efforts are useless. Exhausted, he breaks down, but realizes he must escape and that the window is the only chance.

He climbs through the window and slowly starts on his dangerous path down the steep castle wall. His hand loosens a stone and he falls.....

FADE OUT

FADE IN- England... Count Dracula's plane arrives just before sun-up. He unloads the coffins in the house next to Dr. Seward's home. He conceals the plane in a big barn on the old country estate, and then enters the house just as the sun rises in the East.

Nobody has seen the peculiar procedure of his arrival. The only sign of anything unusual going on in the neighborhood is heard through the loud howling of the dogs. The howls disturb the quietness of the morning and cause Mina and Lucy to waken.

Lucy seems very nervous, but the more sensible Mina tells her that the noise is only caused by neighborhood dogs, howling for no reason at all. But Lucy explains that her nervousness has not been caused by that alone..she has had a terrible dream... Mina points to the beauty of the sunrise, and Lucy soon quiets down..when suddenly the laughter of a maniac is heard. It is Renfield, who has again escaped his attendant.

In the library, Dr. Seward is busy over some studies as Renfield bursts in. He demands from the Doctor a bird, saying that he is sick and tired of spiders and flies. Questioned as to why he wants a bird, he explains that at first he wanted flies, then spiders, because spiders eat flies... and that birds eat spiders, and so - as the Doctor can plainly see - a bird has more lives than the other insects -- and lives is what he wants. When the Doctor refuses Renfield the bird, he curses him and Dr. Seward is unable to quiet the raving Renfield.

Lucy and Mina enter the room. When Renfield sees Lucy, he bows courteously and addresses her - "Oh, my beautiful bride!" The appearance of Lucy has changed a raving maniac into a man as mild as a lamb, and when the attendant enters to get his escaped patient, Renfield follows him without a struggle. Lucy is almost sick with fright. Dr. Seward compliments her on the power she seems to possess over Renfield. She shudders at this compliment, but the Doctor pats her on the shoulder and says, "Don't be afraid. That poor lunatic, properly handled, is like a child."

FADE OUT

FADE IN. It is two weeks later and Dr. Seward is seated at his desk, writing a telegram to his friend and prominent scientist, Professor Van Helsing. He writes:

"My dear Friend:
Grave happenings have befallen my house. Lucy, the girl friend of Mina, and a guest here in our home, has just died of a mysterious illness which I cannot analyze. Now my own child, Mina shows the same symptoms. I beg of you to come at once.
Urgently,
Seward."

As the Doctor finishes this unpleasant task, the butler announces Count Dracula, who enters immediately. He addresses the Doctor and introduces himself as Count Dracula. He says he has been his neighbor for two weeks and that he has heard of the terrible misfortune that has befallen his house...he desires to express his sympathy, and also offer his services in case the Doctor may need them... He explains that he has had some experience in the Far East with mysterious diseases and pleads that he may be shown the patient, Mina.

The Doctor thanks him for his courtesy and kindness and asks him to follow to the drawing room where Mina lies on the divan, pale and ill. The Count is introduced and it is plainly seen that his presence works wonders on the almost lifeless Mina. She seems to regain some of her vitality and her old vivacity while in his presence. He even succeeds in making her laugh.

At last the Count retires. Dr. Seward has not words sufficient to thanks the Count, who also offers, in case the necessity should arise, his blood for a transfusion.

Immediately after the Count leaves, the howling of a wolf is heard and a big bat flashes past the window...and the pleading voice of Mina is heard asking for the Count. FADE OUT

FADE IN: The next morning as Prof. Van Helsing arrives. Mina's condition is worse. Dr. Seward explains to his old friend the pitiful symptoms which have caused the death of Lucy and which are now painfully apparent in Mina...great nervousness, fear and dread of sleep...terrible dreams and...mysterious loss of blood. Outwardly, the symptoms are those of Anemia, but two blood transfusions have not helped her condition. Mina's case is also aggravated by the fact that she has not heard from her fiance, who is away and was expected to return over a week ago.

The Doctor also tells Van Helsing of the mysterious little marks on the girl's throat which he says might have been caused by a pin -- and that they were also to be seen on the throat of Lucy before she died. Dr. Seward is frantic. Van Helsing becomes very serious. Before he can answer, Renfield rushes into the room. This time he demands a cat. As he is led away by the attendant, Van Helsing seems to have dismissed the cause of Mina's illness and his interest is concentrated on Renfield and his symptoms. He asks the Doctor many questions.

Presently he asks to see Mina. At first she refuses to allow him to examine the little points on her throat, but when he has finally persuaded her and has looked at them through his microscope, he grows more serious than ever, and demands to see Renfield again.

The two men return to the Doctor's office where Renfield is brought in by the attendant. Professor Van Helsing takes something out of his bag and holds it in front of Renfield, who, with a scream, stumbles back and shudderingly covers his face with his nervous hands. Renfield is led out again.

Dr. Seward asks for an explanation. Van Helsing tells him that the herb is Wolfbane, a preventative medicine, but he refuses to explain further, demanding that the Doctor leave everything to him. He requests that Renfield be watched secretly. He must leave immediately to prepare and arrange certain matters to prevent any further danger for Mina. He takes from his bag a lot of garlic-blossom and instructs the Doctor to place this blossom around the neck of Mina, and also above her head at night when she retires, and under no circumstances to permit anybody to remove the herbs. Doctor Seward considers all this rather foolish and asks for an explanation, but Van Helsing, who is very sincere, refuses explanation and asks again to be trusted. He also warns against the lunatic, Renfield, having any liberty.

Just as Van Helsing is leaving the house in a motor-car, a scream is heard. The Doctor rushes into the house recognizing the voice of Mina. Going to her bed, he finds she has fainted away and is holding a newspaper clutched in her hand. The article which Mina has been reading, says-

"The Hampstead Horror.
Attack of small children has been committed after dark by a beautiful woman. Nobody seems to know her. Narratives of three small girls, all under ten years of age, tally in essential details - each child speaks of a beautiful lady in white who

37

gave them chocolates, enticed her to some secluded corner and there kissed and fondled her and bit her slightly in the throat. The wounds are trivial. The children suffered no other harm and do not seem to have been frightened. Indeed, one small girl told her mother she hoped she might see the beautiful lady again."

Dr. Seward is dumbfounded by the mention in the article of the same marks which have appeared on the throats of Lucy and Mina.

While he still holds the paper in his hand, Mina wakens from her faint and moans - "Oh ,no, Lucy -- don't! Don't!" But when her father questions her, she refuses any explanation. She only tells him that she does not know why she has fainted. She does not remember, when her father reminds her, that she has mentioned the name of Lucy. Mina's body seems to have shrunk to almost nothing, and it is plain that the crisis of her illness has arrived.

Dr. Seward, in his need for help, rushes over to Dracula's home to summon him for assistance, but does not get any response at the door, either from Dracula or any of his servants. The Doctor is slightly puzzled and as he rushes back to his own place, the hideous laughter of Renfield is heard coming through the window where he has been observing the Doctor.

He cries - "You will never find the Master! You will never find the Master!" His maniacal laughter follows the distressed Doctor into the house... FADE OUT

FADE IN.....It is evening again. Sadly, Dr. Seward stands at his office window watching the sun disappear behind the mountains. It is the time of each day when Mina's condition always grows worse.

Suddenly, a terrific scream pierces the silence.

The Doctor recognizes his daughter's voice. He rushes to her room. A great bat is sitting on the window sill, and Mina is almost convulsive with fright. When Dr. Seward chases the bat away, the howling of dogs (resembling the howl of wolves) is heard. This weird howling increases the girl's nervousness. The attendant enters and reports to Dr. Seward that his "pet luny"(sic), Renfield, has again mysteriously escaped. Dr. Seward, at his wit's end, and still attending his fainting daughter, is interrupted again by the maid's entrance. She announces Count Dracula.

The name of Dracula works an immediate change in Mina for the better, and when the Count enters the sick room, she seems to become herself again.

Dr. Seward thanks Dracula for his kindness in coming over, and asks him to excuse him for a few moments as he has to recapture a patient who has escaped.

Dracula assures him he is delighted to stay with the patient.

Dr. Seward and the attendant leave in search of Renfield and track him to the house of Dracula. They find him at the entrance, but Renfield refuses to leave the spot. He curses and snarls at them and says the Master will make them pay for taking him away. At last he is overpowered and brought back.

As the reach the gate of the Sanitorium, the car of Professor Van Helsing drives up. He inquires what has happened and Dr. Seward starts to explain. We leave them as Dr. Seward starts to relate the events which have occurred during the Professor's absence, and CUT TO

Mina's room, where she and Count Dracula seem to have become great friends in the short time they have been together. Using the excuse of desiring a glass of water, and after pretending to ring for the maid, who, of course, does not answer, Dracula leaves the room. He finds the maid in the ante-room asleep. She awakens with a start and excuses herself for not having heard the bell, and says that so much disturbance and mystery in the house of late has caused her loss of sleep. She also complains of a headache.

Dracula tells her he can cure her headache and offers her his help, which she accepts. He takes advantage of her submission and hypnotizes her, commanding her to obey him in all things. He orders her to remove the garlic blossom and the wolfbane which will be placed around the person of Mina that night, and to open the windows of her room. He then returns to Mina's room.

Ban(sic) Helsing and Dr. Seward have now entered the Doctor's office where the Doctor is still relating what has occurred during the absence of the professor. He tells about the almost constant howling of dogs which resembles more the howl of wolves; about the article in the paper. Van Helsing tells him to wait as he hasn't sufficient proof to back up his suspicions yet. In the meantime, he would like to meet Count Dracula. The words are scarcely out of his mouth when Count Dracula enters.

Clever repartee follows between Van Helsing and Dracula, pointing to the suspicion which Van Helsing has. Van Helsing is playing with a pair of paper scissors, which are on the desk. He cuts himself and as the blood comes out of the wound, Van Helsings gives a slight exclamation of pain and holds up the finger which is oozing blood. Dracula, seeing the blood, makes a spasmodic start for Van Helsing, and then with great effort, regains control of himmself. He turns away to avoid seeing the blood.

Van Helsing watches him closely for a moment, then holds the bleeding finger in front of Dracula. Dracula makes a sudden snap at the finger, but Van Helsing turns quickly away, covering the blood with a handkerchief. Dracula apologizes , saying he only wanted to look at the injured finger.

Suddenly, a loud pounding is heard at the entrance to the house. A voice demands to be admitted. Van Helsing and Seward rush out. The Count remains in the Doctor's office. As soon as the two men are gone, he quickly disappears through the door which leads to that part of the house used for the sanatorium.

The man demanding entrance is John. His clothes are torn and his general appearance indicates that he has gone through many hardships. Quickly he explains that his client in Hungary must have been a maniac - that he had disappeared in a plane for England and left John a prisoner. In his attempt to escape from the castle, he had fallen and injured himself severely. A band of roving gypsies had picked him up and nursed him back to life. As soon as he was able to travel, and without money, he had made his way back to England as fast as possible to prevent the maniac from committing more crimes. He tells them he has already inspected the house he had secretly purchased for Count Dracula and has found it empty. The only evidence of the presence of Count Dracula is the aeroplane in the barn, and to prevent Dracula's escape, he has wrecked the engine.

John is informed that Dracula is at present a guest in the house -- and Dr. Seward assures him that he must be mistaken regarding Dracula as he has found him to be a perfect gentleman, and also to have a very soothing effect on Mina, who is quite ill.

Before the Doctor has finished the sentence, Van Helsing breaks in excitedly - "Come, come! -- Before it is too late! That fiend is after Mina!"

When they reach Mina's room , they find Dracula gone and Mina lifeless -- seemingly dead. Van Helsing counts her pulse and orders a quick blood transfusion which may save the girl's life. Upon being questioned, Van Helsing promises to explain everything after the operation....there is no time to lose.

John gives his blood for the transfusion. Mina regains consciousness slowly and as she wakens and sees John, a smile comes over her face, John bends down to kiss her. Over her gentle, sweet face creeps the horrible expression which we have witnessed in Dracula at the sight of blood.

Vividly alert, Van Helsing notices the change, and before Mina's lips can touch John, he tears the two apart. Mina, with a sigh of relief, sinks exhausted on her pillows. John demands furiously an explanation of Van Helsing's action. Before Van Helsing can answer, Mina reaches for his hand, and in her sweet voice, thanks the professor for saving her sweetheart -- and then falls into a deep sleep.

John and Seward are very unhappy and puzzled as they watch Van Helsing arranging the protective blossoms around the person of Mina. As the men pass the maid in the anteroom, Van Helsing tells her that under no circumstances is she to leave her post, and to call for assistance at the slightest noise. They exit to the library.

As soon as they disappear, a curtain moves and the fiendish, smiling face of Dracula appears. He commands the maid to do as he has ordered -- to remove the flowers from Mina.

In the library, Van Helsing tells Dr. Seward and John that his suspicions are confirmed, and that they not only had to deal with a maniac, but with a Vampire -- with an "Undead". But he cannot understand how it is possible for Dracula to exist here in England, as according to rules, the Vampires has to be in a coffin containing the earth in which he has been buried at his natural death, before sunrise of each day.

When John tells him about the seven coffins which Dracula had carried with him in the aeroplane, there is no more doubt about Dracula being a Vampire.

(NOTE: This dialogue can be very brief and still sufficient to explain clearly Dracula's existence as a Vampire and his power over bats and wolves.)

Van Helsing begs John to forgive him for so rudely separating him from Mina a few minutes before, but explains that he had done it to save him from the same fate of Lucy and Mina, and possibly the maniac, Renfield, who has already become the creature of the Vampire. He would also have become the slave of Dracula, had he allowed Mina to kiss him.

John groans as he hears that his Mina is already in the power of Dracula. Van Helsing explains that the only way to free these unhappy creatures from Dracula's power is through the death of the Master Vampire. To do so they must find the coffins and destroy them -- and so, unable to return to his lair, and unable to reach by aeroplane before sunrise the earth necessary for his survival, the Vampire must die -- there would be no possible escape for Dracula tonight.

At this moment the attendant rushes in and says that the lunatic, Renfield, has escaped again. He had been watching Renfield closely in his cell as he talked nonsense to a big bat which had been sitting on the window, when suddenly he disappeared through the window, When he got outside to look for him, Renfield had vanished.

Another horrifying scream is suddenly heard, coming from Mina's room. Rushing to her, they find the maid lying unconscious on the floor of the ante-room and Renfield guarding the door to her room. Renfield puts up an almost superhuman struggle to prevent their entrance, at the same time shouting that the Master does not want to be disturbed.

Finally, John gains entrance. The picture he sees is terrifying. Dracula stands in the middle of the room, his arms about Mina -- sucking blood from her throat.

Dracula repulses John's efforts to free Mina with one arm while he holds the girl with the other. His eyes are burning, sadistic -- and Mina's blood is seen in the corner of his mouth.

John's shirt has been torn open in the fight and the cross of the Rosary is revealed on his chest. As Dracula sees it, he steps back. The terrific fight with Dracula has left John utterly exhausted, but as his hand touches the cross, he gains new strength.

Realizing from Dracula's action that the cross has some undefined power over him, he lifts it and holding it in front of him, moves toward Dracula. Dracula lets go of Mina, who falls to the floor, and backs away from the cross. Unearthly noises issue from his throat, as defeated, he is forced into a corner of the room.

Dr. Seward and Van Helsing, having disposed of Renfield, rush into the room. Dracula sees them and making a flying leap, he passes John and disappears through the window, spreading his cloak like wings.

They make a brief examination of Mina and Van Helsing declares that with God's help there is a chance of saving her, but that another visit from the Vampire will surely kill her. He lays a little gold cross on her forehead which brings the life slowly and sluggishly back through her veins. Removing the Cross, they see it has left its imprint. Van Helsing declares the mark will vanish when the Vampire is killed -- and its disappearance will be the sign that Mina is clean again. John urges them to hasten to Dracula's home.

The flowers are replaced around Mina, and leaving her in care of the attendants and the maid, they hurry in the night to find Dracula.

John, Dr. Seward and Van Helsing, with weapons such as knives and guns, proceed to search the mysterious home of Dracula.

They are astonished to find the house empty. The filthy, dark, mysterious rooms, full of spider webs, do not reveal anything of the Count or his coffins.

The only living things about the place are the bats that are flying about the deserted rooms. After a long search, they finally find, hidden in a dark damp room, five of the coffins, but the other two are missing.

Destroying the five and sprinkling Holy water over the earth they have contained, they continue their search for the other two.

In another room, the only one which seems to have been inhabited, they find another coffin and some things belonging to the Count, such as title deed to the house, clothes, and great stacks of money - notes of the Bank of England.

Footsteps are heard. Van Helsing holds up his hand, warning in a low voice - "Be ready. It is probably the Count." Instinctively the men part - John next to the door, Dr. Seward in front of the window and Van Helsing next to the coffin. They prepare themselves for an attack. Slowly and cautiously the footsteps approach. The Count is evidently expecting a surprise.

Suddenly he leaps into the middle of the room, laughing with a terrible laughter. John, determined to kill the Count at any cost in order to save his sweetheart, springs towards him, swinging a terrific blow with his knife - which would have cut the Count in two, had he not sidestepped it with inhuman swiftness. The Count quickly grabs the bundle of banknotes, but before he can reach the door, Van Helsing has blocked his path, holding the Cross in front of him.

The mysterious power of the Cross forces the monster, eyes blazing in anger and hellish rage, to stop. Dr. Seward follows the lead of Van Helsing, and the two are forcing Dracula into a corner. However, John in his madness, has lost all sense of precaution and jumps in wild abandon at the Count.

Dracula gives him a terrible blow and he falls to the floor, bringing down Van Helsing with him in his fall.

Dracula jumps quickly over the bodies of the two men and before Dr. Seward can prevent him, a loud crash of glass is heard and Dracula jumps through the window and reaches the court below, unhurt. He turns and looks back at the men mockingly, his fiendish, terrifying laughter ringing out - "Ah! You fools! You tried to destroy Dracula! ...I - the Master of the undead! Yes, you found my hiding place, but where is the seventh casket? Fools. to dare me!....Your women are mine and through them, you and others shall be mine! The whole world shall be my creatures!......I will come back."

When the astonished men have regained their senses, Dracula has vanished in a fog and you can see the approach of the new day in the distant sky.

"He will come back," Van Helsing repeats -- "That means he must have returned to Hungary. But how...? He cannot use the trains as the customs office would find his body when they inspect the coffin. He cannot take the chance. His plane is destroyed. The only way he could possibly go is by water -- and in half an hour it will be sunrise. We must be quick to prevent him."

John curses himself for having been the cause of Dracula's escape, but Van Helsing quiets him, saying that Dracula can do no more mischief today as the sun will be up in half an hour, and Dracula must be in his coffin...but they must hurry and reach the harbor before that time.

When they reach the harbor in their car, the first beams of the sun break through and a ship is seen slowly leaving as day breaks. From an old coast guardsman, they learn that the mysterious rental of a small yacht had been made by a stranger during the night before. He had paid the crew and the captain a fabulous sum to ship a heavy coffin-like box to a place called Galatz, on the mouth of the Danube River, where it would be received by someone who would be there waiting. The Captain had at first refused, but the price offered was so large, that he had finally accepted. Then, mysteriously, the stranger had disappeared and returned again just before sunrise, carrying the coffin-like box himself, although later it had taken three sailors to lift it.

After giving very detailed instructions as to where and how to place the box on the boat, and handing over the money to the Captain, the man gave the order to sail exactly at sunrise. A fog settled over the boat and as it cleared away, the mysterious stranger had departed, and as the sun was rising, the Captain, according to his instructions, pulled anchor and sailed away.

"Oh, God!" exclaimed John. "It is my fault -- we are too late! Mina and Lucy are lost forever!"

"Calm yourself, my boy. We have missed him but everything is not lost. We will beat the Count at his own game. We must overtake him before he can reach the castle. If we travel by train, it is possible that we can reach Galatz before the boat. We must take Mina along - we cannot take the chance of leaving her here alone -- and she will perhaps be a valuable decoy in our pursuit of Dracula."

Through LAP DISSOLVE of train and boat, we see John, Mina, Dr. Seward and Van Helsing making their desperate journey - with everything at stake, to reach Galatz before the boat. At last they reach the port, but they are too late. The boat had docked an hour before and they were told by the Captain that a man by the name of Immanuel Hildesheim had claimed the cargo.

In the office of Hildesheim they learn the important information that he had received a letter from London telling him to receive the cargo and to avoid the usual inspection of the customs officer. He transferred the box, according to instructions, to a Slovak by the name of Skinsky, who is a river-trader. He had been paid for his work in English banknotes.

The short search for Skinsky ends when they find him dead on the river bank, with his throat slashed. A woman's voice cries that it is the work of the gypsies who have gone on up the river.

Skinsky's trading boat is gone, and unable to determine whether or not Dracula and his coffin are on board, Van Helsing orders John and Dr. Seward to pursue the boat while he travels with Mina by land to the castle. Seward and John rent a motor launch and the desperate chase starts.

Information they receive from passing boats leads them to believe that the body of Dracula is transported by a band of gypsies, who are sailing like madmen up the river. But each time they reach a given destination where they hope to overtake them, the gypsies have already departed.

Finally, in the distance, they can see the silhouette of the castle. They are gaining on the boat carrying Dracula and his coffin -- have almost reached it, when the gypsies come to a sudden halt and the coffin is transferred to a long litter-wagon. The gypsies divide themselves, part of them mounting horses to rush the coffin to the castle, the others remaining to prevent the Doctor and John from landing.

A terrible fight ensues with John's and Dr. Seward's guns spitting fire.

In the meantime the gypsies, rushing with the coffin on the wagon, are approaching the castle gates where Van Helsing and the trembling Mina are watching the outcome of the battle, the rapid approach of the wagon, and the slowly setting sun.

At last John and Dr. Seward gain the shore. John knocks a gypsy from his horse, mounts, and rides madly after the gypsies and the wagon. They are now over half way to the castle, where Van Helsing with faint hope, stands -- gun in hand -- to prevent their entrance.

Dr. Seward holds the gypsies in check at the boat so they cannot follow John.

Just before the wagon reaches the castle, John overtakes the gypsies and makes an unsuccessful attempt to break into the cortege in an effort to reach the coffin.

Just one more turn in the road and they will reach the Castle gates.

Just as the wagon reaches the gate, it overturns in its mad rush, and the coffin crashes at the feet of Mina and Van Helsing -- shattered to pieces. The corpse of Dracula is exposed just as the sun sinks down in the west.

The gypsies, terrified when they see what they have been carrying, shriek and fly in all directions in moral fear. Mina screams loudly. The howling of wolves is heard in increasing volume.

As the sun disappears on the horizon, the body of the Count slowly comes to life. But John is too quick for the Vampire this time. Using the broken spoke of the wagon as a weapon, he drives it with superhuman force through the Vampire's heart -- his body shrinking to nothing.

Mina faints. Van Helsing and John bend over her as her father comes into the scene. Her body seems lifeless. John cries out --"Oh God --after all, we are too late -- she is dead!"

Before Van Helsing has a chance to answer John, Mina's eyes open and her old sweet smile reappears. She looks up at John, who holds her in his arms, Then her eyes wander questioningly to Van Helsing as John Screams:

"Look, look! The cross has disappeared from her forehead!" Van Helsing, with tears in his eyes, answers:

"Yes, my children. It is all over. You have earned your happiness as none before. Through your love and courage you have given many restless souls peace and perhaps saved humanity from destruciton. God bless you."

John and Mina fall in each others' arms...as we...
FADE OUT.

THE END

(NOTE: I would like to suggest that the attendant at the sanatorium is played for comedy and that his remarks concerning the constant escape of Renfield are made in very dry cockney English. This will afford some relief to the intense and dramatic atmosphere of the story. It may be even advisable to take him along to Hungary and through his clumsiness, make the situation of the chase more interesting.)

Fritz Stephani with Buster Crabbe and Jean Rogers on the Universal backlot during the shooting of FLASH GORDON, 1936 (Stephani directed).

"Return of the Phantom" to be Made By Universal With Full Sound Effects

Carl Laemmle Acquires Full Screen Rights To "Phantom of the Opera" Sequel By Gaston Leroux

THE "Phantom" is coming back. Universal has definitely decided to make a sequel to the famous "Phantom of the Opera," the mystery spectacle of several years ago, which holds the record of the Universal sales department for gross business.

The new picture will be "The Return of the Phantom," and it will be made with full dialogue and sound effects. The full significance of this will be appreciated when it is recalled that the original "Phantom," besides including a brilliant masked ball in the foyer of the big Parisian opera house, and glorious scenes from a popular opera, also was featured by stirring organ playing by the Phantom himself and many scenes of intense drama.

"The Return of the Phantom" is by Gaston Leroux, the famous French mystery writer, who wrote the original "Phantom." When he saw Universal's "Phantom" at the Paris opening he was so pleased that he conceived the idea for a sequel to the story. He died before the new manuscript was completed, but he left the plot well outlined and the story far enough along for Universal to develop it.

Universal has just acquired all screen rights to this manuscript from Madame Leroux, his widow. The rights even include television rights.

No announcement is yet possible as to the cast or director for "The Return of the Phantom." It will be remembered that Lon Chaney created the character of the Phantom in the original. Mary Philbin, Arthur Edmund Carewe, Norman Kerry, Snitz Edwards, Gibson Gowland, Virginia Pearson and others were in the cast. Rupert Julian directed it, with Edward Sedgwick adding supplementary scenes.

"The Return of the Phantom" is regarded by Universal officials as a "natural" for sound and dialogue, because of its unlimited musical and operatic angles and for its dramatic dialogue possibilities. Also, the possibilities of the opera house interiors and the stage effects in technicolor are said to appeal strongly to the Universal production heads as excellent working material.

Meanwhile... In 1929, Chaney's last two films had been released with scores and sound effect tracks. His first sound test had been in 1928 for *The Big City*, also directed by Tod Browning. Universal had been trying to lure Chaney back, knowing that his contract with MGM was nearing an end. They proposed a 3 picture deal, a remake of the earlier Chaney/Browning 1921 Universal film *Outside the Law*, *Dracula*, and *The Return of the Phantom*. It appears that Chaney was considering the offer. Both his brother George and his son Creighton related that Chaney had an excessive fear of poverty stemming from his early show business days. Often he would have to write home for money. Chaney's parents were living comfortably in Colorado Springs and were there to help him and his new wife and baby son. But the memory of those early stage days, travelling the west and midwest, always out of cash, haunted him even when he had millions in the bank and owned several homes. His contract was coming up for renewal, but his benefactor, Irving Thalberg, was losing a power struggle with L.B. Mayer. (Chaney never trusted Mayer. After he saw his friend John Gilbert's career ruined by Mayer, he trusted him even less.) The studio itself was threatened. Marcus Loew, one of the three founders of MGM, had died two years before and his family was no longer interested in the entertainment business. Secretly, Wm. Fox (Fox Studios) had purchased controlling interest in Loew's theater chain from the Loew family and was about to take over the studio. The situation was aggravated in Chaney's mind by the stock market crash in October of 1929. Now he was certainly not about to be left without a contract to secure his future income.

Then unexpectedly Chaney got sick, and for the first time in his picture career took a leave of absence. It was found that he had developed pernicious anemia, following a tonsilectomy and a life-threatening bout with pneumonia caught while filming *Thunder*, his last picture under the old MGM contract. The incision in his throat would not heal properly but he stubbornly went back to work, against doctor's orders, too soon after the operation. Although confident of a fast recovery, he had stated that he could no longer portray characters involving painful makeup devices. Even the five previous pictures, *Laugh Clown Laugh*, *While the City Sleeps*, *West of Zanzibar*, *The Big City* and *Where East is East* were all character parts involving little or no elaborate makeup and certainly Dracula would have been the perfect role, for it would have only involved false fingernails, sharpened teeth and different hair shadings. Browning, in turn, had begun filming an all-talking mystery for MGM titled *The Thirteenth Chair*, with Bela Lugosi portraying a mystic. Upon its completion Browning had signed on with Universal in anticipation of filming *Dracula* with Chaney.

Then several unforeseen events changed the course of film history:

The Fox takeover attempt of 1929 had failed through fast maneuvering in Washington by Louis B. Mayer. The government filed an anti-trust suit against Fox. Shortly after, Wm. Fox was incapacitated due to a car accident, and his own studio was bought out by 20th Century in late 1935. Thalberg and Mayer remained in power and were even stronger allies. So Chaney signed on with MGM for another five years, leaving Browning in a spot. Chaney's first MGM talking picture was announced: a fast-paced adventure called *The Bugle Sounds* (to be directed by Jack Conway).

He was now the nation's number one box office attraction. Knowing that his millions of fans were anxiously awaiting his talking debut, he refused to delay production any longer. But he was too weak to meet the demands of the part of a "hard-boiled Foreign Legion sergeant." Thalberg substituted a less strenuous part by remaking Chaney's 1925 silent hit *The Unholy Three* giving Chaney the chance to talk in five different voices. Jack Conway replaced Tod Browning as director and it was completed in the late spring of 1930.

On June 23, 1930 Chaney was diagnosed as having cancer and put on sick leave by L.B. Mayer. (His illness was extremely underplayed by Mayer, who feared MGM stock would drop and the loan out to Universal would fall through.)

The Unholy Three was released on July 6, 1930 to tremendous reviews while Chaney was in New York seeing specialists.

By the end of July, 1930, Universal was close to acquring the rights to *Dracula*.

Chaney returned to California on the first week of August and went to his cabin for a rest. He returned to Hollywood, but on August 20th was rushed to the hospital.

On August 22 Universal officially obtained the rights to *Dracula*. These rights included the Deane/Balderston play as well as another play version by Charles Morrel.

On August 25 MGM announced that "they were pleased with the reported progress of the actor and declared their belief in his ultimate recovery."

On August 26, 1930 Chaney died alone in St. Vincent's hospital due to internal bleeding in the lungs. The "official" cause of death was termed 'carcinoma of right lower and slight of upper bronchus with Pulmonary hemorrhage not T.B. as a contributing factor.' He was 47.

Universal announced that "almost $400,000" would be spent on the production -- an impressive sum from a studio in financial trouble at a time when half that amount constituted an "A" budget. The worst fears of the New York office were manifested by the death of their bankable name star, Lon Chaney. Browning was devastated. He had already had to complete *Outside The Law* with Edward G. Robinson playing Chaney's role. Now there would be no *Dracula*! (The death haunted Browning throughout production, with his staging and direction a memorial in style to his lost friend.)

The Laemmles had just paid one-tenth of their proposed budget on the screen rights to Florence Stoker. There were sudden lay-offs of many studio personnel and The Universal Weekly, Uncle Carl's most ingenius method of making personal contact with the studio and all the distributors and theater owners, was ordered to close down its publication office. (It was revived in 1932 and continued until 1936.)

Carl Laemmle Jr., however saddened, was undaunted by the second setback due to the death of an artist. He still saw an original and exciting variation of the novel and popular play, surpassing even the famous Universal Western films for action and adventure. He had given the assignment of the screenplay to Louis Bromfield, whose novel, The Strange Case of Annie Spragg, had come to his attention through Richard Schayer, of the Story Department. It was reviewed in New Republic the year before as being "the combinaton of sinister religious influences with intense dramatic situations," just the combination Laemmle Jr. wanted for his *Dracula*.

Louis Bromfield on his farm in Ohio, circa 1937. Within a few short years he was to win a Pulitzer Prize for his writing.

Back on August 7, 1930, Bromfield submitted his first treatment of the screenplay, which has become legendary in the study of film history along with the Florey/Fort version of *Frankenstein*.* In Bromfield's work, which was based primarily upon the book, the film would have been the definitive version of the subject. We present for the first time what would have been Carl Laemmle Jr.'s ideal production of *Dracula* intended for Lon Chaney:

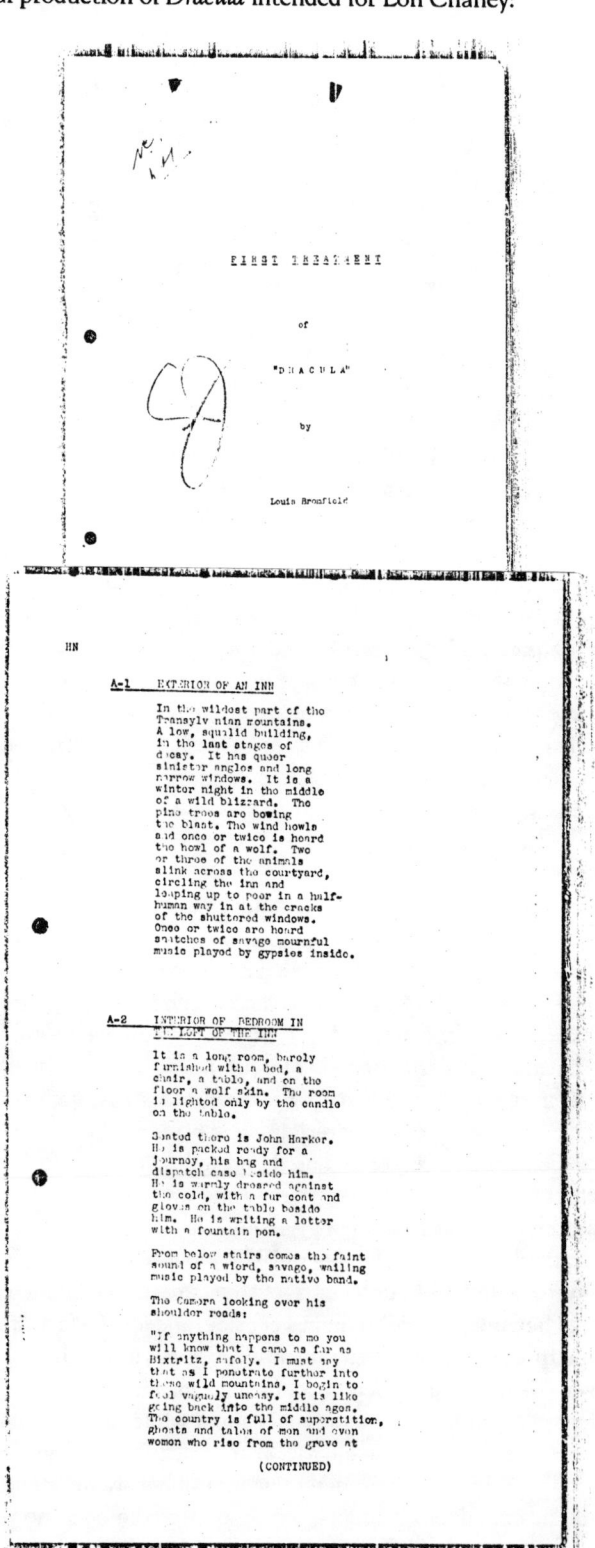

*See Universal Filmscript - Classic Horror-Volume One-Frankenstein for a synopsis and actual pages from the Florey/Fort/Lugosi screen test

HN

A-2 (CONTINUED)

night to take on the forms of
wolves and bats. From here on, I
must journey by any means possible.
Motors cannot traverse the wild
roads. For some reason the natives
regard me as a man already doomed.
Thank Heaven I am a solid, sensible
Britisher not to be frightened by
wild tales of horror. Say nothing
to Mina of what I have written you.
I would not have her frightened
for the world."

He signs the letter, folds it,
places it in an envelope and
addresses it to

"Penthurst, Williams & Harker,
Barristers, Fleet Street, London."

As he folds the letter, the
shutter rattles. Pausing, he sits
transfixed, staring at it. Then
he turns again to write and again
the shutter rattles, half rattle,
half knock. Stealthily he rises
and moving toward it, suddenly
opens the window and flings the
shutters open. There is nothing
there. Below him in the courtyard
he sees a wolf slink off into the
shadows.

Closing the shutter, he returns
to the desk and starts another
letter.

"Darling Mina:

Just a line before leaving for
Castle Dracula. I shall not be
able to write you every day from
there. I am well and in fine spirits,
though I miss you horribly. The
country is interesting and beautiful,
though very savage and the trip is fine
experience, although nothing can take
the place of you. It won't be long
now until we shall never again be
separated. My love to your father,
and to Lucy and her fiance.
If you had not been yourself, I
should have not been fallen in love with her.
I am wearing the little crucifix
which you have me. Nothing will
ever separate it and me. I hope
to finish this mission in short order
and then, when I return, you will be
my wife.

Jonathan Harker

(CONTINUED)

HN

A-3 (CONTINUED)

HARKER

Has the sleigh come yet?

PROPRIETOR (he speaks English
with a broad accent)

No....I think you'll hear
it when it comes.

HARKER (handing him the two
letters)

When will these go?

PROPRIETOR

Day after tomorrow. The
mail coach only comes into
the mountains once a week.

HARKER

They're important. I
trust you to see that they
get off.

PROPRIETOR

You can trust me.

HARKER (looking about at the
peasants who continue
to stare at him)

What's the matter with me?

PROPRIETOR

Its because you're a
stranger, Sir. They have
never been out of the
mountains.

HARKER

They must be used to me by
now.

PROPRIETOR

They're very ignorant, Sir.

An old moustached hag
suddenly comes forward
and throws herself at
Harker's foot. She holds
out a charm toward him
and mumbles excitedly in
Czecholovak.

HARKER (drawing back,
alarmed)

What's the matter? What's
she saying?

(CONTINUED)

HN

A-2 (CONTINUED - 2)

He takes out the crucifix
from beneath his shirt and kisses
it romantically.

Again the rattling of the shutters.
Again, somewhat terrified, he stares
at it. The rattling continues as if
there was an attempt to force an
entrance. Slowly he raises the tiny
crucifix toward the window, calling
out in a loud voice, "Back to the
Devil from whence you came."

At once, the rattling ceases and
with it the howl of the wind and the
wolves.

Harker smiles a half-credulous smile,
seals the envelope, addresses it,
picks up his coat and bag and carrying
the candle, starts toward the door.
The wind begins to howl once more and
with it the distant howl of the wolves.

A-3 THE DRINKING ROOM OF THE INN

It is like the exterior of the
house, ancient, crumbling and
worn. There is a gigantic fireplace in one corner and in the
opposite corner a crazy stairway
leading to the rooms above. The
whole room is distorted like
something seen in a dream.

In the room are seated, drinking
and carousing, a villianous
assortment of Transylvanian peasants.
In one corner are two or three
savage peasants playing the music
that has been heard up to now.
The proprietor, a lean, sallow
fellow of great height and fierce
black moustaches, is seated behind
a sort of till.

At the top of the stairs Harker
appears. One of the peasants
sees him, then another and another.
They all stop drinking. The music
stops. They all stare at him in
pity and terror, as he slowly
descends the stairs. One or two
cross themselves.

Harker advances slowly across the
room until he reaches the till
where he addresses the proprietor.

(CONTINUED)

HN

A-3 (CONTINUED - 2)

PROPRIETOR

Take it.
(indicating the object
she is holding out)
It's a charm against the
evil forces.

Harker takes it. The
old woman, crossing
herself, seizes his
knees. He frees himself.

HARKER

What's she saying?

PROPRIETOR

Perhaps I ought not to
tell you.

HARKER (angrily)

Tell me. I'm not a fool
or a coward.

PROPRIETOR

I didn't mean that, your
Excellency.
(hesitating)
She is saying that tonight
is the Eve of St. George's
Day.

HARKER

Yes!

PROPRIETOR (hesitating)

At midnight all the evil
things in the world will
be loosed.

HARKER (laughing)

Yes! And what are they?

Proprietor doesn't
answer.

HARKER (again)

What are they?

PROPRIETOR (evasively)

Demons - werewolves -
vampires. It is evil to
even speak of them.

(CONTINUED)

HN

A-3 (CONTINUED - 3)

HARKER (laughing)
Well, if it's not any more than that, I shan't worry. I fancy I'll be safe in the castle of my friend, Count Dracula. It's walls are thick enough.

The proprietor crosses himself.

HARKER (looking at him seriously)
What? You believe too?

The clock begins striking midnight slowly.

PROPRIETOR
You can never tell -- I've seen things --

HARKER
What things?

PROPRIETOR (after a pause)
You had better keep the charm the old woman gave you.

HARKER (laughing)
Our friend, the coachman is late.

PROPRIETOR
I think he never meant to come before midnight.

The sound of horses' hoofs are heard. They both listen. In the background the peasants grow terrified. A wolf howls. The clock finishes striking. There is a knock, made by the butt of a whip, on the door.

The Proprietor makes no effort to unbolt the door. He has placed himself with his back against the wall, motionless. All the peasants are struck dumb and appear terrified. Harker looks at him and then unbolts the door himself.

(CONTINUED)

HN

A-4 (CONTINUED)

He fires once or twice as they draw near, but the mysterious coachman rising in his seat, turns and cracks his long driving whip in the direction of the wolves, who instantly vanish. Again Harker is both astonished and frightened. The coachman appears to take no notice of the extraordinary happening and Harker settles back as the sleigh dashes on.

A-5 A LONG SHOT OF CASTLE DRACULA

It is an immense and crumbling ruin of the ages, silhouetted against waning moon, which appears now and then thru the storm tormented clouds. The sleigh drawn by the black horses sweeps into the courtyard, before an immense doorway, which is also a kind of porch where Harker is sheltered from the storm. He gets down from the sleigh again, bearing his luggage and dispatch case. Again no word is spoken between him and the mysterious coachman. Suddenly the sleigh dashes off. Apparently whisked to invisibility by a wild gust of wind and snow. Harker is left alone, standing in the fitful moonlight before the great door.

On the door is an immense iron knocker with which he hammers again and again, against the moldering iron-studded oak. For a long time there is no answer. The wolves begin to howl again, their howls coming nearer and nearer, until, as they rush into the vast courtyard. There is a metallic sound of chains and bolts, the great door opens, apparently of its own accord, and he steps inside and the door closes again. He finds himself confronted by an immensely tall man in old-fashioned, very worn, footman's livery. He silently takes up the baggage of Harker and without a word leads the way. Harker follows.

(CONTINUED)

HN

A-3 (CONTINUED - 4)

HARKER
Goodnight. I'll return here when my visit is finished.

PROPRIETOR (in a low voice)
May God bring you safely back.

Harker opens the door. The wind blows in. A wolf howls. He closes it and the Proprietor flings himself on it, bolting it and making the mark of the cross in chalk.

A-4 THE COURTYARD AND ROAD OUTSIDE THE INN

It is roughly paved and lighted only by the lantern above the inn door.

As Harker steps to the door under the light it is banged behind him. In front of him stands a sleigh drawn by four coal-black horses, prancing nervously. For a moment he stands taking in the sight and then notices the extraordinary figure of the coachman.

He is a big man, wrapped in furs with a scarf hiding the lower part of his face like a mask, beneath the wolf-skin cap. The only visible part of his face are his eyes, which are large, black and brilliant. As they regard Harker they seem to dilate and take on an expression of gloating. For a moment Harker stands staring at him with an expression of amazement and then alarm. The wolves howl louder and nearer. Without speaking a word Harker climbs into the sleigh and is whirled off. At the same time the wolves appear from the bushes close in pursuit. Harker, alarmed, half rises from beneath furs which he has thrown over himself and drawing his pistol turns to face the wolves.

(CONTINUED)

HN

A-5 (CONTINUED)

The hallway is an immensely high, narrow, vaulted passageway and is lighted only by the candlestick, very rich and very beautiful, bearing six candles, which the man-servant has given to Harker to carry while he himself brings the baggage. The candle-light throws fantastic shadows against the walls.

The long hall terminates in an immense stone stairway, which appears to lead up and up indefinitely. It is likewise completely bare and as the two figures climb up and up they grow smaller and smaller, until in a turning of the staircase, they are lost to sight.

A-6 AGAIN AN IMMENSE HIGH VAULTED ROOM THE STONE FRONT ROOM ONE SIDE

It is dark, except for the moonlight which comes in by a small window. A great door opens and a man-servant comes in followed by Harker carrying the candlestick, which illuminates the room for the first time. This room, too, is virtually bare, save for a group of furniture, crude and massive, gathered about an immense fireplace filled with burning logs.

The man-servant leads the way to the fireplace, where he puts down the luggage, bows, and goes out without a word. Harker, left alone, takes off his fur coat and looks about him. He notices suddenly that the chairs and table are covered thickly with dust and traces, with his finger a faint design on the surface of the table. On the table lie bread, cheese, fruit and a bottle of wine. A place is set for one person. While waiting, he wanders about the room going presently to one of the windows which he unfastens with difficulty.

HN

A-7 SCENE BENEATH THE WINDOW
     SEEN FROM AN ENORMOUS
     HEIGHT

Half blotted out by the snow
lies a mountainous landscape
threaded by a river. Beneath
the window there is a sheer
drop of castle-wall and
precipice of a thousand feet.
The wall of the castle is
broken only by another window
a hundred feet lower down.

A-8 INSIDE THE ROOM

Harker draws back from the
window, dizzy by the great
height. Behind him the howl
of wolves is heard. He bangs
the window shut and a moment
later a voice is heard coming
out of the shadows.

              VOICE
     It is a long drop,
     nearly two thousand feet.

Harker, turning toward
the voice, sees the figure
of a tall man, dressed in a
misty, unpressed, trousers
and morning coat. He has a
very pale face with drooping
white mustache and long, unkept
white hair. Yet he has a
distinction of bearing. He wears,
also, a long black cape, which
floats about him as he moves forward
to greet Harker.

As he comes into the firelight
it is the eyes which Harker sees
first - large, black and
burning. Suddenly Harker
sees, in his mind at the same
time, the eyes of the wild
coachman and the sinister
footman. The eyes of all
three are the eyes of the
same man.

              HARKER
     Count Dracula?

                              (CONTINUED)

A-8 (CONTINUED)

              DRACULA (he speaks with a
                       foreign accent)
     I am Dracula. I bid you
     welcome. My servants have
     gone to bed. Let me see
     to your comfort myself.
     I pray you, be seated
     and sup when you please.
     Excuse me if I do not join
     you, I never sup.

They seat themselves and
Harker brings out
papers and lays them on
the table.

              HARKER
     I will present my
     credentials.
              (taking up dispatch
               case)
     And I have the leases
     laready to sign.
              (He brings out the
               papers)

              DRACULA
     I make my apologies for
     having brought you all the
     way from London into this
     wild country - Please eat,
     while I talk --

              HARKER
     I have not much appetite,
     but I will have a little
     wine, it will warm me
     after my journey.

              DRACULA
     Your nerves are shaken by
     the wild ride. I
     apologize, it is a wild
     country.
              (wolves howling)
              (Dracula grins showing
               suddenly two very
               prominent canine
               teeth, very long and
               pointed.
     Listen to them -- the
     children of the night.
     What music they make.

Dracula sits with his
hands on the edge of the
table, and all the time
he is talking, Harker with
an evil fascination, regards
them and the various features
of his face.
                              (CONTINUED)

HN

A-8 (CONTINUED - 2)
              (All this may be shown in
              close-ups in and out of the
              speech.) One by one Harker
              examines them. (1) the hands,
              coarse and covered with hair
              almost like the bristles of
              an animal. The nails are long
              and pointed in needle-like
              fashion. As one hand turns
              over you see hairs growing
              out of the palm. (2) the
              eyebrows, very dark and bushy.
              (3) The ears, very pointed at
              the tips with a suspicion of
              hair on them.

              DRACULA
     I was forced to make you
     take this long trip because
     it was impossible for me
     to leave my castle. Now
     it seems, owing to sudden
     developments, I shall be
     able to leave shortly to
     occupy the house you have
     bought for me in England.
              (he leans toward
               Harker laying a hand
               on his shoulder)
     Ah! You are a stout
     young fellow - young and
     full of life. There is
     nothing like youth - youth
     and young blood.
              (he looks at Harker,
               who, a little
               frightened, draws
               away)
     You are young and full of
     young blood. Yes....yes.
     full.
              (for a moment he seems
               in a trance. Then
               he draws away and
               recovers himself)
     Yes - if you will give me
     the papers, I can sign
     them now at once. I shall
     be busy during the day
     tomorrow and not able to
     see you. I have the
     necessary checks which I
     can pay you at once.

Harker produces the papers.
Dracula draws over to him an
inkwell with a quill pen and
proceeds to sign. He holds
out the checks.

                              (CONTINUED)

HN

A-8 (CONTINUED - 3)

Throughout the scene Count
Dracula alternately wavers
between behavior, which is
all that is polished and
polite, and a sudden sinister,
gloating over Harker, which he
seems unable to control.

              HARKER (with an air of trying
                       to make conversation)
     I trust, Sir, that you will
     find your stay in England
     agreeable.

              DRACULA
     It will be a change. I
     have lived so long in this
     wild, lonely country -
              (slowly, as if to
               himself)
     So long, so many, many
     years, and now I'm going
     to a new, fresh world.
              (slowly)
     A world full of opportun-
     ity.
              (coming to himself
               again)
     You will, I am afraid, be
     forced to stay here for
     several days, as there is
     no coach coming from the
     village before Friday. I
     trust you will be able
     to amuse yourself during
     the day. I am occupied
     during the daylight, but
     I shall be able to see you
     in the evening.
              (rising)
     And now, let me conduct
     you to your room.

He rises and takes up
Harker's baggage.
Harker protests, but
he insists. Leading the
way, Dracula conducts
Harker to a door on the
opposite side of the
room.

45

HN

A-8 A SMALL ROOM WITH A
     SINGLE WINDOW

The window looks out over
the valley. The room is
simply furnished.

The two enter and Dracula,
with an air of a servant
opens Harker's bag on the
bed and begins to unpack
for him

                    DRACULA
             You will allow me, I
             trust, inasmuch as all
             the servants are in
             bed.

Harker protests and begins
to unpack himself. Among
other things, he takes out
a large, round-shaving
mirror. He turns to hang
it on the wall. Dracula
quietly slips the revolver
he finds in the bag into
his own pocket. Meanwhile
Harker, engaged in hanging
up the mirror, notices
that in it there is no
reflection of Dracula.
Puzzled, he deliberately
holds the mirror so that he
can have in it a full view
of Dracula. To his
astonishment no reflection
of Dracula appears. Dracula,
discovering what he is up to,
leaps toward him, seizes the
mirror and dashes it to bits.

Then, recovering himself
sharply, he becomes suave
and polished once more.

                    DRACULA
             I beg your pardon. I have
             an uncontrollable hatred
             for all mirrors. They are
             symbols of the vanity of
             mankind.
                    (he bows)
             And now, Sir, I will leave
             you. I have only one
             request to make. The post
             in these wild mountains is
             very irregular and uncer-
             tain. I would like to have
             you write three letters --
             one dated the third,
             written from here, saying
             that you have arrived.

                    (CONTINUED)

HN

A-8 (CONTINUED)

                    DRACULA (continued)
             are comfortable and will --
             one written on the sixth
             saying that you are leaving
             and one dated the ninth
             from Bucharest saying that
             you are on your way to
             London.
                    HARKER
             Well, I need not trouble
             you with that, I can send
             them myself.
                    DRACULA (looking at him with
                              sinister meaning)
             You understand it would be
             much safer if you left
             them to me.
                    (bowing his way out
                     the door)
             I will expect to find the
             letters tomorrow. Good-
             night, and may you have
             pleasant dreams.

He closes the door behind
him. The clinking of
chains and bolts is heard.
Harker rushes instinctively
to try the massive door and
finds it securely bolted.
He is a prisoner. He goes
to one window and looks out.

A-10 VIEW OF SHEER WALL AND
      PRECIPICE

It is the same view of the
sheer wall and precipice
you have seen before.

A-11 VIEW OF OTHER WINDOW

He rushes across the room
to the other window. Here
too, the walls fall
abruptly to the great courtyard by which Harker has
entered a little while ago.
In the courtyard there appears
to be a great activity.

                    (CONTINUED)

HN

A-11 (CONTINUED)

The storm is still raging.
But, in the courtyard are
two great carts and horses
and a number of wild looking
gypsies. Some are carrying
lighted torches, others are
carrying from the depths of the
castle, great coffin-shaped
boxes, of immense weight, loading
them upon the carts. Harker
watches for a moment and then
closes the window. He tries the
door again. Searches for his
revolver and finds it missing.

A-12 AN IMMENSE FLIGHT OF STAIRS

An immense flight of stairs
leading down, down, down into
the depths of the castle.
Dracula, his cloak wrapped
about him, bolts the door to
the large room where Harker
has recently had supper and
descends the stairs. The
camera follows him on the
end of descent until he comes
out into an immense vaulted, chapel-
like room filled with coffins and tombs.
Here, a half dozen wild-looking
gypsies are at work shovelling the
earth into a coffin-like box. Dracula
stands watching them until it is filled
and placed on the shoulders of six men
who bear it out.

A-13 AGAIN IN HARKER'S ROOM

He has taken off his collar
and put on a dressing gown to
make himself comfortable, but
has not undressed. Again he
goes to the window overlooking
the valley and looks out. This
time the storm has ceased and
in the moonlight appears a cloud
of mist, which moves toward him
assuming fantastic shapes. He
closes the window quickly and
turns to his bed and lies down.
The mist begins seeping in the
cracks of the window and fills
the room until nothing in it is
visible.

                    (CONTINUED)

Hn

A-13 (CONTINUED)

Then quite slowly it dissolves
and in the room are three women,
wild and beautiful, in the
costumes of three different
periods of history. Hypnotized,
Harker on the bed, is unable to
move. The three women move
toward him bending over laughing
in an evil way. One of them
attempts to bare his throat, but
at that moment, Dracula himself
appears suddenly and orders them
to go, bidding them not to touch
Harker. He drives them through the
door which is already bolted and
disappears. Harker rises, not
sure whether or not he has been
asleep and again tries the door,
which he finds closed. Again
he goes to the window overlooking
the valley and opening it, looks out.

A-14

This time, far below Harker, is an
extraordinary sight. Dracula, in
his black cape, comes out of the
window, headfirst and proceeds to
climb down the wall head-first,
edging a little side-wise at times.
His great black cloak spread out
about him and clinging to the wall
like the wings of a bat.

Harker watches, then calculates for
a moment the distance from his window
to the window from which Dracula has
just disappeared. Then he sets to
work making a rope with the bedclothes
and with this he climbs out of the
window and makes his way down to the
lower window, slipping into another
empty room. Then he goes through
endless rooms finding his way back,
at last, to the corridor thru which
he entered the house. He opens the
door but as he steps onto the porch
a score of wolves, all howling, rush
across the courtyard towards him and
he slips the bolt into place as they
leap against the door.

Wandering back, he comes again to the
great staircase which leads down, down,
down into the bowels of the castle.
On his way down, he peers out of one
of the narrow barred windows and sees
the sun rising over the mountains.
Continuing downward he comes at last

                    (CONTINUED)

A-14 (CONTINUED)

to a chapel-like crypt. There, with a candle, he feels his way about. Coming at last to three small tombs in a row. The lids of these have all been tumbled off. As he holds the candle higher he sees in them the three women who have entered his room in the mist. They are lying dead in their coffins. The three tombs each bear birth and death dates that are generations apart, all more than 300 years ago. Beyond them is a more pretentious tomb from which the lid is likewise been lifted. It bears the name "Dracula", and the date 1204 to 1298.

On the ground all about the tomb are scattered picks and shovels and freshly dug earth.

In the big tomb lies Dracula himself, wrapped in his black cloak. Harker stares at him for a moment and then seizing one of the shovels, swings it with all his force at the head of the monster. But as he does so the head of the corpse turns over so slightly, the eyes open and fix him with a horrible stare. His arm falters. He drops the weapon and turning, runs up the long stairs and down the corridor to the door which unbolts.

It is daylight now. He runs out into the storm. There are no wolves. He, too, disappears in a great whisp of flying snow.

B-1 THE EXTERIOR OF DR. SEWARD'S NURSING HOME AT CARFAX, NEAR LONDON

It is a big, quiet, ivy-grown house, set in a walled garden. It is night. By the light above the gate one can read the dignified brass plate sign.

"CARFAX NURSING HOME
AND SANITARIUM FOR
THE CARE OF NERVE
DISEASES.

EDWARD SEWARD, D.S.C.M.D.

On the wall a signal -

"LONDON 30 MILES"
"CARFAX 20 MILES, etc."

A tall man wearing a black cape approaches, opens the gate and enters. The camera follows him and he approaches the door, rings and is admitted. The prolonged howl of the wolf heard in the last scene continues until the door is opened. A servant admits him. The camera follows him into the drawing room.

The drawing room is a large comfortable room with tall curtained windows. In the center of the room more people are playing bridge - Dr. Seward, a thin nervous man of about 50 with greying hair, his daughter Mina, a pretty, voluptuous young woman who is John Harker's fiancee, Lord Godalming, fiance of Mina's sister, Lucy, and Mrs. Triplett (Alison Skipworth) a woman of fifty, but coquettish and rather silly. She is a neighbor who can play bridge and has forced them into a game. As the servant announces the Count de Ville, they all turn toward the door where the man in the cape still stands with his back to the camera.

The four faces at the bridge table register various expressions - Mrs. Triplett, coquettish and beaming with delight, Dr. Seward polite interest, Lord Godalming the same, only Mina betrays herself for a moment by a look of horror. Dr. Seward and Lord Godalming rise from their chairs.

SEQUENCE "B"

DR. SEWARD — A distinguished man of 50, Proprietor of Carfax Sanitarium for persons with nervous diseases.

MINA SEWARD — His daughter, and the fiancee of John Harker. She is young, plump, voluptuous and appetizing.

LUCY SEWARD — Also Doctor Seward's daughter. She has once been like Mina, but is now wasted and pale from some mysterious disease which none can diagnose. She is the fiancee of Lord Godalming.

MRS. TRIPLETT — A rich neighbor of the Sewards. She is a fat, silly, coquettish woman of about fifty who behaves as if she were still attractive to men. She is a good deal of a fool.

COUNT de VILLE — A handsome, youthful foreigner. Hungarian in origin - physically attractive to both girls and to Mrs. Triplett. He has beautiful hypnotic eyes which are like the eyes of Dracula.

RENFIELD — A patient in Doctor Seward's sanitarium. Thin, gaunt, morbid, about thirty years old.

VAN HELSING — A celebrated Dutch Scientist. Short, plump, solid and bearded with an academic manner.

B-1 (CONTINUED)

As Doctor Seward rises to greet the Count de Ville you see the Count for the first time. He is Dracula, but miraculously altered. His hair and moustache, instead of being grey, are black. He appears young, very good looking, vigorous and attractive. There is only a look of the sinister in him, which appears to expand whenever his gaze is turned toward the pretty voluptuous Mina.

After the greetings are exchanged, he seems as he has dropped in for a moment to inquire about Lucy. Dr. Seward says she is about the same, very pale and very weak, and in a sort of coma. Dr. Seward tells him that both he and Lord Godalming have submitted to transfusions in order to help her condition. The Count gallantly offers himself for a blood transfusion. He asks if she is well enough to receive visitors and is told that she is too weak, although Mrs. Triplett says that she always seems brighter and more cheerful after seeing the Count. The Count says that he will go now and not interrupt their bridge, but they, politely say it does not matter, because Mina can't possibly go on playing. They have been playing simply to pass the time, and because Mrs. Triplett dropped in. Mina is too wasted a girl, and says she is too sad and depressed to go on pretending she is enjoying it. Mrs. Triplett asks the Count if he will drop her at home. She has walked over from her house. He gallantly agrees, and as they go out, the Count manages to take Dr. Seward aside and ask if there is any news of Miss Mina's fiance, John Harker. He confides in the Count that he is afraid some fatal accident has happened to him. It is three months since they have heard from him. The Count expresses sympathy, and conducts the too tearful Mrs. Triplett out of the house. In the

(CONTINUED)

IH   B-2 (CONTINUED)

way out he turns and
asks "when is your friend,
Van Helsing, arriving?"
Dr. Seward says "we expect
him tonight". And then
looking sharply at the Count,
asks, "how did you know that
he was coming"? The Count
replies, "I heard you speaking
of it the other day".

Back in the drawing room Mina
is very nearly hysterical.
She declares she cannot bear
the Count, and that his presence
near her, fills her with dread.
Dr. Seward admits there is
something strange about him.
How does he know that Van Helsing
is on his way from Amsterdam. He
is certain that the subject was
never discussed in front of him.
At that moment a maniacal laugh
is heard. Mina very nearly
faints. Lord Godalming snatches
away the curtain and standing
there, leering at them is discovered Renfield, a patient in
the sanitarium.

Dr. Seward, alarmed, asks him
what he is doing there and bids
Godalming to ring the bell for
the keeper at once. From Renfield comes only insane clatter.
He is at the moment, completely
mad. The keeper appears to drag
Renfield away and Renfield makes
a speech begging to be allowed
a single night of freedom. He
is hysterical and pitiful. Dr.
Seward, to humor him, tells him
"yes, but later on". Renfield,
jittering to himself is dragged
away by the keeper. As he
leaves the room he emits a long
wolf-like howl. The howl is
answered distinctly from the
outside. Godalming observes
that Renfield has started all the
dogs in the neighborhood to howling.

Godalming urges Dr. Seward to send
Renfield away because he is growing
violent and his screams and yells
must be disturbing to the sick
Lucy. Mina leaves them, saying
that she is going up to see her
sister, Lucy, and as she leaves
a servant enters bringing the mail.
There is a letter bearing the stamp
of John Harker's law firm. Seward
opens it hastily hoping that
perhaps it may contain news of John
Harker. Godalming watches while he
reads.

IH   B-3 (CONTINUED)

While they are bending
over her the long howl
of dogs is heard again.
They turn fearfully to-
ward the window. The
outline of a bat is seen
there again. Again Godalming
goes to the window and frightens
away the bat, which flies out
into the moonlight. Again they
bolt the window and this time
draw the curtains across it
shutting out the moonlight.

Godalming beckons silently
for Mina to leave the room.
They go out quietly, closing
the door after them.

B-4   THE HALLWAY OUTSIDE LUCY'S BEDROOM

Godalming says that he is
going with his rifle to shoot
the cursed bat. He is one
of the best shots in England
and cannot miss it. Mina
says she will remain outside
the door. She takes Harker's
letter from her pocket and
begins to read it all over
again.

B-5   THE DRAWING ROOM AGAIN

A servant enters and
announces Dr. Van Helsing.
The Doctor comes in and
between him and Seward
there is a warm greeting.

DR. SEWARD

Thank God, you've come.
I'm at my wits end. We
cannot discover what is
wrong with Lucy. She
grows weaker every day,
and has all the symptoms
of anemia. But when her
blood is analyzed it is
normal. We have given
her three infusions -
gallons of blood, but it
has simply vanished.

Van Helsing says that all
the details of the case
fascinate him. He has
many theories, none of
which he will discuss now.
He is very grave and
(CONTINUED)

IH   B-3 LUCY'S BEDROOM

It is an old-fashioned room
with a low dormer window
looking out on the park.
It is moonlight and the
room is lighted only by
the window and a night light.
The door opens and Mina
comes in. She moves softly
to the foot of the bed and
stands for a moment looking
down at her sister.

Lucy, lying on the bed, looks
pale and shaken. She is
wearing a bed-jacket and a
scarf wrapped around her
throat. She is moaning in
her sleep and talking to herself. Presently she opens
her eyes and recognizes
her sister, who falls on her
knees beside the bed and
takes Lucy in her arms, asking
her how she feels. Lucy in
a daze, answers her brokenly.
Suddenly, with an odd look
of unearthly joy, she points
to the window and says, "look,
there he is, come back. Let
him in." Turning, Mina sees
against the window pane the
outline of a huge bat.

Mina regards the sight with
horror and taking up a
candlestick as a weapon
advances toward the window.
Courageously she opens the
window. As she does the bat
flies off into the moonlight.
Closing the window Mina bolts
it firmly.

Returning to the bed she finds
that Lucy has slipped into
unconsciousness again. She
does not rouse her. There is
a knock and Lord Godalming
comes into the room. As he
enters Mina places her fingers
to her lips but Godalming advances and says softly, "John
has been found." She asks
fearfully if he is alive and
he says: "Yes". He draws
her outside the door where
he tells her the truth and
hands her the letter. "John",
he says, "is on his way home.
He will arrive in two weeks."
While she reads the letter
he goes inside and bending
over, kisses Lucy's hand gently.
Lucy stirs, wakens and looking
at Lord Godalming cries out,
"No - don't touch me! I'm
unclean! Go! -- Leave me in
peace!" She sinks back again
on the bed, unconscious.
(CONTINUED)

IH   B-5 (CONTINUED)

mysterious about the
disease.

A howl is heard. Van
Helsing listens for a
moment with an expression
of deep interest, and then
says in a low voice,
"the howl of a wolf. Have
you a caged wolf in the
park?"

SEWARD

No - that is one of the
patients. A man called
Renfield. Lately he
has taken to howling
like that.

VAN HELSING

No living man ever made
that sound.

SEWARD

You shall see for your-
self. I will take you to
see him. He is a most
interesting case. That
is described as zoo-
phagous. He tries to
eat life by eating spiders
and flies and even
sparrows which he lures
to his room.

VAN HELSING   (gravely)

I should, indeed, like to
see him. Indeed I think
it will be necessary.

B-6   DRACULA IN THE HALLWAY

Mina, lying on the sofa,
reading. Presently,
she hears low moans from
Lucy's room and rising,
she goes slowly to open
the door. Softly so as
not to disturb Lucy.
As she opens the door a
look of frightful terror
crosses her face. She
screams and falls in a
faint.

As she faints in the doorway,
Dracula, emerging from the
room seizes her, carries her
inside and locks the door.
(CONTINUED)

IH B-6 (CONTINUED)

Then with a look of obscene and loathsome gloating he seizes her unconscious body, presses back her head, bares her junctental(?), and baring her throat presses his mouth to it with an unholy passion.

(N.B. In his unnatural)
(unearthly manifestations)
(the Count de Ville as-)
(sumes the insane wolfish)
(appearance of Dracula.)
(His eyes grow dilated)
(and his canine teeth)
(appear to grow much)
(longer.)

The howl of Renfield is heard again, and then cries of "Lucy" and "Mina" are heard and a pounding on the door.

B-7 OUTSIDE THE DOOR AGAIN

Van Helsing and Seward trying desperately to enter. They smash open the door with a chair and as they enter a pistol shot is heard outside.

B-8 INSIDE THE ROOM

Lucy lies on the bed, unconscious, the scarf torn from her throat. On the floor, partly lying on the sofa, lies Mina in the same condition. A wisp of mist seems to hang about the locked and curtained window. Van Helsing and Seward bend over Mina, trying desperately to rouse her. Slowly she comes to, saying: "Where am I? What has happened?" Then hysterically, "go to Lucy - save Lucy."

Dr. Seward goes to Lucy and Van Helsing bends over Mina, lifting her up and speaking to her.

VAN HELSING
Save her from what? Speak to me! From What? From what? What have you seen? What was it?

Mina only moans and murmurs "I don't know - I don't know."

B-9 A CORNER OF THE PARK SURROUNDING THE SANITARIUM

Again the figure of the Count de Ville, in a long cape, is seen advancing in the moonlight under the trees. On the door step he encounters Lord Godalming carrying a rifle. The Count bows gravely.

COUNT (with a sinister smile)
Shooting at night, Lord Godalming?

GODALMING
I was trying to get a bat which has been annoying Miss Seward, by trying to enter her room. I shot at it and I'm sure I hit it, but it did not fall. I searched everywhere.

COUNT (awed)
A bat at this time of the year! Possibly it came from Carfax Abbey. The old ruin is filled with bats.

GODALMING
Will you come in and have a drink before going to bed?

COUNT
I meant to drop in. As I was passing, I heard a scream. I thought it might have something to do with Miss Lucy.

GODALMING (in wild alarm)
A scream! Miss Lucy! I heard nothing. Oh, my God!

He turns and runs toward the house. The Count follows him slowly.

IH B-10 AGAIN THE DRAWING ROOM

As Godalming rushes into the room still carrying the rifle, a servant, in agitation, rushes to him and tells him that something has happened in Miss Lucy's room. Godalming rushes up the stairs and as he exits the Count, still in the cape, crosses the room slowly.

B-11 LUCY'S BEDROOM

Mina lies on the sofa with her head in the pillow, sobbing hysterically. Seward and Van Helsing bend over Lucy.

VAN HELSING (rising slowly)
I have come too late, and only a moment too late. She is dead.

Van Helsing bends down and peers, with a magnifying glass, at Lucy's throat. There are two small marks like the teeth-marks of a bat. He draws back slowly and says: "I was afraid I might find those marks".

Godalming enters. Dr. Seward rises and breaks the news to him. He becomes almost hysterical and kneels by the bed, kissing Lucy's hand and begging her to speak to him.

The Count appears in the doorway, bows, expresses his sympathy and begs pardon for the intrusion. Van Helsing turns and sees him. For a second in closeups he and the Count regard each other with a long, fixed and hostile look.

The Count begs them to call upon him if there is anything he can do to help. As he bows his way out, the howl of Renfield is heard again.

VAN HELSING (gravely)
That is the howl of no living man.

B-12 AGAIN THE FIGURE OF THE COUNT IN THE CAPE

Moving under the trees. This time toward the Carfax Abbey, the ruin where he lives. It is dawn. The sun is rising. He approaches a great studded iron door, and as he advances toward it the door swings back of its own accord. He enters a vaulted stone hallway. The door closes behind him and he bolts and chains it and picking up a candle, advances along the corridor to a stair-way which, like the great stairway in Castle Dracula, appears to descend down and down into the bowels of the earth. He disappears from sight around a turn in the stairway.

SEQUENCE "C"

C-1 AGAIN THE DRAWING ROOM OF DR. SEWARD'S NURSING HOME.

In the room are Lord Godalming, Dr. Seward and Van Helsing. Dr. Seward is dressed in black clothes. Godalming in a grey suit with a black mourning band on his arm. Van Helsing is in an old rumpled tweed suit. All three look worn, distracted and weary.

In a three-cornered conversation Van Helsing slowly explains to them the real cause of Lucy's illness and death. They are incredulous and he at last convinces them that the menace with which they are dealing is no earthly one.

In the middle of the conversation Mina enters. She looks pale and worn and sinks into a chair with weariness. She also is in mourning, dressed to go out and wears about her throat a scarf.

She is going to meet Harker, her fiance, at the railway station. He is returning, having lost his memory, to try to take up again the threads of a life which is already dead.

Dr. Seward thinks she ought not to go alone. She is not strong enough and the meeting with Harker will necessarily be painful, and too much of a strain in her weakened condition.

Godalming protests also, but points out that the greatest danger lines in her being out of doors after nightfall. Mina, however, insists. She points out that the meeting will also be painful for Harker and that she loves him so deeply but she wants their first meeting to be alone. Perhaps, she says, the sight of her will bring back his memory. Van Helsing says that perhaps she is right, but he insists upon her wearing about her throat, underneath the scarf, a wreath of wolfsbane, which he says, half in jest, is a partial cure for her illness.

(CONTINUED)

C-1 (CONTINUED)

She must, he says, never go anywhere without it until she has recovered. He suddenly grows very serious about it. She sets off alone in the motor for the station.

When she has gone the conference continues. Van Helsing explains that he has sent to Russia, by telegram, for the wolfsbane, which has just arrived. The smell of it is reputed to be abhorred by the evil forces with which they are beginning to battle. Van Helsing says that the battle will be a terrific one and they will need all the help possible against the terrific forces arrayed against them.

Godalming suggests that they enlist the advice and aid of Count de Ville, their friend and neighbor, inasmuch as the Count comes from Hungary where the legends and traditions of the forces they are fighting is centered. Dr. Seward supports him, but Van Helsing is doubtful. He has, he says, suspicions of the Count and does not wish to call in his aid until he has tried him by a proof which he has planned. Van Helsing says that their first step must be to question the maniac, Renfield, and try to get at the root of the strange transformation which has taken place in his character. He points out that it began at the same time as Miss Lucy's illness, and that both things may be due to the presence in the neighborhood of the same evil spirit.

Dr. Seward rings for the keeper and bids him send for Renfield.

C-2 A CORNER OF THE RAILWAY STATION AT CARFAX VILLAGE

The train arrives and John Harker descends from it. He is shockingly altered in appearance, looking older, nervous, and with streaks of white in his dark hair. He gets down from the train and looks about him. Mina comes toward him full of delight and joy, but he only stares blankly at her until she says she is Mina Seward. Then he knows that this is the girl to whom he was engaged before his mind went blank.

(CONTINUED)

C-2 (CONTINUED)

She conducts him to the automobile and they get in and drive away. There is a touching love scene between them in which Mina tries desperately to make him remember all that has passed between them and in which he desperately and shyly, tries to behave as he should toward her. And although he is attracted to her, and in a way, in love with her at first sight, he cannot quite feel at ease with a woman who is almost a stranger to him. They begin slowly to come together into an understanding.

C-3 THE DRAWING ROOM AGAIN

Renfield is brought in by his keeper and questioned by Van Helsing. At first he answers sensibly and then slowly he begins to talk jibberish about the presence of "the master". He again begs Dr. Seward to let him free for a single night. He will, he says, return again, on his word of honor. Dr. Seward says he will allow him freedom if he will speak openly of what he knows. He begins to speak, revealing more than he should, in the hope of saving his soul. While he is speaking a bat flies in at the window, circles the room and goes out. At once Renfield falls hysterically upon his knees, addressing the air as "Master", begging for mercy and declaring that he has betrayed nothing. He becomes completely mad and is lead away by the keeper.

No sooner has he gone than Van Helsing says he is convinced that there is some close relationship between Renfield and the force they are battling.

The same moment Mina and John Harker come in from the station. She seems happy and flushed, but John is still puzzled, as he recognizes neither Dr. Seward nor Godalming, and has, of course, never seen Van Helsing. Mina says that now John has returned everything will be alright and that she will recover, but Van Helsing only shakes his head and says that it will not be as easy as that and that she must still obey his smallest instructions.

(CONTINUED)

C-3 (CONTINUED)

She must wear the herbs about her throat and must never leave the house alone after nightfall, nor be alone for an instant. He summons her maid and tells her that she must never, under any circumstances leave Miss Mina alone. The maid promises.

The Count de Ville is announced suddenly and Van Helsing says to have him come in. He enters as usual, suave and charming and inquires after Mina's health. He is of course, introduced to John Harker. Harker, of course, does not recognize him, but is fascinated by the eyes which interest and hold him, for reasons which his poor brain does not fathom. There is an awkward moment while they stare at each other and the Count clearly attempts some hypnotic power.

Then he recovers himself and says that he must be off, as he is leaving for London by the ten o'clock train. Van Helsing suddenly asks him if he will not dine and play bridge on the following evening. The Count hesitates and then replies that he will be delighted. All the while Harker regards him like a bird fascinated with a snake. The Count leaves and when he has gone Harker, putting his hands over his eyes, groans and says that he knows the face and the eyes from somewhere, but can remember nothing.

Mina tries to comfort him tenderly and says that he ought to retire and lie down for a time before dinner.

Mina, accompanied by the maid, goes out with John to show him his room. Again, for an instant, there is a love scene between John and Mina in the corridor in which John kisses her. John tries desperately to find his way back to the memory of what happened before he wakened in the Transylvania Hospital.

C-4 THE GUEST ROOM

Mina shows John the room, arranges the flowers, does everything to make him comfortable. She says, she too, is exhausted, and when John questions her about her illness and how pale she looks, she replies evasively and says that

(CONTINUED)

EJP

C-4 (CONTINUED)

it is nothing, and says that she will go now and lie down for a while. The maid is still with her. While they are talking a lone howl is heard. Harker, alarmed, asks what it is. Mina, affected, is forced to sit in a chair.

A strange look comes over her face and she replies, with some effort, that it is only the howling of the maniac, Renfield. She rises slowly and tells John and Lucy that she will see him at dinner and leaves the room. On the way out she pauses for a moment as if overcome by dizziness. When she recovers herself she bids the maid go downstairs and fetch her a book from the library, which she describes.

The maid protests that she has been ordered not to leave her. Mina, outside Harker's door, becomes like a person possessed and with a strange craftiness, says that she will wait here until the maid returns. The maid goes. There is again a lone howl, and Mina, as if hypnotized, moves down the corridor out of sight.

C-5 AGAIN THE DRAWING ROOM

Downstairs, the fat, silly, Mrs. Triplett arrives. Van Helsing explains to her that they asked her to come in on her way home from London because there were questions they desired to ask her about the Count de Ville, who occupies the semi-ruin on the edge of her estate, known as Carfax Abbey.

She is very coy about the Count, and hints that there is a romantic attachment between herself and him. Van Helsing, however, keeps her to the point and questioning her finds out a great many interesting facts about the mysterious de Ville.

(CONTINUED)

C-5 (CONTINUED)

She has leased the place to him for 99 years in order to raise money for the income tax. It was all arranged by lawyers. She did not see him until he called on her the day of his arrival. The house, she explains, had not been occupied for nearly 80 years; ever since her grandfather's time. Most of it was a ruin. In the part that was livable there was a little furniture. The Count did not object to this. There was, however, a stipulation in the lease that so long as he lived the place was not to be visited by the proprietor or any other person without his express permission.

C-6 THE GLOOMY PARK BETWEEN DR. SEWARD'S SANITARIUM AND CARFAX ABBEY

The Count, wrapped in his cloak, stands in the shadow of a tree. Thru the trees approaches the figure of a woman. As she comes nearer she turns out to be Mina wrapped in a coat. She is walking in a perfectly straight line with the same queer hypnotic look in her eyes. The Count de Ville in his long black cape, follows her at a little distance. He comes nearer and nearer to her.

C-7 THE DRAWING ROOM AGAIN

Mrs. Triplett still being questioned by Van Helsing. He asks her if she has ever noticed anything unusual about Carfax Abbey. She answers that the only unusual thing seems to be that there are no servants and that no furniture has ever been moved in, unless it came in the coffin-shaped boxes which she saw arrive one afternoon while she was riding thru her own park.

(CONTINUED)

EJP

C-7 (CONTINUED)

At the mention of the boxes, Van Helsing becomes greatly excited, and presses Mrs. Triplett further. She says they appeared to be very heavy and it required several men to lift them. Her gardner, who talked to the carters who brought the boxes, said the boxes were labelled "earth for experimental purposes."

C-8 THE HALLWAY OUTSIDE HARKER'S ROOM

The maid approaches without the book. She listens for a moment at Harker's door, then knocks. Harker, himself, opens the door and when she asks if he knows where Miss Mina is, he says he does not. Alarmed, they both start to search the house. The maid will go to Mina's room and Harker is to search elsewhere.

C-9 A CORNER OF THE GLOOMY PARK

Mina, still in a hypnotic trance, moves forward as the Count comes out of the shadow. In a strange voice she addresses him as "Master". In a dreadful love scene he reproaches her for yielding to the advice of his enemies and begs her to remove from about her throat the circlet of wolfsbane. She obeys him and he kisses her passionately. The scene culminates and he bares her throat and presses his mouth against it.

C-10 THE DRAWING ROOM AGAIN

The maid, hysterical, rushes in and explains that Mina is missing. There is great confusion and they all rush out to search the park, with Mrs. Triplett left astonished and alone.

mrk

C-11 THE PARK OUTSIDE

They are all searching frantically thru the shrubbery under the gloomy trees, calling out Mina's name. It is John Harker who comes upon Mina lying across a bench, unconscious, in the moonlight. As he discovers her, a bat flies up, circles about and vanishes in the moonlight. Again there are three long wolf-howls. John Harker, picking up Mina is joined by the others and they bear her back into the house.

C-12 THE OPERATING ROOM OF THE SANITARIUM

Godalming, Van Helsing, Dr. Seward and Harker all enter. Mina is placed on the operating table and examined by the two doctors, who say "thank God, it is not too late", "but she must have a transfusion at once." John Harker at once offers himself. Van Helsing says he must see Renfield at once, and bids Seward to take charge of the transfusion while he interviews the maniac.

C-13 A LONG CORRIDOR WITH PRIVATE ROOMS FOR PATIENTS OPENING FROM EACH SIDE. WHERE THE STRETCHER IS

At one end the keeper sits at a desk asleep. His head on his arm. Van Helsing, in great excitement, rouses him and asks him to open the door of Renfield's padded room. The keeper says that Renfield has been very quiet all evening, not a sound from him. They peer in the small grating of the door and call out his name, but there is no answer. They open the door quickly. Inside it is dark. The keeper, using an electric torch, searches the room. It is in dreadful disorder with the furniture smashed and splintered.

A dreadful sight meets their eyes. Partly on the floor and partly on the cot, and in a

(CONTINUED)

mrk

C-13 (Continued)

pool of blood, lies the mangled body of Renfield. Van Helsing cries out, "help me Arm, the poor devil into the light".

They drag him into the corridor where Van Helsing makes a hasty examination. He exclaims "his back and neck are broken". "This is the work of a fiend". Renfield, still conscious, opens his eyes and murmurs, "Master, I have not betrayed you," and dies. Van Helsing goes at once to the telephone at the end of the corridor and asks for the railway station. There he questions the station-master. "Has the Count de Ville, who lives at Carvax Abbey, taken the train for London?" The station master replies that a left on the train at 9:30, he himself saw him get aboard. Van Helsing hangs up the telephone receiver baffled.

C-14 THE OPERATING ROOM AGAIN

Godalming, Dr. Seward and John Harker are gathered about Mina. She is slowly regaining consciousness. Van Helsing enters and observes that she is all right and has regained consciousness. He again says that she must not be left alone for an instant and that they each must take turns to keep watch over her, day and night. He proceeds to make a wreath of wolfsbane which he fastens about her throat and then takes from his pocket a small black velvet bag from which he extracts a wafer. Breaking off a piece of it he fastens it with surgical gauze about her throat. Godalming asks him what it is and he replies that "it is the Host". I have a dispensation. Against it all the forces of evil have no power, but we must watch her least he induces her to remove it.

He replaces the remains of the wafer in the black sack and puts it in the pocket over his heart.

(CONTINUED)

mrk

C-15 (Continued)

and suspicion. The Count is now playing a hard and in closeups, Harker becomes fascinated by the Count's peculiar hands. They are, as in the first sequence, claw-like with fearful cruel nails and covered with wolfish black hair. Something begins to dawn slowly in Harker's mind. Presently one hand of the Count rests on the table, palm up, and Harker sees the black hairs growing on the palm. He presses his hands to his head trying vaguely to recall where he had seen this before.

The rubber is finished and Mrs. Triplett takes out her vanity case to powder her nose. She holds in her hand a small square mirror. Suddenly, with a stealthy movement, Van Helsing takes the mirror from her and holds it up opposite the Count. In the mirror there is no reflection. The Count turns very slowly, catches Van Helsing making the test, and seizes the hand holding the mirror in his own claw-like paw. In his grasp the mirror is shattered and cuts Van Helsing's hand. At sight of the blood the Count becomes transformed suddenly into Dracula, with fangs and wolflike ears. At sight of him Mina screams and faints, recognizing in him the creature who visited her in the night. He leaps to attack Van Helsing, as John Harker, with a look of revelation on his face cries, "Dracula". Everything has come back to him.

Van Helsing snatches from his pocket the black velvet bag containing the "Host" and holding it before him, forces Dracula, still snarling, step by step backward toward the window, crying out "begone monster!" Dracula passes thru the closed and curtained window and vanishes.

Mrs. Triplett screams and covers her face with her hands.

John Harker, his memory restored in a flash, now recognizes Mina as his fiancee and remembers all his love for her.

(CONTINUED)

mrk

C-14 (Continued)

John Harker, in excitement, begs him to tell him the truth and say what it is that is destroying Mina. Van Helsing replies that he must have faith and that tomorrow they will perhaps know the truth. The thing they are fighting is more powerful than all of them together. They must not let it gain an advantage by acting before they are sure of themselves. John Harker, despite his weakened condition, insists upon sitting up all night to guard Mina.

C-15 AGAIN IN. SEWARD'S DRAWING ROOM

A bridge game is in progress. At the table are seated the Count, Dr. Seward, Mrs. Triplett and Lord Godalming. The Count and Mrs. Triplett are partners. Beside them is a chaise lounge. On it reclines Mina dressed in a negligee with a scarf wrapped about her throat. She looks feeble and ill. Beside her on the chaise lounge sits John Harker. On the other side of the table sits Van Helsing. They all are watching the game.

As the dialogue develops, it proves that the Count is an uncanny player, that he not only plays expertly, but reads the minds of the other players and has a hypnotic influence on the silly Mrs. Triplett, his partner. Presently John Harker gives a word of advice regarding a play to Mrs. Triplett, at which the Count looks at him with sudden alarm and says: "I thought you didn't play bridge. How do you know about that play?"

Harker replies "I used to know how to play before I was ill, and forgot everything. It is slowly coming back to me. I am beginning to remember fragments of all sorts of things." The game proceeds but the Count still watches Harker with fear.

(CONTINUED)

mrk

C-15 (Continued)-2

He attempts to raise her from the sofa in his arms and is about to kiss her when she opens her eyes, and with a cry of horror, cries "No! No! You must not kiss me! I am unclean!" Van Helsing seizing Harker, exclaims -- "She is right, you must not!"

They bring Mina to her senses and as they do so she sees John and recognizes him and says: "poor John" and strokes his head with her hand. Then she takes from her bosom a newspaper clipping which she silently hands to Van Helsing, who reads it.

It is the strange account of a happening in Bloomsbury, where, on several occasions, small children have been lured by what they describe "a beautiful lady". After being missing for some hours they have returned, bearing on their throats two small marks, apparently like the marks on the throat of Lucy and Mina.

Van Helsing finishes reading the article and murmurs, "So soon". Mina covers her face with her hands. As Dr. Seward reads the clipping Godalming exclaims with horror, "It is not true -- such things cannot be." Van Helsing replies: "I fear it is Lucy, but there is a way to discover. We will go to the graveyard at dawn. If it is Lucy we shall see her return to her tomb."

Mina, half hysterical, exacts from them the promise that they will tell her nothing of their plans. She and Van Helsing explain that already she is partially in the power of Dracula, and that thru her he can learn of their attempts to destroy him.

Dr. Seward takes Mina away leaving Mrs. Triplett and the three men alone. Mrs. Triplett, hysterical, says she will now return to her own house and Van Helsing bids her stay and guard Mina, while they carry out the work which must be done. She goes to join Dr. Seward and Mina.

(CONTINUED)

mrk

C-15 (Continued)-3

John Harker tries a drink to give him strength to go on with the story of what happened to him in Transylvania, which he now remembers. He begins to recount it to Van Helsing and Godalming.

C-16   THE HALLWAY

Mrs. Triplett making her way upstairs towards Mina's room. She hears steps coming along the corridor and hides herself, in terror, in an alcove. At the same moment the howl of a wolf is heard. The steps come nearer and it turns out to be only the keeper. She calls out to him and begs him to accompany her to Mina's room. She is too terrified to go alone. As they enter the room Dr. Seward orders the keeper, a burly fellow, to sit up with Mina and Mrs. Triplett. Mina is on the bed but not sleeping. She can no longer sleep at nights, but only sleeps in the daytime. At that moment a sound is heard at the window and looking toward it they see the outline of a great bat against the moonlight. They fling open the window and the keeper fires at it with his pistol and as he hits it, it turns into a cloud of mist.

C-17   THE DRAWING ROOM AGAIN

John Harker is finishing his story. He says: "I raised the spade to crush his head and the corpse turned in the coffin and stared at me. After that I can remember nothing." Van Helsing says: "The boxes are the same as those described by Mrs. Triplett. They are the earth to which the vampire must return at sunrise. We must find them and in one of them, after sunrise, Dracula is certain to be found. If they find him thus he will be helpless. They can then drive a stake thru his heart and destroy him forever."

Van Helsing has obtained Holy Water to sprinkle upon the earth in each of the boxes.

(CONTINUED)

C-17 (Continued)

If this is done the vampire cannot return to them.

Dr. Seward comes in and Van Helsing bids them prepare for the expedition to search for the boxes in haunted Carfax Abbey. Godalming suggests a pistol, but Van Helsing points out that these would be of no use. Instead he gives them each a fragment of the "Host" to wear in a pocket against their hearts. It is no use trying to capture Dracula until sunrise, as he will not return to his box of earth until then.

He says that before then they must go to the graveyard and wait to see whether Lucy returns to her tomb. If they discover that she is still "Undead" they must, likewise, put her at peace by driving a stake thru her heart.

C-18   THE ABBEY CHURCHYARD — THE TOMB IN THE FIRE

The four men enter thru the gateway among the tombstones. Again there is a howl of a wolf, and in the darkness are seen the burning eyes of scores of animals which appear to hate no bodies. The four men plan their action in entering Carfax Abbey and searching it, and as they are taking Van Helsing cries out suddenly — "look -- it is true". Thru the trees, among the tombs, appears the figure of Lucy. She is dressed all in white, but is transparent and is carrying something in her arms. They watch her with a horrible fascination. Van Helsing restrains Godalming, who starts to cry out and to go forward. Lucy puts down what she is carrying beside a gravestone and moves on, vanishing suddenly thru the closed door of the tomb.

The four men advance toward the tomb in which the ghostly figure of Lucy has just entered. Van Helsing takes a key and unlocks the door, saying, "Come, now we shall have the final proof".

(CONTINUED)

---

mrk

C-18 (Continued)

Godalming is overcome and John Harker says, "do not ask this dreadful thing of him". Van Helsing answers that he may wait outside with Dr. Seward, if John Harker will accompany him and do what they must do. John replies that he will do anything that will save Mina, or anything which will save the soul of poor Lucy. They go inside.

C-19   INSIDE THE TOMB

The only illumination comes from the electric torches which they carry, and from the blow-torch which Van Helsing has with him and which he lights. Then he unscrews the top of the coffin and rips open the lead covering. By the light of the electric torch they discover Lucy lying unchanged, looking perfectly alive. John Harker exclaims "she is not dead, she is living." To which Van Helsing replies, "Nothing can restore her to life. She is one of the undead. There is only one way to save her soul and give her peace. Are you strong enough to help me?"

Harker, after a moment of hesitation and horror, replies that he is. Van Helsing, taking up the sharpened stake they have brought with them, begins charring the end of it.

C-20   OUTSIDE THE TOMB

Seward and Godalming wait for the dreadful sound which will mean the end of the gruesome task performed by Van Helsing and Harker. The red eyes of phantom wolves still glimmer in the graveyard and now and then a howl is heard. Suddenly they hear a child crying. Following the sound a little way they come upon a small child lying beside a tombstone. Picking it up they carry it back to the door of the tomb, where Dr. Seward tries to comfort it.

(CONTINUED)

C-20 (Continued)

NB. There is no especial dramatic value in using the child. On the contrary, it rather clutters up the action and may annoy the censors.

C-21   INSIDE THE TOMB AGAIN

Van Helsing has prepared everything for his dreadful task. The stake is sharpened with the end charred. He takes out from a surgical case a long scalpel, which he lays on the edge of the coffin. Then he says to Harker, "you must hold the stake in place just over the heart." Harker closes his eyes with horror, holds the stake in place, and Van Helsing picks up a great stone lying near, using it as a hammer to drive the stake thru Lucy's heart. As he raises the stone

CUT TO:

C-22   SEWARD AND GODALMING-OUTSIDE

It is growing light. They listen and suddenly there is a wild scream wail from the inside of the tomb. Godalming attempts to enter the gate but is held back by Seward, and then covers his face with his hands in horror.

Van Helsing and Harker come out of the tomb, closing the door and locking it.

Van Helsing sees Godalming in suffering, and says: "That wild cry was not the cry of Lucy, but of the evil spirit which infested her body. Lucy is no longer undead. She is now at peace and her soul is saved. If you could see her face, you would believe me."

"Now for Carfax Abbey. The sun has risen and with luck, we shall find the monster sleeping in one of the coffins."

(CONTINUED)

mrk

C-22 (Continued)

where he must rest by day. We shall put this - (holding up the second stake) thru his heart and so destroy him and save our lovely Mina."

They move toward the ruined Abbey, which is on the other side of the graveyard.

> N.B. If they still have the child, it could be sent to the gardner's cottage with Seward.

C-23 THE IRON-STUDDED DOOR OF THE ABBEY.

With some difficulty they batter down the door and find themselves in a long corridor, thru which we have already seen Dracula disappear at the close of the second sequence.

They come, by the light of the torches, to a stairway which leads apparently into the bowels of the earth. They descend this, the camera accompanying them, down - down - down, until they come into a great vaulted chamber, like that which Harker has already seen in the Castle Dracula.

> N.B. Weird sounds and what-nots can accompany this descent.

On the floor of the vaulted room are four coffin-like boxes. The place is filled with bats and in the back, at bay, glitter the red eyes of innumerable rats.

Van Helsing, holding the Host before him and murmuring in Latin, advances into the unholy place. Harker exclaims, "there is no doubt, these are the same boxes I saw leave Castle Dracula, but there were five of them."

Van Helsing bids them tear open the boxes. In one of them must be the undead body of Dracula, himself. The rats advance toward them as they begin work. Van Helsing, with the Host before him, drives

(CONTINUED)

---

mrk

C-24 (Continued)

Suddenly Mina wakens and recognizes John and Van Helsing. John attempts to embrace her. Again she cries out, "do not touch me, I am unclean". Van Helsing, straightening up, says, "we must act at once. Dracula is in that box. He is escaping and we must pursue him. He cannot escape so long as he is on a ship. A vampire cannot cross open water. Our chance of capturing him is when he lands between sunrise and sunset."

In excitement Van Helsing shakes the keeper awake and orders him to bring a newspaper with the shipping news at once. The keeper obeys and steps out on the errand.

John Harker, charged also with excitement, calls Seward and Godalming and excitedly breaks the news to them. They all plan to depart at once in pursuit. They set about preparing to go. Mina, rising in the bed insists that she accompany them and Van Helsing agrees with her. It is the only way to protect her in case Dracula has played them a trick of some kind. She must never be out of their sight.

The keeper returns with the paper. Harker turns frantically to the ship news and finds that the "Black Eagle" has sailed at daybreak for Costanza, at which he cries out, "he is fleeing to Castle Dracula." Van Helsing says, "If he gets there before us, everything is lost. He can hide himself away and sleep a hundred years, until we are all dead. We must catch him while he is still chained to that box of earth.

END OF SEQUENCE "C"

---

mrk

C-23 (Continued)

them back. He says he will keep them at bay while the others perform the work. One by one they rip open the boxes. All are filled with earth, but none contain the form of Dracula. In dismay, Van Helsing exclaims, "he has escaped and hidden the fifth box elsewhere as a refuge. Unless we find it he has escaped and Mina is doomed. He has already put his stamp upon her. Unless we destroy him, he will claim her."

Harker, in despair, cries, "What must we do? What can we do?" To which Van Helsing exclaims, "Only God, or a miracle can help us now. We must go at once to Mina."

C-24 MINA'S BEDROOM AGAIN

The burly keeper and Mrs. Triplett have both fallen asleep in grotesque attitudes. On the bed Mina, half unconscious, is moaning incoherently. The door opens gently and Harker and Van Helsing enter the room. Harker bends over her and is about to take her hand when Van Helsing says, in a hoarse whisper, "wait... listen!"

From the mutterings of Mina a few words become distinct. She murmurs, "Oh Master, don't leave me. Do not put the water between us. Do not go away".

Van Helsing, in a fierce, excited whisper says, "Wait! Perhaps we have found a way to capture and destroy him. Perhaps God has delivered him into our hands."

Bending over Mina, Van Helsing begins to stroke her forehead and to question her. In a low voice he asks, "what do you see?" And in a hypnotic trance, Mina describes a ship with the name "Black Eagle" lying against the wharf, which they recognize from her description as the "Chelat Pier".

The ship is weighing anchor just as a coffin-like box is borne on board.

(CONTINUED)

EJF

SEQUENCE "D"

Sequence four is the race between the gypsies who are transporting the fifth box of earth, containing Dracula and the party consisting of Harker, Mina, Van Helsing, Godalming and Seward.

It is a race against time to capture the body of Dracula and put a stake thru his heart before sundown, when he can escape from the box and find refuge in his castle.

It is essentially a chase with very little dialogue and a great deal of action, ending in a fight with the gypsies just as they reach the door of the castle. When the box is captured it is opened and Dracula is found inside. A stake is driven thru his heart, the body crumbles into dust and Mina is saved, and for the first time is taken in Harker's arms with safety.

NB: It is well to note that an added suspense is given to the chase by the fact that each hour counts in saving Mina, who, as each hour progresses, draws a little nearer toward her complete transformation into a vampire.

The Hollywood Filmograph reported on August 2, 1930 that Bromfield, Murphy and E.M. Asher, Universal's Associate Producer on the project, had traveled to Oakland, California to see Lugosi in the play.

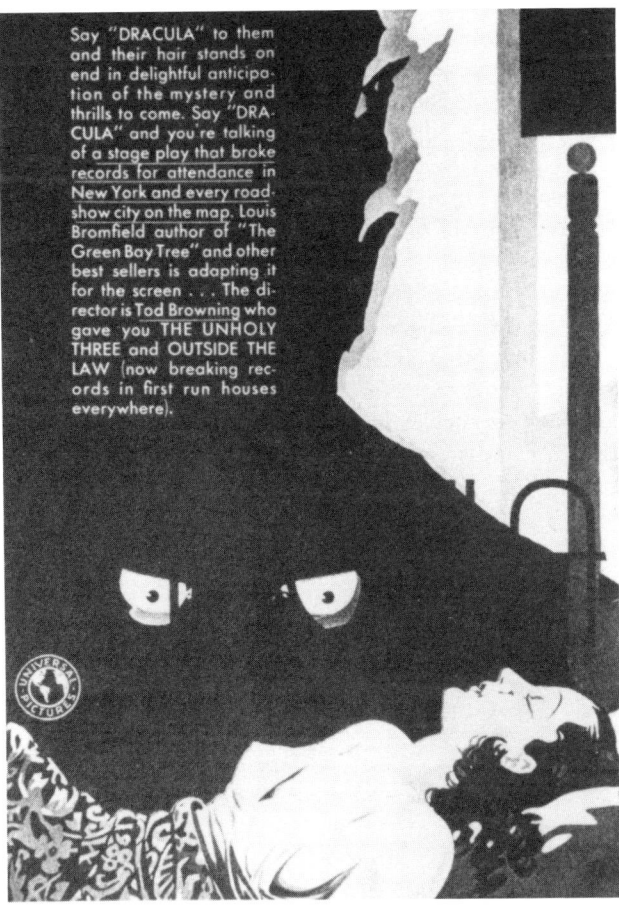

In this advance ad to distributors, Universal announced Bromfield as the writer even before Lugosi was given the part.

Conrad Veidt (1893-1943), Laemmle Sr.'s first choice for Count Dracula.

Tod Browning had now officially been announced as director, but without Chaney, the New York office became nervous. Universal's earlier attempt to replace Chaney in its successful gothic dramas had been mildly successful. Conrad Veidt, who performed superbly in several Universal silents between 1927 and 1929 - including the marvelous *The Man Who Laughs* and the part-talking *The Last Warning* - had returned to Germany when faced with the prospect of making talking pictures in English. There is no question but that Veidt would have been ideal for the role, but he was not disposed to leave Europe at the time.

Passing over Lugosi as not being sufficiently well known, the studio also considered the darkly handsome Ian Keith, a brilliant actor then in disfavor because of a drinking problem; and the distinguished stage actor, William Courtenay.

The next step in the development of the script was the assignment of Dudley Murphy to work with Bromfield to produce a workable script that could be produced within the limits of the budget. The Studio was becoming cautious and leaning more towards the Deane/Balderston play than the 30-year-old gothic novel.

Screenwriter Dudley Murphy

Unlike Bromfield, Dudley Murphy had years of experience in not only filmwriting but also directing and producing. He was born on July 10, 1897 in Winchester, Massachusetts. Ephraim Katz's Film Encyclopedia lists him as the son of a Harvard professor who became a journalist and assistant drama editor before turning to films in the early 20's. His last film was made in 1944 at his Mexican Studio.

The completed Bromfield-Murphy script was submitted to Carl Laemmle Jr. on September 8, 1930. This version dropped much of Bromfield's action and more closely remembled the Broadway play with touches of Murnau's *Nosferatu*. Murphy had seen the German version while in France where he was producing Fernand Leger's experimental work *Ballet méchanique*.

Restored was the ship's sequence, Renfield now takes the trip to Transylvania, and the Count's name remains unchanged. The remaining action now takes place, as in the play, on the grounds of the two estates - Dr. Seward's Sanitarium and Carfax Abbey.

After reviewing the script Carl Laemmle Jr. was still not satisfied. In his personal copy of the script the following comments were written:

(As Renfield's coach stops at the Inn)

Scene: A-17 - "Have action take place in long afternoon shadows."

(Inside the Inn a fellow traveller - an older Englishwoman in a black hat - is travelling with a simple-minded servant girl named Sara. Both characters appear in the final film, but Sara's only lines are reading about the Borgo Pass from a travel guide. This scene was shot but cut.)

Scene: A-21 - "Keep comedy in picture down - Maybe better..open picture simply."

Scene: A-30 - (Renfield is waiting at Midnight for Dracula's coach which is described as a fantastic cabriolet at top speed) - Laemmle notes: "Why is this fantastic?? Should be realistic!"

Scene: A-42 - (Renfield is left in the Castle grounds - the door opens with no one there - all is shot from inside the door using a long tunnel-like Hall-Truck shot.)

Laemmle comments: "This might be a cumbersome shot if you are going to use the columns and catacombs from the Phantom."

Scene: A-69 - (Renfield has fallen asleep in the den against Dracula's warnings. The three vampire woman find Renfield and their hands are seen in a closeup on Renfield tearing open his shirt and biting him on the neck.)

Laemmle writes: "Maybe eliminate! Women vampires very gruesome..."

Scene: B-14 - The wreck of the Varna has just arrived at the harbor and the captain is found dead at the wheel.

Laemmle's comments: "What happened to the crew? Explain in dialog? How? ...Dracula should go only for women and not men."

Scene: B-16 - Renfield is discovered in the hold of the ship: Laemmle notes: "How could Captain be killed by Dracula when he wore a crucifix?"

Later in the same scene when Renfield is found in the hold he is found eating flies off a small lump of sugar.

Laemmle's comment: "Awful strong.."

Following in the same scene the men burst in and find Renfield who takes his attention off the fly and says to the dock warden, "I almost had him and now you have frightened him away." He then sees another fly, licks his lips and sneaks toward it to the horror of the other men.

Laemmle's notes: "Sequence not right - What happened to Dracula? Can eliminate this sequence...."

There were only three more comments on the first draft script: first, he wanted the shots of Dracula walking through the fog after attacking the flower girl removed; he also ordered one of the most famous lines of the film cut where Dracula says:

"To really die - to be really dead - that must be glorious." Mina is shocked and says, "Why, Count Dracula," and Dracula sadly replies, "There are far worse things waiting for man than death."

Fortunately Browning must have talked him out of the cuts, for they are some of the best scenes in the film. However, the next scene numbered D-9 in the first draft would never have made it past the censors at the time:

D-9 LUCY CLOSEUP

She has given up reading and is lying back, her eyes closed as if dreaming of something. A slight smile plays on her lips. She breathes evenly and as her head lies back on the pillow we see her beautiful white throat and a suggestion of her well-formed bosom. The camera pans slowly down the bed and we see Dracula standing at the foot of the bed, looking intently at Lucy. Slowly he moves toward the head of the bed, nearer, nearer. As he does so, the scene includes Lucy. Dracula's long hands reach out, his lips part and his head bends nearer to her throat. The teeth seem to have almost a canine appearance as his mouth is about to touch her neck.

DISSOLVE ......

The only other comments written in Laemmle's script were that he wanted the term "looney" eliminated and that some locations were not clearly established as sets to be built or already existing. There is a strong indication that financial pressures from the New York office were starting to win over the artistic desires of Jr.

(Above) Director Tod Browning on the set.

It was then given to Tod Browning and writer Garrett Fort for the final polish. The final "polish" turned the script into a film version of the stage play, far removed from Fritz Stephani's action-packed horror drama. Bromfield's name was dropped from the writing credits. Bromfield and Hollywood did not get along well, as is the case with many noted novelists. In the late 1930's he left Hollywood and moved to his farm in Ohio, where in the next decade he was to win the Pulitzer Prize for Journalism.

During the rewrites, Lugosi was finally called to Universal for a screen test. Two scenes were shot in a few hours and then rushed to the projection room for review by Laemmle Jr.

Writer Garrett Fort from a an earlier New York portrait

Ayres, however, was finishing up his commitment to Fox Studios and had just completed *The Spirit of Notre Dame* (with William Bakewell, his comrade-in-arms from *All Quiet On The Western Front*) for Universal. He was replaced by David Manners, whose Canadian accent and charming screen presence fit more into the British character of the Universal-play version. Lew Ayres was assigned to co-star with Jean Harlow in Tod Browning's next Universal film, *The Iron Man*, released a few months after *Dracula*. Laemmle thought the jump from football player to English solicitor (Real Estate Salesman) and then back to a lightweight prize fighter might be too much for the public to accept.

David Manners had also been receiving glowing reviews, as in The New York Times: "an actor whose excellent diction and personal charm are an asset to any film."

It was announced in the press on September 20, 1930 that Lugosi had won the part! Edward Van Sloan, Herbert Bunston and Dwight Frye signed to repeat their stage roles and Lew Ayres and Helen Chandler were to play the "two lovers."

The romantic leads, David Manners and Helen Chandler

Lew Ayres - from a Universal Studios 1930 portrait

Abraham Van Helsing, Edward van Sloan

Renfield, Dwight Frye

Lucy, Frances Dade

Dr. Seward, Herbert Brunston

Innkeeper, Michael Visaroff, greets Mr. Renfield

Nurse, Josephine Velez

Martin, Renfield's attendant, Charles Gerrard

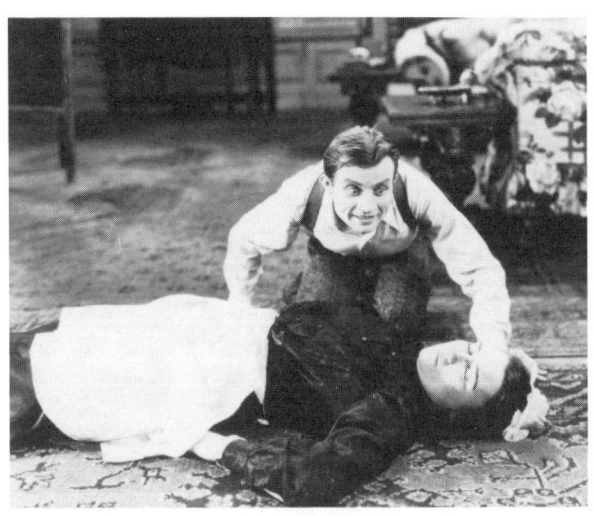
Maid, Moon Carroll
(The end of this scene was cut from the final release - note what happens in the script.)

Count Dracula - Bela Lugosi

Karl Freund, ASC, the most celebrated cinematographer of Germany's "Golden Age" of expressionism, was assigned to *Dracula*, his first American film. His German credits included *Variety, Metropolis, The Last Laugh, The Golem, Symphony of a City*, and other revered classic of imaginative cinema. Born in Bohemia in 1890, he had been a movie technician and cameraman since 1906. He was also an inventor, owned a film lab in Berlin, and was a director and producer for Fox Film in Germany. When he came to America in 1930 to tout a color process in which he had a proprietary interest, William Stull, ASC secretary, informed him that "...at the last meeting of the Board of Governors of the American Society of Cinematographers, you, as Europe's foremost cinematographer, were unanimously elected to Active Membership in that society."

Freund gravitated to Universal, which he had visited in 1924 while *The Phantom of The Opera* was being made there. Arthur Edeson, ASC, then Universal's top-ranking cinematographer, championed him as "a great photographer" and Carl Laemmle Sr., who was extremely loyal to his native Germany, welcomed him with open arms. Freund ingratiated himself quickly by suggesting the perfect ending for *All Quiet On The Western Front* that had eluded the writers.

Universal's supervising art director, the very British Charles D. Hall, made a number of idea drawings for key sets, including the much imitated cellars of Dracula's London home, with its massed groined arches and monumental stairway. He was assisted by two remarkable artists, Herman Rosse and John Hoffman. Rosse, a noted stage set designer from the Netherlands, had come to Universal with Broadway director John Murray Anderson for the spectacular *King of Jazz*, which won him an Academy Award for 1929-30. It was Rosse who saved a chunk of the set budget for *Dracula* by designing the spectacular facade of Castle Dracula to be pieced together with portions of disassembled Medieval sets from the silent days. Hoffman was one of those brilliant but little known artists who worked behind the scenes at the major studios. Hoffman designed sets for several early talkies, but later switched to directing, special effects photography, and, most notably, to creating montage sequences.

Herman Rosse

Karl Freund, ASC, March 1955

To call the short, rotund Freund "colorful" would be to understate the case. He could be gracious and charming at one moment, cool and distant the next. When directing, he proved to be a hard-boiled, Prussian-styled taskmaster in the tradition of his mentor, Fritz Lang. A handful of directorial assignments from 1933 to 1935 (*The Mummy, Moonlight and Pretzels, Uncertain Lady, The Count of Monte Cristo,* and *Mad Love*, all of which were realized with speed and resourcefulness) prove him to have been a brilliant and imaginative director.

Carl Laemmle Jr. at age 21, 1929

Budgeted at $355,050 and scheduled for 36 working days, principal photography was begun September 29 on the back lot country inn set. It was completed Novermber 15, after 42 working days, at a negative cost of $341,191.20. Added scenes were shot on December 13, and retakes on January 2, 1931.

The actual final cost (not including exploitation and talent) was a reported $441,984.90.

A Spanish language version, utilizing the same sets but with a different cast, producer, director and crew, was begun on the night of October 23, 1931.

Production Schedule from DRACULA (English and Spanish)

62

Scenes from the Spanish Production of *Dracula*

Tod Browning visits the set of the Spanish DRACULA: (Top of stairs), Writer Fernandez Cue, Director George Melford; (with script), Carlos Villar (Dracula); Barry Norton (seated), Pablo Alvarez Rubio (hand on Dracula's arm), crew member, Manuel Arbo, unidentified, Eduardo Arozamena, Cinematographer George Robinson on crane with crew; (bottom, far right), Paul Kohner and Lupita Tovar look up from below.

The producer was Paul Kohner, who later founded a leading talent agency but at the time was head of Universal's foreign department. Born in Czechoslovakia and educated in Vienna, the tall and personable Kohner had been a production supervisor at Universal for years and was the producer of an excellent silent spectacle, *The Man Who Laughs*, in 1928.

Kohner had fallen in love with Lupita Tovar, a beautiful actress from Mexico who was playing small parts at Universal.

"Lupita told me she couldn't make enough money at Universal and she was going back to Mexico," Kohner said in 1988. "I lay awake all night trying to figure a way to change her mind. I went to Uncle Carl and told him that I could make Spanish versions of his pictures for about $35,000 each by using the same sets after the regular company had quit for the night. He agreed to give it a try with THE CAT CREEPS. I put Lupita in Helen Twelvetrees' role, the picture was a great success, and she decided to stay in Hollywood."

Following a triumphant tour of Mexico, the petite actress was assigned the feminine lead in the Spanish *Dracula*. (She also became Mrs. Kohner. The marriage was happy and enduring.)

George Melford, a veteran director of the hard-boiled school who was best known for the Rudolph Valentino silent *The Sheik*, directed. The cinematographer was George Robinson, ASC, undoubtedly one of the most underrated artists in his field. The adaptation was the work of the scholarly Baltazar Fernandez Cue, who did most of the Spanish language screenplays made in Hollywood. In the cast were Carlos Villar as Dracula, Lupita Tovar as Eva (Mina), Barry Norton as Juan, Eduardo Arozamena as Van Helsing, Carmen Guerrero as Lucia, and Pablo Alvarez Rubio as Renfield. Villar somewhat resembled Lugosi and obviously patterned his portrayal after him.

• • • • • • • • • • • • • • •

(Above) Count Dracula (Carlos Villar) invites Mr. Renfield (Pablo Alvarez Rubio) to dine. Robinson's camera angle makes much greater use of the eerie gothic decay of the castle even in the "Cheerful atmosphere of the dining hall."

(Below) Villar leaves Carfax to drain the blood of his victims.

Edwardo Arozamena (Van Helsing), Lupita Tovar (Eva),
Jose Soriano Viosco (Dr. Seward), Juan Harker (Barry Norton)

Juan and Eva are confronted by Dracula as a bat.

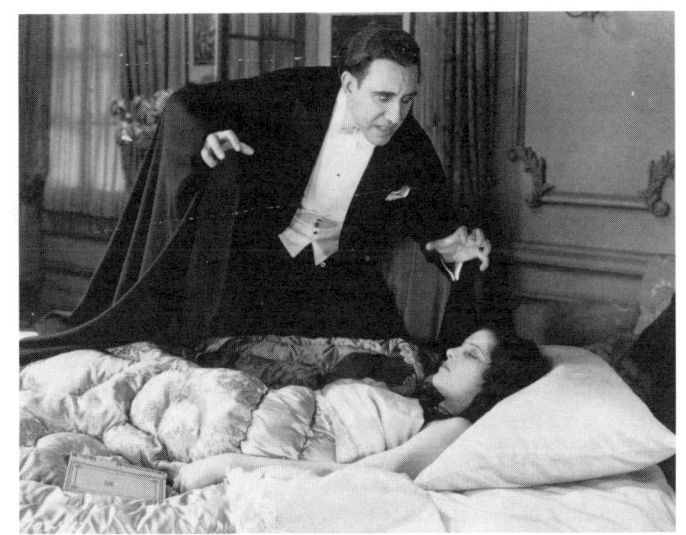

Villar and the beautiful Lupita Tovar
make a much more sensual version of this scene.

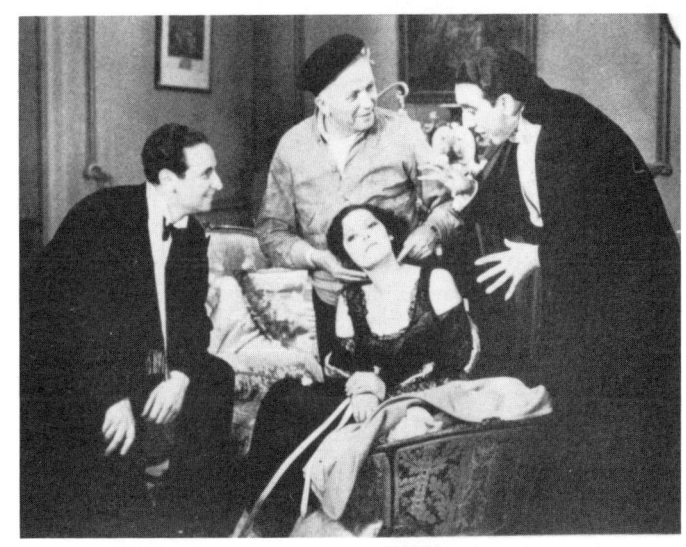

Paul Kohner watches as Director George Melford playfully point out
Lupita Tovar's jugular vein to Carlos Villar in this production shot.

Castle Dracula

Both versions of *Dracula* open with glass shots, which were photographed by Frank Booth, of a horse-drawn coach coming at breakneck speed down a mountain road in the wilds of Transylvania. Swirling mist is superimposed over the scenes, which were made northeast of Los Angeles at Vasquez Rocks, whose angular hogback formations blend flawlessly into the artist's towering peaks.

Renfield is met by Dracula's coach.

Dracula's wives (changed to sisters by the censor). The identity of these three actresses remains a mystery.

The inn, yard, corral and peasant hut were constructed on a back lot hill (now the site of the Universal Tour gift shops and Tour shows) around the curve of a deeply rutted old wagon trail. A large wooden cross, jutting from the brow of the hill, and other Old World props left over from *The Hunchback of Notre Dame* and *All Quiet On The Western Front*, lend versimilitude to the setting.

There are other glass shots of the castle and the coach in the mountains and an excellent miniature of Castle Dracula perched atop the crags. The camera roams the ruined cellars, where rats, armadillos and other animals scurry among skeletons and debris. There are several coffins. The lid of one raises slightly and a man's hand snakes forth. The hands of the women emerge from three other coffins and a gigantic beetle crawls out of another. Then Dracula and his wives are shown standing majestically beside their coffins. (In the Spanish version a heavy mist spreads from each opened coffin, followed by a burst of light, then by the standing figure of the vampire.) Subsequent night for night scenes, representing the midnight meeting point in Borgo Pass, were photographed at a mountainous junction in the west part of the lot. These unreal but eerily effective shots are backlit from below, the light beaming up through the mist, presumably from a town in the valley. The journey to the castle is handsomely photographed, particularly in a stunning pit-shot as the team and carriage hurtle over the camera in a thunderous roar and vanish into the castle grounds.

The vaulted hall is introduced in a glass shot that expands the impressive set to enormous proportions. It perfectly conveys decaying grandeur and an atmosphere of dread. A fallen tree thrusts its branches through tall windows.

Bats flutter and screech beyond breaks in the walls, and the place is littered with fallen stones, decaying tapestries, cobwebs and dust. The deep shadows cast by the full moon and evil scurrying sounds (actually aided by the primitive recording method) suggest unseen menace at every hand. One of the three cutting continuities calls for the introduction scenes in Dracula's Castle between Dracula and Renfield to be tinted a blue-green to enhance the full moon effect. This, as in Murnau's *Nosferatu*, creates a totally different and literally hair-raising mystique and tone missing in today's prints.

The "cheerful" bedroom is also large, with a fireplace of heroic proportions, windows that extend above the frame, ornate pillars and massive furnishings. This room is exploited to better effect in the Spanish film, in which the players move more freely and the flaming fireplace becomes more than a backdrop. Browning had moved his actors away from the fireplace because the crackling of the fire interfered with the dialogue.

The ship which takes Dracula and Renfield to England is depicted first as a minature. Full scale shots of the seamen fighting to keep the ship afloat are undercranked, suggesting stock footage from a silent film. The investigation of the derelict is imaginatively executed, the camera roving over the deck, taking in the details as the voices of the unseen men come over. In Browning's version, the director himself is heard saying, "Captain dead - tied to the

exterior scenes, however, are fascinating because of excellent night for night lighting and fog effects.

The Melford/Robinson sequences are better visually, being made up of a greater variety of shots, including a fine glass shot of Carfax Abbey overlooking the real ocean. The sets are decorated more colorfully for the Latin audiences, with added frills and filagrees, and the lace negligees worn by Tovar and Guerrero are considerably more eye-catching than the more British nightwear of Chandler and Dade. The one thing lacking is the magical ensemble work that Lugosi, Frye and Van Sloan gave to Browning.

The climax occurs in Carfax Abbey, a magnificently decadent setting, and in these scenes much of the excitement of the opening reels is regained. Although the elaborate camera moves that were a Freund hallmark are absent in the English version, the

wheel. Horrible tragedy - Horrible tragedy." Next Browning is actually seen as he bends to open the hatch and again can be heard reciting the lines, "They must have come through a terrible storm. (Renfield is heard laughing) What's that? Why - it's come from that hatchway. (Shot of Renfield at the bottom of the stairs) Why, he's mad - Look at his eyes! Why, the man's gone crazy!" The scene gunning down at Renfield is quite subtle; the madman's shadow produces an illusion that he has additional arms jutting from his lower body, lending him an appropriate insect-like appearance.

The scenes inside the sanitarium are photographed straightforwardly in rather long takes, showing little of the imagination that distinguishes the Transylvanian action. The action proceeds in the manner of a stage play, with some key material happening off-screen (the werewolf episode, for example). It is generally believed that Browning had to hurry through this part of the picture because he had fallen so far behind schedule. The several

lighting of the catacombs and a huge vault with a long, curving, unbalustraded stairway show artistry of a high order. Here again, however, Melford and Robinson take the palm with some stunning camera moves, especially when they utilize the unique "Broadway Crane" to carry the action onto the high stairs. In the Spanish version Dracula flings Renfield over the side of these steps instead of Frye's more dramatic tumble down two flights.

In the original release the end title was interrupted as Van Sloan stepped in front of the screen to make a brief curtain speech, which was taken from the New York play, in which it was spoken by Dracula rather than the professor.

§

Music
After the editing was completed, the next step in this new media of talking movies was music.

In his article "Music for the Monsters--Universal Pictures' Horror Film Scores of the Thirties" (published in the <u>Quarterly Journal of the Library of Congress</u>, Fall, 1983), film music historian William H. Rosar recounts:

Born in Milwaukee on May 1, 1901, Roemheld had been a concert pianist and studied composition in Berlin with Hugo Kaun, a rival of Richard Strauss. Roemheld was discovered in 1925 by Carl Laemmle Sr. at Milwaukee's Alhambra Theater.

The popular Victor Concert Orchestra recording the accompanying music for Universal's Newspaper Newsreel. The addition of such excellent music to Graham McNamee's newscasting makes the newsreel triply entertaining.

Rosario Bourdon, conductor of the Victor Concert Orchestra, in his study

In the fall of 1930, when Universal finished its production of Bram Stoker's *Dracula*, the place of music in sound films was the subject of ongoing controversy. In question were such issues as the amount of music there should be in a film, where the audience would think the music was "coming from" if they did not actually see musicians performing it, and whether or not to have music during dialogue scenes. The outcome of this debate was that, aside from main and end titles, there was very little music in most early sound films.

With these prevailing attitudes toward film music in 1930, it is perhaps not surprising that the only music in *Dracula* is heard during the main title and in the concert hall sequence where there is some "source" music (coming from an on-screen source). There was no music at the end of the film, only chimes.

Dracula is one of the few films of that time containing long stretches which are not only without dialogue but which are virtually silent, leaving ample room for music!

Supervising what little music there was in *Dracula* was the responsibility of Heinz Roemheld, who was general music director of Universal's Music Department at the time. He composed music for a number of Universal's films in 1930, including the nondialogue version of *All Quiet on the Western Front*, the musical *Captain of the Guard*, and the main title music for *The Cat Creeps*.

Roemheld was music director and conducted the pit orchestra which accompanied the silent films. Laemmle was very impressed by Roemfeld's musical treatment of *The Phantom of the Opera*, for which the latter staged a musical prologue featuring opera stars singing arias from Gounod's *Faust*. Because of this, Laemmle gave him a four-year contract, first appointing him music director of the Rialto Theater in Washington, D.C. for two years and then sending him to Germany, where he managed Laemmle's two theaters in Berlin. In 1929 Laemmle brought Roemheld to California to be a composer in the Music Department at Universal. Roemheld succeeded David Broekman as general music director of the department in the summer of 1930 (Broekman had been appointed in early 1929). Roemheld had definite ideas about music in films, one of which was to use the classical songs of Schubert, Schumann, and others to offset the more-or-less exclusive use of songs by Tin Pan Alley songwriters which he regarded as being mostly second rate.

The main title of *Dracula* consists of an abbreviation of scene 2 from Tchaikovsky's *Swan Lake* ballet suite, edited to fit the length. There is no record if this was Roemfield's idea, but it was the first time the piece was used in a Universal sound film (and it appears to have had a history of usage in silent films as a mysterioso, and may have been chosen for *Dracula* for this reason).

Heinz Roemheld

The original arrangement of Swan Lake used in the main titles

Presumably the version used in the recording of *Dracula* was the *Swan Lake* suite published by Fischer, arranged for theater orchestra by Charles Roberts, since it would have been the only one readily available in those days.

Any number of classical selections were used in the scores for Univeral's nondialogue versions because they did not cost anything (being in the public domain), and were known to be dramatically effective by those who compiled the score.

It is interesting to note that the classical excerpts heard in the concert hall sequence (supposedly Albert Hall in London), the prelude to Wagner's *Die Meistersinger* and Schubert's *Unfinished Symphony*, almost seem to follow the action: a declamatory phrase from Schubert's symphony as Count Dracula enters the lobby of Albert Hall; the majestic coda of Wagner's *Meistersinger* prelude as the Count is ushered to his seat; and after the intervening intermission scene, a solemn figure in low strings from Schubert's symphony as the lights dim and the Count exclaims, "There are far worse things awaiting man than death!" The illogical order in which the excerpts are heard in this concert hall context suggests that they were chosen and arranged in this sequence for dramatic effect.

In addition to the information in his article, Mr. Rosar adds:

Of the 70 measures comprising "Scene" from the *Swan Lake* suite, only 38 are heard in *Dracula*. Also, there is an interesting idiosyncracy in the performance of "Scene".

In the middle of the piece there is an abrupt increase in tempo not heard in recent performances or recordings of "Scene". When I brought this to Roemheld's attention, he remarked that he thought the music was marked "doppio movimento" at that point (twice as fast as the preceding tempo). He was apparently aware of the inconsistency in performances, and said that "conductors don't know what to do there," though in his opinion, the tempos heard in *Dracula* were correct.

Consistent with Roemheld's recollection, in the Carl Fischer edition published in 1917, arranged by Charles J. Roberts for theater orchestra (the only edition listed in a card catalog in Universal's music library), the time signature change to <u>alla breve</u> marking is absent. Presumably, the performance heard in *Dracula* is of the Fischer edition, since Universal used Charles Roberts' arrangements of the classics published by Carl Fischer because the studio orchestra of those days was about the same size as a theater orchestra (about 20 to 30 players).

(Mr. Rosar is founder of the Society for the Preservation of Film Music in Los Angeles.)

Count Dracula in front of Albert Hall

In the September 8, 1930 script by Bromfield and Murphy, Dracula, after feeding on the unfortunate flower girl, pauses in front of the theater. He sees Mina, Lucy, Dr. Seward and John getting into a cab. Upon hearing their destination Dracula then enters his own cab and follows them back to the Sanitarium grounds. The dialogue takes place almost exactly as heard in the final release version, however it takes place in Dr. Seward's living room instead of Albert Hall. Mina is heard playing the piano in the background until Dracula makes his famous entrance as announced by the maid.

The final Browning-Fort version takes place in the concert hall, giving a much grander shade to the scene than "just a piano," which audiences in 1930 associated with silent films. It also gave the audience their "source" as Mr. Rosar has noted as being the neccessary element for allowing music to be heard in an early talking film.

(Above) David Manners and Helen Chandler listen to Bela Lugosi's words "There far worse things than death.." to Francis Dade, as the music from Schubert's Unfinished Symphony enhances the Count's last words (shot on the old Phantom Stage #28).

(Below) The sound technician records the dialogue and music on a Vitaphone disc.

The Spanish *Dracula* was previewed in January at the studio. The Hollywood Filmograph (January 10):

If the English version of Dracula, directed by Tod Browning, is as good as the Spanish version, why the Big U haven't a thing in the world to worry about...The other evening, before a capacity theatre on the lot there was screened a preview...which was witnessed by Bela Lugosi and to use his own words the Spanish picture was 'beautiful, great, splendid.'

The English *Dracula* was announced to open at the Roxy Theater in New York on February 13, 1931.

Tod Browning took out an ad (having it set to look like a telegram) dated February 7th:

> DEAR ROXY: DON'T BLAME ME BUT I WAS BORN SUPERSTITIOUS - STOP- JUST HEARD YOU ARE OPENING DRACULA FRIDAY- STOP- THAT BAD ENOUGH BUT FRIDAY THE THIRTEENTH IS TERRIBLE - STOP- I HAVE PUT EVERYTHING I HAVE INTO THIS PICTURE AND AS A FAVOR TO ME CAN'T YOU OPEN YOUR PRESENTATION THURSDAY - STOP - BEST REGARDS TOD BROWNING

Rothafel, going along with the publicity, promptly set the date back one day to the 12th.

S.L. Rothafel, owner of the famous Foxy Theater in New York City

The reviews were sensational, and firmly established Carl Laemmle's faith in his son as studio production manager.

The New York Times: *Mr. Browning is fortunate in having in the leading role in this eerie work, Bela Lugosi. What with Mr. Browning's imaginative direction and Mr. Lugosi's make-up and weird gestures, this picture succeeds to some extent in its grand guignol intentions. This picture can at least boast of being the best of the many mystery films.*

The Herald Tribune: *Lugosi's performance is even more effective than he was on the stage, which is something of a tribute.*

The Film Daily: *Bela Lugosi gives a convincing performance and creates one of the most unique and powerful roles of the screen.*

The New York Daily News: *It is superbly photographed, and presented to audible screen audiences at the capable movie direction of Tod Browning--megaphoner of so many mysteries that he knows every trick of the type. Carl Laemmle Jr. counts Dracula among his productions for the season, and the boy's done well again. He chose director, cast, and story wisely. Bela Lugosi's performance as Count Dracula is a repetition of his stage role. He's simply grand.*

The picture was photographed in full silent frame aperture for sound on disc presentation and for a subtitled silent version with intercut dialogue titles. When the sound on film prints were made (the Vitaphone was rapidly becoming obsolete), the picture area was masked to Western Electric standards to allow for the sound track and some masking at the top and bottom. This operation shifted the optical center and changed the compositions noticeably. The visuals gain considerably when seen at full aperture (available only on MCA/Universal laser disk). The silent version differs from the talking film only in the cutting in of dialogue titles, which are like telegraph versions of the spoken words -- i.e., "To die -- to be really dead! That must be glorious! There are far worse things awaiting man than death," becomes: "To be really dead -- that must be glorious! There are far worse things than death." And the Spanish version - "Morir de verdad....estar realmente muerto...debe ser sublime! Algo peer que la muerte, acecha a los mortales. "(To really die...to be really dead...must be wonderful! At the end of one's life there are things more horrible than death!)

And what of the Spanish version? An incomplete print exists in the United States' Library of Congress in Washingon, D.C.; a complete print in the Cuban Film Archive is listed at 102 minutes -- a full 27 minutes longer than the standard version. It is easy to agree with the El Cine Espanol critic Fillipe Veracoechea, who said in 1931 that "Spanish American audiences will receive *Dracula* as the most fascinating picture made." There was, however, one complaint from the Spanish speaking audiences - the clash of different dialects spoken by actors who hailed variously from Spain, Mexico, and Central and South America.

Bela Lugosi was now a star. But the role of Dracula became synonymous with his own name - with tragic results for this great Hungarian actor. In fact, almost everyone associated with Dracula, from his creator Bram Stoker to the present day, seems to have fallen under it's overpowering force.

In early Summer of 1931, Universal began production on *Frankenstein*. Lugosi was cast as Dr. Frankenstein by Director Robert Florey. Lugosi agreed, seeing a classic literary character in the role of the Doctor. However, Junior saw Lugosi as the new Lon Chaney, and insisted on his portraying the Monster when James Whale took over production. Lugosi passed, to avoid being typecast. It didn't work! He told writer John Sinclair, a few months after the release of *Dracula*:

Circumstances made me the theatrical personality I am, which many people believe is also a part of my personal life. My next picture, Murders in the Rue Morgue, will continue to establish me as a weird, gruesome creature. As for my own feelings on the subject, I have always felt I would rather play say, Percy Marmout roles than Lon Chaney types of things.....

I will never play the role of Dracula again.......

(For an in-depth study of the shadow of Dracula that touched the lives of many connected with the name, may I recommend: *Hollywood Gothic 1* by David Skal, published by W.W. Norton, 1990 -- PJR)

Dracula

English Version

STUDIO: Universal
PRODUCER: Carl Laemmle Jr.
A Tod Browning Production presented by Carl Laemmle
DIRECTOR: Tod Browning
ASSOCIATE PRODUCER: E.M. Asher
BOOK: Bram Stoker
ADAPTED FROM THE PLAY BY: Hamilton Deane and John L. Balderston
PLAY SCRIPT: Garrett Fort
CONTINUITY: Louis Bromfield
ADDED DIALOGUE: Dudley Murphy
ADAPTATION: Louis Stevens
TREATMENT: Fritz Stephani
SCENARIO SUPERVISION: Charles A. Logue
ART DIRECTOR: Charles D. Hall
CINEMATOGRAPHER: Karl Freund
FILM EDITOR: Milton Carruth
SUPERVISING FILM EDITOR: Maurice Pivar
SET DESIGNERS: Herman Rosse, John Hoffman
PHOTOGRAPHIC EFFECTS: Frank J. Booth
RECORDING SUPERVISION: C. Roy Hunter
MUSICAL CONDUCTOR: Heinz Roemheld
MAKEUP: Jack P. Pierce
SET DECORATIONS: Russell A. Gausman
COSTUMES: Ed Ware, Vera West
CASTING: Phil M. Friedman
RESEARCH: Nan Grant
ART TITLES: Max Cohen
WESTERN ELECTRIC RECORDING:
Running time, sound on film and disc versions, 78 minutes; Running time silent version, 78 minutes.
Premiered at the Roxy Theater, New York City, February 12, 1931.

CAST

Count Dracula	Bela Lugosi
Mina	Helen Chandler
John Harker	David Manners
Renfield	Dwight Frye
Van Helsing	Edward van Sloan
Dr. Seward	Herbert Bunston
Lucy	Frances Dade
Briggs	Joan Standing
Martin	Charles Gerrard
Maid	Moon Carroll
Nurse	Josephine Velez
Innkeeper	Michael Visaroff
Surgeon	Wyndham Standing
English Passenger	Daisy Belmore
Transylvanian Passenger	Nicholas Bela
Sara (coach passenger)	Carla Laemmle
Passenger	Donald Murphy
Harbor Master	Tod Browning

Spanish Version

STUDIO: Universal
PRODUCER: Carl Laemmle Jr.
ASSOCIATE PRODUCER: Paul Kohner
DIRECTOR: George Melford

ADAPTED FROM THE PLAY BY: Hamilton Deane and John L. Balderston
SCREENPLAY: Garrett Fort and B. Fernandez Cue
ART DIRECTOR: Charles D. Hall
CINEMATOGRAPHER: George Robinson, ASC
EDITORIAL SUPERVISION: Maurice Pivar
SOUND SUPERVISOR: C. Roy Hunter
FILM EDITOR: Arturo Tavares
MAKEUP: Jack P. Pierce
WESTERN ELECTRIC RECORDING SYSTEM

Running time, 102 minutes, Released January, 1931

CAST

Count Dracula	Carlos Villar
Eva	Lupita Tovar
Juan Harker	Barry Norton
Renfield	Pablo Alvarez Rubio
Professor Van Helsing	Eduardo Arozamena
Lucia	Carmen Guerrero
Dr. Seward	Jose Soriano Viosco
Martin	Manuel Arbo
Marta	Amelia Senisterra

ART DEPARTMENT

The Great Hall of Dracula's castle as drawn by John Hoffman (Courtesy, U.S.C. Cinema Library - Universal Collection).

The miniature Castle Dracula - seen only for a few seconds in the film.

Another variation of the Great Hall from Hoffman's scrapbook, and the same scene as filmed by Browning.

Behind the Scenes

Bela Lugosi and Tod Browning are visited by Broadway producer Horace Liveright (facing Lugosi) and writer Dudley Murphy (far right).

Garrett Fort working on rewrites

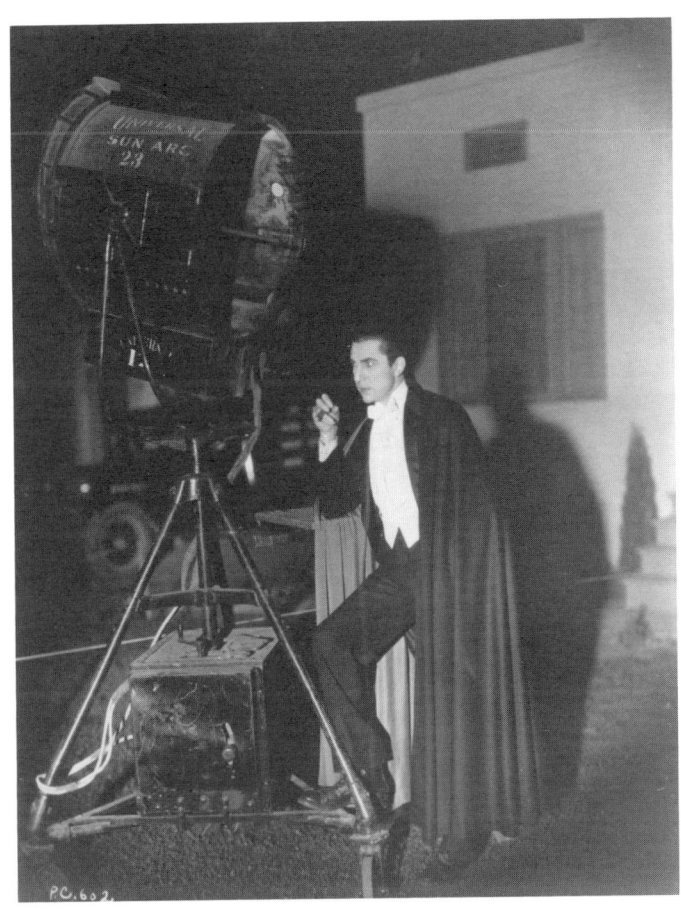

Bela Lugosi poses during a break next to a kleig light (above) and a wind machine (below).

Dracula's identity has been discovered by Van Helsing. (Note chalk marks on floor in foreground)

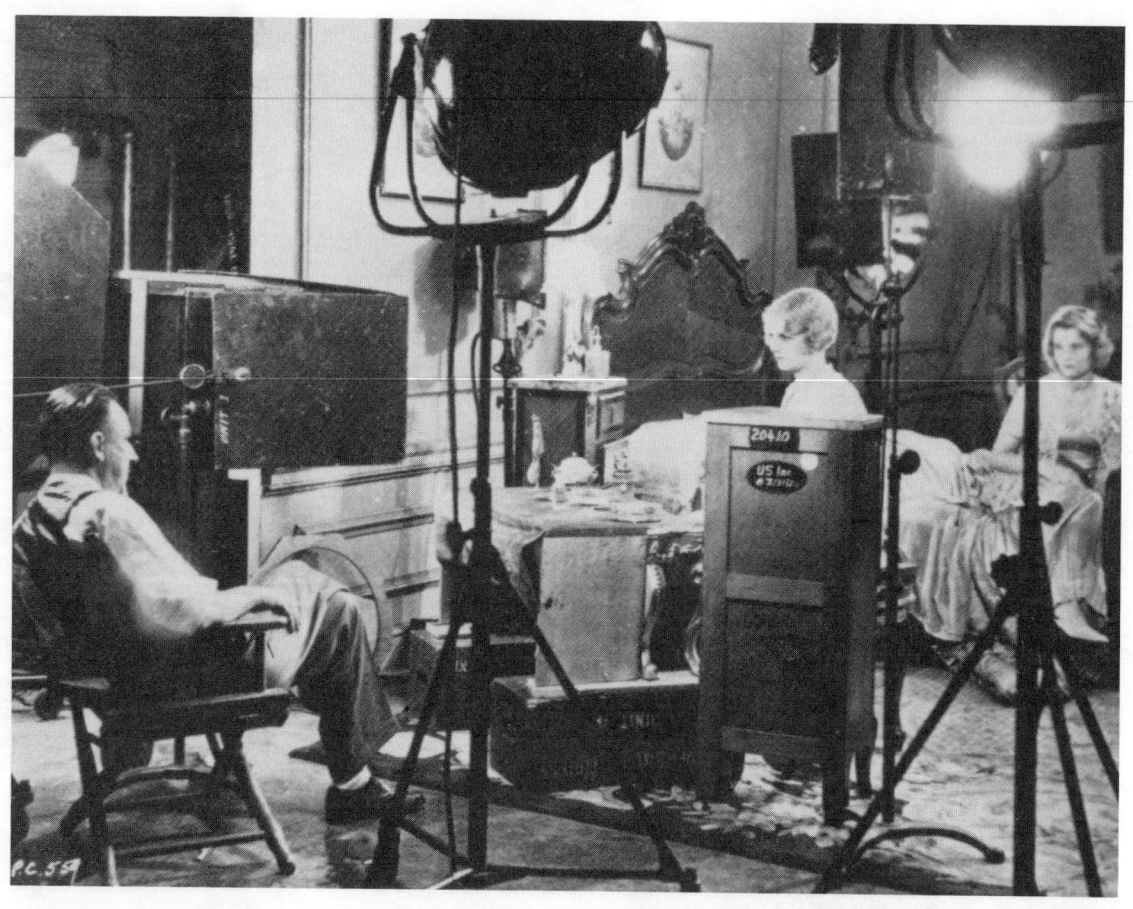

Director Browning (far left, in chair) watches the actions of Lucy and Mina after they return from the Albert Hall Sequence.

(Above left) Bela Lugosi and his wife Lillian arrive in Hollywood. (Right) Bela with his dog on a ski trip in the Sierras. (Below) Back on the set, posing with Edward van Sloan for publicity pictures.

79

Director Browning stops to pose during an interview.

Writer Fort studying his script (in 1929).

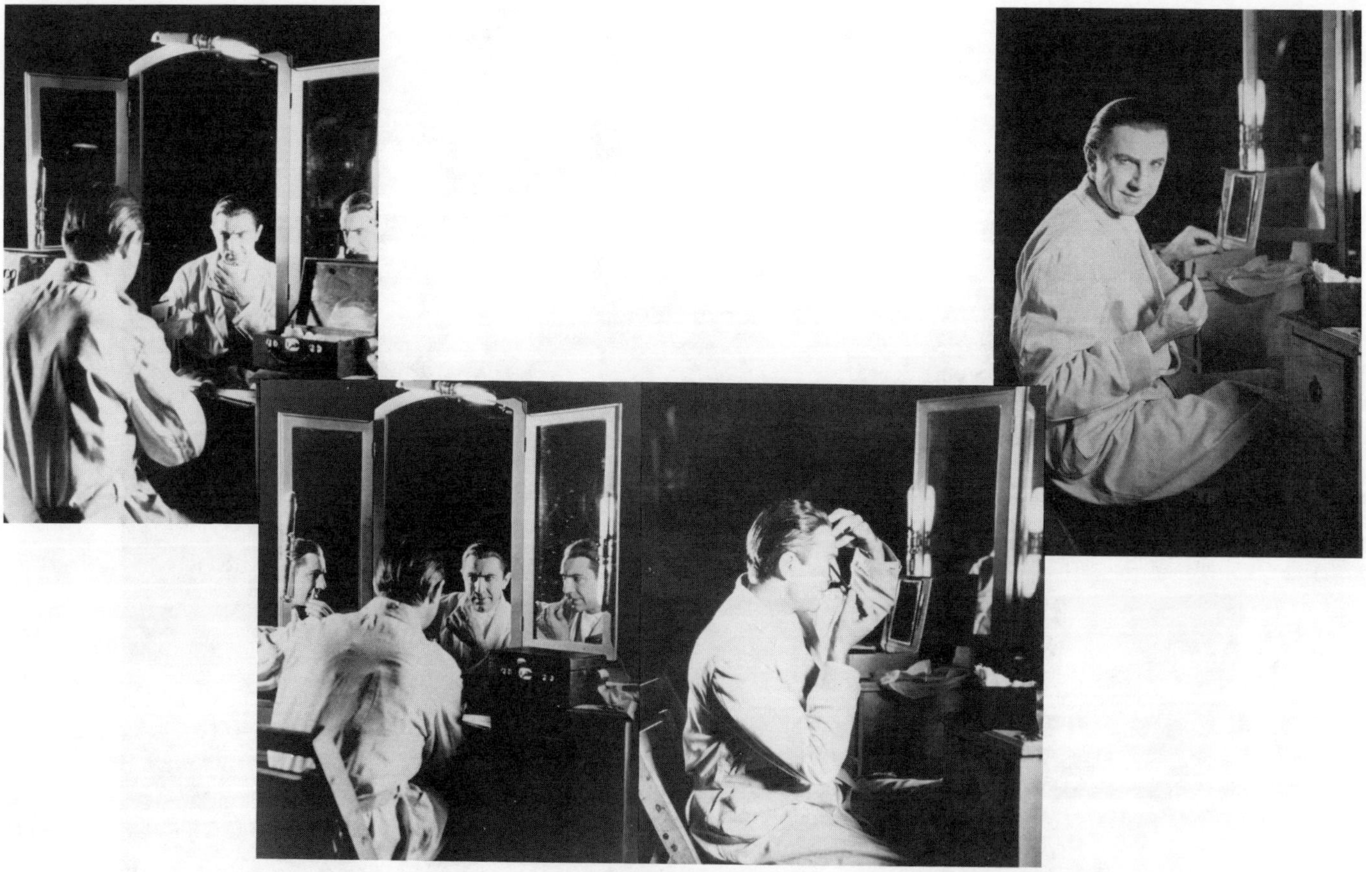

Bela Lugosi insisted on putting on his own makeup after playing the role for four years on stage.

Scenes cut from the final Release

(Above) The Gypsies watch as Count Dracula's coach takes Renfield to the Castle.

(Below) Note the cardboard behind Dr. Seward.

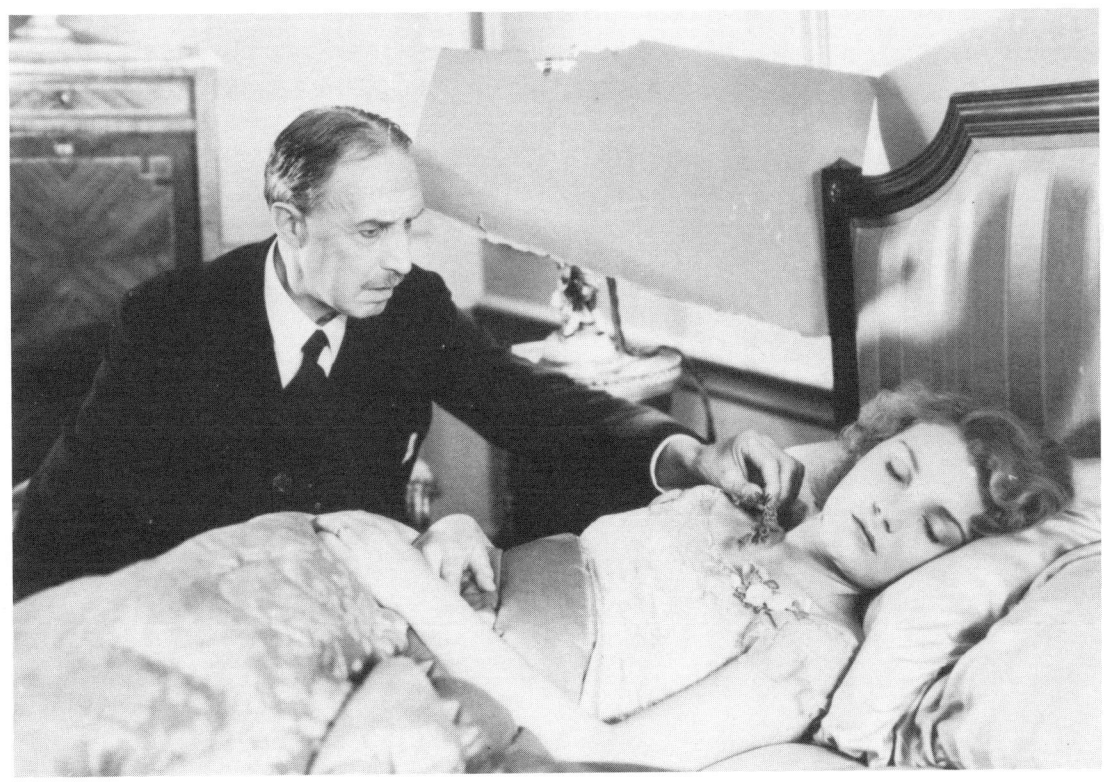

After Renfield is put under Dracula's power, he helplessly watches as Dracula loads his coffins on the carriage to take them to England.

Dracula is seen disposing of Renfield's possessions.

Dr. Seward and Van Helsing go in search of the last three boxes and discover a note left by Harker. These scenes were to precede the chase back to Transylvania that were cut when the budget was trimmed. (The final cost of DRACULA, not including publicity, was $441,984.90.)

Van Helsing delivers the famous "There are such things...!" speech at the end of the original release print.

Memorabilia

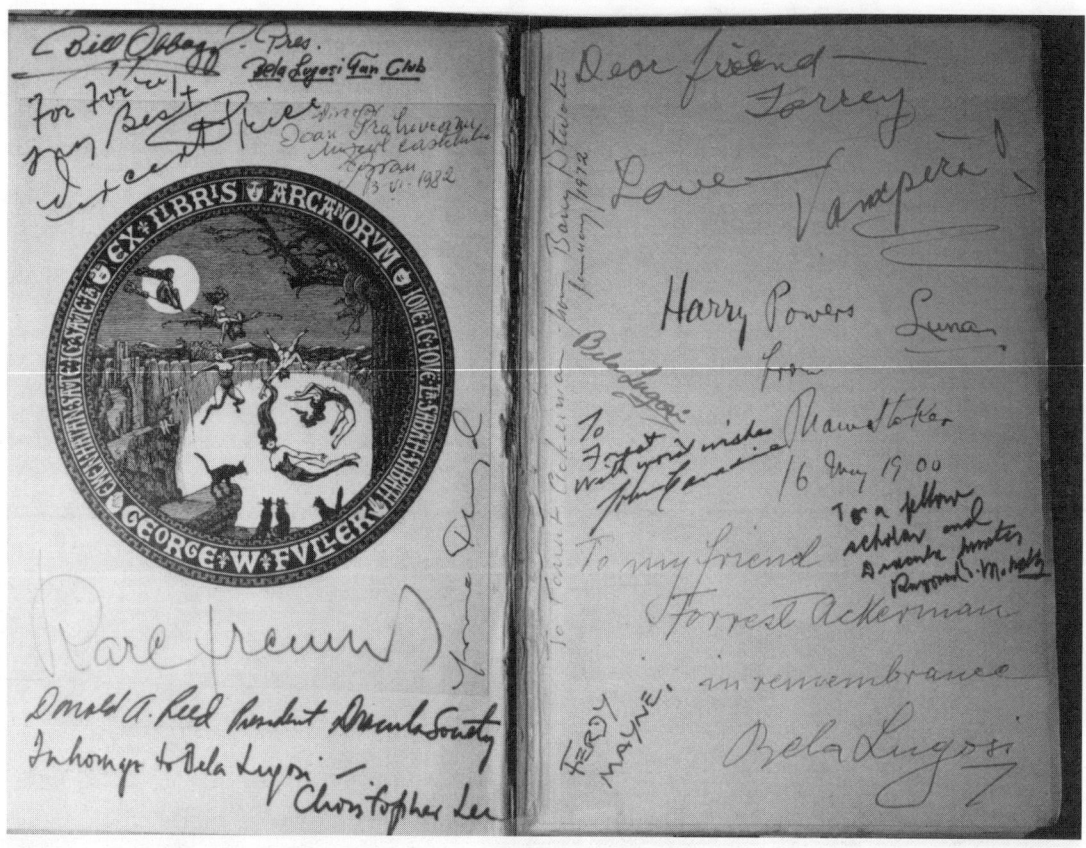

Perhaps the rarest first American edition of <u>Dracula</u> in existence belongs to Forrest J Ackerman. It is signed by: Bram Stoker, Bela Lugosi, John Carradine, Vincent Price, Christopher Lee, Karl Freund, Dr. Donald Reed, Carroll Borland, Vampira, Barry Atwater, Dr. Raymond McNally and Bela Lugosi Jr.

Carl Laemmle Jr.

Tod Browning

Edward Van Sloan

Helen Chandler

David Manners

Charles D. Hall

Art Director, John Hoffman

Writer, John L. Balderston

Carl Laemmle

Wyndham Standing

David Manners swats the prop bat.

The same bat today at the Museum of Natural History in Los Angeles.

The script that you are about to read was the final shooting script used in the making of the film. On screen, Tod Browning was not given credit as a writer. You will find it interesting to note the changes made as the production evolved into the classic Universal film that we know today. Portions of this script are from Bela Lugosi's personal copy which was incomplete. The remaining script was made up from Karl Freund's and Paul Kohner's personal copies.

Universal Pictures Corporation

CARL LAEMMLE
PRESIDENT

(APPROVED BY CARL LAEMMLE, JR.)

"D R A C U L A"

(The following credits are tenative only)

From the Book "Dracula" by Bram Stoker

Adaptation and Dialogue
By
Tod Browning and Garrett Fort

Continuity By
Dudley Murphy

E. M. Asher -- Associate Producer

(4th DRAFT-------FINAL)

PICTURE NO: 109-1

DIRECTED BY: TOD BROWNING

Send Lugosi c/o Hollywood Athletic Club

SEPTEMBER 26, 1930

"DRACULA" A Universal Production MADE IN U.S.A.

Béla Lugosi   *Count Dracula*

(APPROVED BY CARL LAEMMLE, JR.)

"D R A C U L A"

(The following credits are tenative only)

From the Book "Dracula" by Bram Stoker

Adaptation and Dialogue

By

Tod Browning and Garrett Fort

Continuity By

Dudley Murphy

E. M. Asher -- Associate Producer

(4th DRAFT-------FINAL)

PICTURE NO: 109-1

DIRECTED BY: TOD BROWNING

SEPTEMBER 26, 1930

Date_____

No._____

is loaned to you for the benefit of acquainting you with the story. It is valued at $25.00 as a penalty for its safe return in proper time.

UNIVERSAL PICTURES
CORPORATION

Universal City, Calif.

This Scenario must be returned to Scenario dept. for the files.

"DRACULA" A Universal Production MADE IN U.S.A.

FC

SEQUENCE A

A-1 FADE IN TO:
EXT. LONG SHOT MOUNTAIN PASS
LATE AFTERNOON

Process shot of a narrow mountain pass in the wilds of the Carpathians - sheer cliffs rise to jagged summits above the barely passable roads. The character of the surrounding scenery is fantastic, eerie. In b.g., the sun is just setting. Through pass and approaching camera dashes a stage-coach of fifty years ago, a ramshackle weather-beaten affair that looks as if it would hardly hold together - four horses draw it at top speed as the driver leans forward, gripping the reins and urging them to greater speed.

DISSOLVE THROUGH TO:

A-2 EXT. SEMI CLOSE SHOT

Shooting towards driver on box. He is lashing his horses and shouting something unintelligible in Hungarian - pauses briefly to glance aloft with anxious eyes at the descending sun and lengthening shadows.

DISSOLVE THROUGH TO:

A-3 INT. COACH

Two seats running lengthwise in coach. The passengers consist of a mannish-looking Englishwoman in tweeds; her secretary, a little mouselike creature with a perpetually worried air; two natives of Transylvania, a husband and wife; their little four-year-old girl; and Renfield. The latter is a quiet-looking, well-bred type of young Englishman. The passengers are being jostled about uncomfortably as the coach charges at breakneck speed over the rutty road. The Englishwoman, however, a lady with

(CONTINUED)

A-3   (CONTINUED)

>   a mind of her own, has her
>   foot braced against the seat
>   opposite, and is stoic in her
>   lack of visible concern. Her
>   secretary is trying to read
>   from a Baedeker.

SECRETARY (reading)

" - approaching Bistritz, the road leads through the very heart of the Carpathian Mountains, one of the wildest and least known parts of Central Europe - "

> As coach lurches and she is
> shot across the aisle into
> Renfield's lap; with an em-
> barrassed air, she recovers
> her balance, Renfield aiding
> her.

RENFIELD

Allow me -

> Hands her back into her seat.

SECRETARY (gulping)

Oh! Thank you!

> Renfield makes a deprecatory
> gesture and sits back, on
> guard. The Englishwoman, who
> has apparently been paying not
> the slightest attention to all
> this, says crisply,

ENGLISHWOMAN

Where are we, Sara?

SECRETARY (fumbling with her book)

"-- - wildest and least - known parts of Central Europe - "

ENGLISHWOMAN

Continue, Sara.

SECRETARY (drawing deep breath)

"Among the rugged peaks that frown down upon the Borgo Pass, are found crumbling castles of a bygone age - "

(CONTINUED)

A-3   (CONTINUED) -2

>   Again the coach lurches, and
>   she sails across into Ren-
>   field's lap. Renfield repeats
>   his routine with a tired smile
>   and having restored the blushing
>   secretary to her seat, thrusts
>   his head out of the coach window
>   and calls,

             RENFIELD

>   I say! A bit slower up
>   there!

>   At this, the two natives
>   exchange quick, frightened
>   glances; and the man grabs
>   Renfield by the arm, sputter-
>   ing excitedly,

             NATIVE

>   No, no! We must reach the
>   inn before sundown!

>   The Englishwoman turns cold,
>   fishy eye upon him.

             ENGLISHWOMAN (coldly)

>   And why?

>   The man leans forward with
>   a superstitious light in his
>   eyes, and lowering his voice
>   to a hoarse whisper, says,

             NATIVE

>   It is Walpurgis Nacht - a
>   night of evil - nosferatu -

>   The wife tries to clap her
>   hand over his mouth, but
>   he pushes her away, and
>   continues,

             NATIVE

>   - the undead who leave
>   their graves at night, and
>   feast on the blood of the
>   living!

>   Sara gives a little startled
>   exclamation, eyes wide. The
>   Englishwoman sniffs openly
>   and exchanges a look with Ren-
>   field as if to say, "What can
>   one except from these stupid
>   peasants?" The native, quick
>   to understand her slighting
>   attitude, says,

                             (CONTINUED)

A-3   (CONTINUED) - 3

                              NATIVE   (earnestly)
                         If in these parts you lived,
                         you would not sneer!. On
                         this night, madam, the
                         doors they are barred, and
                         to the Virgin we pray -

         As he is speaking,
         DISSOLVE THROUGH TO:

A-4   INT. PEASANT HUT
        CLOSE SHOT AT WINDOW

         Picking up an old peasant
         type, clad in the picturesque
         garb of the region, hanging some
         strange-looking herb (wolfbane)
         from the lock. As he moves away,
         CAMERA PULLS BACK and follows him
         to door - he places lighted oil
         lamp before the little figure of
         the Virgin above the door - door is
         barred by a stout cross-bar.
         CAMERA CONTINUES MOVING BACK TO
         WIDE ANGLE, picking up figure of
         an old woman, seated at fireplace,
         telling her rosary in Hungarian.
         The low mumble of her voice is
         the only sound heard throughout
         the action. Over a peasant cradle
         on the other side of fireplace,
         a young mother, in picturesque bodice
         and skirt, bends down and picks up
         a young baby. She slips a crucifix
         about its neck, and replacing it
         gently in cradle, Xes towards shrine
         above door and kneels, the old man
         following suit. . .The lighting of
         this scene should be rich and dim,
         like that of an Old Master.
         DISSOLVE THROUGH TO:

A-5   EXT. COURTYARD OF INN
        DUSK. WIDE ANGLE

         Shooting through gates, in
         in fore. The gates are large,
         ramshackle wooden affairs which
         swing inward. A rustic porter   Sound: of horses' hoofs
         has just opened them and   approaching.
         stands waiting with an air of
         excited expectancy. As he
         hears the coach coming, he
         turns and yells something

                                           (CONTINUED)

A-5   (CONTINUED)

> towards inn, which is a low building of stone, with a thatched roof. The general feeling of the inn and the background as a whole is one of eerie remoteness - the sort of a setting against which anything might happen. Behind the inn, a cliff rises sharp and sheer - behind it we see the last rays of the dying day.
>
> At the signal from the porter, the door of the inn opens and the proprietor emerges. As he does so and stands waiting, the porter ducks back - the clatter of hoofs sound nearer, and the coach, in a cloud of dust, whirls into sight and through the gates. The porter immediately starts closing the gates behind the coach, as we
>
> DISSOLVE THROUGH TO:

A-6   INT. COURTYARD FAIRLY
       WIDE ANGLE AT INN ENTRANCE

> Picking up action as coach drives up in front of door and comes to an abrupt stop. There is immediate flurry of activity- natives and servants come out of the inn, attracted by the arrival of the coach. The driver gets down from his box and opens the coach door and the passengers start to climb out - first native man and wife, who are greeted by the Proprietor's and exit into inn, a torrent of excited Hungarian trailing in their wake. As the Englishwoman and her secretary start to get out of the coach, we CUT TO

A-7   MED. SHOT PROPRIETOR AND DRIVER

> Driver is talking excitedly in Hungarian as he points off towards Renfield, explaining something to the Proprietor.

A-8   MED. SHOT AT SIDE OF COACH

> Renfield climbs out and stands stretching his legs and looking around as a porter from the inn places a little step-ladder at side of coach and climbs up and starts to remove luggage from top of coach. Renfield watches him idly for a moment and then as porter starts to remove Renfield's luggage, Renfield says,

RENFIELD

> Don't take my luggage down - I'm going on to Borgo Pass tonight -

> The porter looks at him oddly and descending step-ladder, scurries out of scene with a couple of bags. As he does so, Proprietor enters scene and addresses Renfield with an apologetic air.

PROPRIETOR

> The driver - he iss afraid - Walpurgis Nacht - a good fellow he iss - he wants me to ask if you can wait and go on after sunrise -

> Renfield shakes his head and says pleasantly,

RENFIELD

> I'm sorry, but there's a carriage meeting me at Borgo Pass at mid-night.

> The Proprietor's eyes become suspicious. For a moment, he hesitates as if almost afraid to ask - he says,

PROPRIETOR (in constrained tones)

> Whose carriage?

RENFIELD

> Count Dracula's -

A-9   EXT. ENTRANCE OF INN.

> Where driver is standing with two or three natives - show their startled reaction to the

(CONTINUED)

FC

A-9   (CONTINUED)

name of Dracula - They huddle
closer together in super-
stitious awe and look again
towards Renfield with a
frightened air. Camera
PANS QUICKLY to another group
just inside doorway, also
getting over their alarmed
reaction.

A-10   MED. CLOSE SHOT
        PROPRIETOR & RENFIELD

Proprietor, speechless for
a moment, finally manages
to gasp,

                PROPRIETOR

            Castle Dracula -!

        RENFIELD (mildly)

            Yes - that's where I'm
            going -

ES

A-11   EXT. LONG SHOT CASTLE DRACULA

This is a glass or miniature shot - a wierd, unearthly setup, showing the crumbled castle of Dracula as it perches high on its mountain eyrie in the moonlight - a place of dark shadows and fearsome shapes.

DISSOLVE THROUGH TO:

A-12   INT. LONG SHOT - CRYPT IN CASTLE
        DRACULA - NITE

CAMERA MOVES FORWARD TO CORNER OF A HEAVY BOX, and PANS UP A LITTLE to include the lid. As it does so, we see the fingers of Dracula's hand appear from under the lid, prying it loose,

CAMERA MOVES QUICKLY AWAY TO WIDE ANGLE OF CRYPT showing the rest of the room, excluding boxes. It is a high-ceilinged, vaulted affair, with tiny Gothic windows set high in the wall. A glimmer of moonlight comes down and strikes the damp wall nearby, creating a sharp, fantastic shadow born of the traceries in the high window.

CAMERA MOVES BACK TO FULL SHOT, picking up Dracula, as we discover him with his back to Camera, bending over and closing the box from which he has just emerged. Beside the box from which he has come, are two others, lids off, piled high with earth. Dracula straightens up and Xes to the two boxes - surveys them carefully, his back still to camera. Then he turns facing camera for the first time, and, moving into fore, towards stairs, starts to ascend. This movement brings his face into camera until the entire screen is filled with the menace of his inhuman eyes, and we CUT TO

(LONG HOWL OF WOLF, WHICH
CARRIES OVER INTO NEXT SCENE)

A-13   EXT. ENTRANCE OF INN, FAIRLY
        WIDE ANGLE - EVENING

The light has gone and the dusk has deepened - inside the inn we catch the glimmer of light from the lamps, showing the group

(CONTINUED)

A-13   CONTINUED

of figures in doorway in sharp
relief. At one side, the coach
is waiting - lanterns on coach
have been lit - there is a general
air of excicement and anticipation,
and we see through windows at one
side of entrance door the faces
of several natives pressed close
against the panes, watching what
is going on outside. Renfield,
the proprietor and his wife, and
the timid little secretary form
a group in the doorway. Driver
is climbing up to his seat on
coach and sits there, the reins
in his hands, glowering sullenly
down at Renfield.

CAMERA MOVES FORWARD TO MED. CLOSE
SHOT AT DOOR, as we hear Renfield
talking. He is addressing the proprietor and his wife in faintly
apologetic sentences - trying to
impress upon the necessity for his
going on without giving offense.

      RENFIELD

    But this is all super-
    stition -

He looks at proprietor and
wife, who stare back at him
without speaking - continues
with an air of embarrassment,

      RENFIELD (Continuing)

    I mean, in mountainous re-
    gions like this, I cannot
    understand how -

then breaks off again, and
realizing that further explanation is useless, and
that he is taking up val-
uable time, he continues

    -after all - what I'm try-
    ing to say is, that I'm
    not afraid - I -
     (turns and points to
     driver)
    explained to him that it's
    a matter of business to me-
    I've got to go - really.

As he says this, he smiles
again in apology to proprietor and wife and exits out of
scene toward carriage, the eyes
of the timid little secretary
following him and growing wider
and wider - she has been looking from one to the other, determined not to miss anything.   CONTINUED

A-13   CONTINUED - 2

The Proprietor turns and looks
at his wife with an eloquent
shrug - his attitude is that
if this young Englishman is
resolved to disregard their advice, there is nothing they can
do. The proprietor's wife nods
slowly, still staring after Renfield - her hand moves unconscious-
ly up to her throat, comes in contact with a small, Gold crucifix
suspended on a black ribbon around
her neck.

CAMERA PANS TO MED. SHOT AT
CARRIAGE. Renfield is about to
step into carriage, when the proprietor's wife (offscene) is
heard to cry,

              PROPRIETOR'S WIFE
                  Wait!

Renfield turns, one foot
in the step. Proprietor's
wife hurries in to scene -
she has removed crucifix
from around her neck and
now holds it up to Renfield,
saying in frightened tones

              PROPRIETOR'S WIFE
                  If you must go - wear this -
                  wear it for your mother's
                  sake. It will protect you!

Renfield looks down at the
Crucifix with a half shy,
half indulgent air - then
when he sees that the proprietor's wife is in deadly
earnest, he takes it from
her with a whimsical smile
and, tucking it away in his
pocket, says graciously,

              RENFIELD
                  Thank you -

Turns again with a smile
and starts to get into the
coach, as we CUT TO

ES

A-14   EXT. MED. SHOT DOORWAY

The proprietor comes into scene, having given instructions to driver - the little secretary turns to him and says, (round-eyed) her voice sinking to a strained whisper,

SECRETARY

Tell me - do you really believe there are vampires who leave their graves at night and go about looking for blood?

As she says this, the Englishwoman comes up from behind her just in time to catch her last words. Proprietor turns to secretary and says

PROPRIETOR   (darkly)

I haf seen their victims -

ENGLISHWOMAN (with a sniff)

Rubbish!

She takes Sara by the arm, indicating interior of Inn and with a movement of her head, says

ENGLISHWOMAN

Come, Sara -

As Sara turns to follow her into the Inn, there is the sound of a crack of a whip - clatter of wheels on cobble-stones, the sound of horses' hoofs.

A-15   EXT. COURTYARD
       WIDE ANGLE

Shooting from angle of those watching from door of inn. As the coach starts off at a gallop, it goes tearing through the gates out of sight.

A-16   MED. CLOSE SHOT
       ENTRANCE OF INN

       Proprietor and those in
       doorway watch the coach
       drive away, with an air
       of grave misgiving -
       proprietor's wife crosses
       herself devoutly!

       CAMERA PANS QUICKLY TO CLOSE
       SHOT AT WINDOWS, showing
       faces of the frightened
       natives peering out, flattened
       against the pane. On panes
       of window, we see several
       crosses marked.

       CAMERA CONTINUES QUICKLY
       PANNING ALONG TO NEXT WINDOW,
       without a break, showing more
       frightened faces peering out
       into the night.

                              DISSOLVE THROUGH TO:

A-17   EXT. WIDE ANGLE
       ON ROAD - NIGHT

       Shot from elevation.
       Coach dashing along.

                              (GALLOPING HOOFS - CRUNCH
                               OF ROLLING WHEELS OVER SCENE)

       - there are queer, gro-
       tesque-looking trees,
       with twisted black branches,
       huge misshapen rocks, that
       in the moonlight, seem to
       take on fantastic shapes -
       the whole area through which
       the coach is passing has a
       grim, macabre quality, as if
       taken bodily from a Dore steel
       engraving.

                              DISSOLVE THROUGH TO:

A-18   INT. COACH

       Through the window the
       light of the coach lamp
       shines on Renfield's face,
       casting shadows in the in-
       terior. Renfield is sitting
       forward on the seat, watch-
       ing the passing landscape
       with interest. The mists
       are rising, and each time we
       cut to an exterior, they seem
       to be closing more and more about
       the coach.
                              CUT:

A-19   EXT. APPROACH TO BORGO PASS
        LONG SHOT

> Of a narrow defile bending
> out upon a little plateau,
> (just the type of country found
> near Redrock Cannon). Behind
> the ragged crest of the hills,
> we glimpse a moonlit sky filled
> with omnious-looking clouds
> against which the mist is drift-
> ing.
>
> (GLASS SHOT)
> The road winds up to the
> very entrance to the pass,
> which is flanked with steep,
> precipitous cliffs.

                              DISSOLVE THROUGH TO:

A-20   EXT. CROSSROADS BORGO PASS
        CLOSE SHOT SIGNPOST

> One sign labelled - "BISTRITZ" -
> the other "BORGO PASS". The
> mists are swirling about as we
> pull our camera quickly back
> to wide angle, revealing Dracula's
> carriage waiting at the cross-
> roads beneath the sign. It is a
> fantastic-looking carriage, all
> in black, drawn by two black ill-
> fed looking nags - the man on the
> driver's seat wears a hat pulled
> down over his face and is muffled
> to the eyes in a great dark cloak.
> Over scene comes the sound of
> approaching horses' hoofs.

                              (HORSES'S HOOFS)

> The coach containing Renfield
> drives up from b.g. - as it
> approaches camera, horses sud-
> denly start to rear on their
> hind legs. Driver has some dif-
> ficulty in controling them, but
> finally manages to quiet them.
> Renfield gets out - the driver
> throws his bag down to him and
> drives off down the road at a
> mad gallop, leaving Renfield
> standing there all alone. Ren-
> field shouts after him, but the
> coach goes on, heedless, and dis-
> appears around the bend. Ren-
> field picks up his bag, starts
> slowly towards carriage which is
> waiting for him. Renfield ap-
> proaches Dracula's carriage, and
> looking up at the driver, who
> sits in stolid silence on the
> seat, asks a little nervously,

                                        CONTINUED

A-20   CONTINUED

                             RENFIELD
                         - The coach from Count
                           Dracula?

A-21   EXT. CLOSE SHOT DRIVER

         Shooting up from Renfield's
         point of view. He is almost
         completely hidden in the folds
         of his great cloak, and has a
         hat pulled down over his face
         so that nothing of him is visible
         save a pair of bright, almost
         feverish eyes. He nods in reply
         to Renfield's uncertain words,
         and without speaking, indicates
         that Renfield is to get in the
         coach.

A-22   EXT. MED. CLOSE
         SHOT COACH

         Matching action as driver
         points to door of coach.
         It is closed. Renfield
         reaches down, picks up his
         portfolio and valise and
         hands them up to driver.
         As he does this, the door,
         unseen by him, swings open
         of its own accord. He turns
         to find it open. With a little
         air of misgiving he climbs in
         and closes it behind him.
         Immediately the driver flicks
         his whip at the horses, and
         the coach lunges forward.

A-23   EXT. ROAD WIDE ANGLE

         Matching action as coach
         starts off with a jerk -
         swings around almost on
         two wheels, and goes dash-
         ing back along the winding   SOUND: of horses' hoofs.
         road from whence it had ap-
         peared. As it disappears around
         the bend with a clatter of
         horses' hoofs, we CUT TO:

A-24   INT. COACH

Renfield is being hostled
around inside - he tries to
brace himself against the   SOUND: of horses' hoofs.
sides - is too frightened
to yell out to the driver.

A-25   EXT. NARROW ROAD - SIDE ANGLE

Coach dashes past.

A-26   INT. COACH

Renfield, being jolted
about beyond all endurance,
sticks his head out of the
window to yell to the driver...

                    RENFIELD

               Hi - driver - !

As he cranes his neck, he
suddenly falls silent in
stupefication, as he sees -

A-27   EXT. CLOSE SHOT
         DRIVER'S SEAT

As seen from Renfield's
point of view. A slight
mist seems to cling to the
seat. The driver is missing -
the reins are hanging limply   SOUND: of horses' hoofs
over the dashboard. Above the   continued
horses' heads flies a great
bat.   THROUGHOUT

                                 THESE

                                 SCENES

A-28   INT. COACH

Renfield withdraws his head
sharply and sinks back into
a corner of the coach. He
doesn't know what to think -
what to do.

ES

A-29   EXT. LONG SHOT ROAD
       FLASH

        Coach hurtling along
        through the night, driver-
        less. The country around   SOUND: wolves howling.
        has grown more gloomy, more
        forbidding, than ever. There
        is the howl of a wolf - then
        silence for a moment, when
        the howl is taken up by another,
        at some distance - and then still
        another, getting over the idea
        that an ever-narrowing circle of
        wolves is drawing about the
        plunging coach.

                                  DISSOLVE THROUGH TO:

A-30   EXT. LONG SHOT - DRACULA'S CASTLE

        This is a glass or miniature
        shot of the castle, shot as
        if from some neighboring peak,
        it rears itself in evil majesty
        against the milky sky, where
        a pale moon strives to pierce
        the drifting, streamerlike mists
        that blanket it....The castle is
        grim and eerie, but there is
        nothing about it to suggest any
        sort of fantastic, unreal archi-
        tecture - nothing of the impres-
        sionistic Caligari school. It
        looks centuries old - remote -
        crumbling - part of its ancient
        battlements are in ruin and stand
        in sharp silhouette against the
        night sky. On three sides the
        mountain walls descend sharply to
        abysses hundreds of feet below -
        and in these abysses heavy whorls
        of mist are creeping, like groping
        fingers of wraiths seeking to
        clutch at the decaying glories of
        a house long dead.

        In fore., very tiny against the
        imposing walls of rock, the coach
        is seen traversing a narrow ledge
        which threads a dangerous chasm.

                                  DISSOLVE THROUGH TO:

A-31   EXT. DRACULA'S CASTLE

        This is a set, or the lower
        part of one, glassed in above.
        The predominant features are   CONTINUED

A-31   CONTINUED

            the massive oaken gates, which
            sag on their moldering hinges,
            half open. The fore-court is over-
            grown with weeds and filled with
            tumbled rocks.

            The coach approaches slowly,
            horses picking their way with
            some difficulty. As they near
            the gates, they hesitate for a
            moment, and then pass on through,
            there being just sufficient room
            for the coach to pass without
            grazing the sides.

            CAMERA MOVES AROUND TO GATES, and
            shooting through, we see the coach
            proceeding on across a wide court-
            yard towards the main entrance door
            of the castle. The courtyard is in
            the same state of decay and desola-
            tion - the walls of the castle cast
            deep shadows across it in the moon-
            light. A ruined fountain, the edges
            of which have fallen away, stands in
            the center of the courtyard. There
            is no sign of life whatever, nothing
            to indicate that a human footstep has
            trod the grass-grown flagstones for
            centuries. A faint mist hangs over
            all.

                            DISSOLVE THROUGH TO:

A-32   EXT. MAIN ENTRANCE DOORS
         OF CASTLE

            Matching action as coach pulls
            up before the doors, which are
            approached up a broad flight of
            broken stone steps. The door opens
            and Renfield steps gingerly out,
            looking around. He looks up at the
            driver's seat - there is no sign
            of driver.

A-33   EXT. CLOSE SHOT RENFIELD

            Reacting to this he shivers a
            little - then turns to the entrance
            doors. One of the great doors opens
            slowly, although there is no one
            visible, and swings back, revealing
            darkness and silence beyond, except
            at what seems to be end of a long
            passage, where a faint shaft of
            moonlight is seen. Renfield starts
            to enter - CUT TO:

A-34   INT. HALL - LONG SHOT

We see that the hall is a huge, square affair, in the manner of ancient feudal castles, with a long, impressive-looking stair-case at the back. There is no furniture of any sort - the hall is absolutely bare. Dust is piled thick on every side - cobwebs - mold - broken architraves - bits of crumbling masonry which has fallen from the roof. On one side, half way up, the walls are in almost complete ruin - through them, we glimpse the night sky and the mists. The moon, struggling through the haze, casts a feeble, murky light over everything. Three or four bats flutter down from above, then whisk past camera.

CAMERA CONTINUES ACROSS TOFOOT OF STAIRCASE which leads up into the other part of the castle. Here it comes to a sudden stop, as across the steps a little way up from the first landing, is a giant, dust-covered spider-web, just in front of the web Dracula is walking slowly down towards camera, a huge taper in hand.

He is a tall, thick-set man of distinguished appearance. His lips are pale, but his large, luminous eyes burn with an unholy light, and upon closer inspection can be identified with those of the mysterious driver of the coach. He is wearing formal attire, and wears a decoration. His manner is invariably suave - his bearing one of distinction. As he comes slowly down the stairs, CAMERA SWOOPS UP TO LARGE CU (Crane Shot) and he pauses, looking down at Renfield:

A-35   INT. MAIN HALL
       MED. SHOT RENFIELD

As seen from Dracula's point of view. He is staring up at Dracula, open-mouthed and startled.

A-36   INT. LARGER CLOSEUP
       DRACULA

He bows and smiles as he says,

A-36   CONTINUED

                    DRACULA

                        I am Dracula –

A-37   INT. MED. CLOSE
        RENFIELD

    He is too frightened for
    the moment to say anything –
    he looks around nervously and
    then looks back at Dracula.

                    RENFIELD

                        It's really good to see you—
                        I – I don't know what hap-
                        pened to the driver and my
                        luggage -- and -- with all
                        this – I thought I was in
                        the wrong place –

A-38   INT. MED. SHOT

    As Dracula with an apolo-
    getic flourish of his hand,
    and says,

                    DRACULA

                        The walls of my castle
                        are broken – the shadows
                        are many – but, come – I
                        bid you welcome –

    Turns with taper and starts
    up the stairs – Renfield
    follows him slowly. As he
    arrives on the landing he halts.
    From outside comes the howling
    of wolves. Dracula also pauses,
    listening – then turns to Renfield
    with a smile, pointing,

                    DRACULA

                        Listen to them – children
                        of the night! What music
                        they make!

    Listens once more, but the
    howling is not repeated –
    turns and continues up the
    steps, approaching web.

ES

A-39   INT. CLOSEUP RENFIELD

Shooting down at him, as he
walks up the steps after
Dracula. Again he stops and
stares up after his host.

A-40   INT. MED. SHOT DRACULA

Shooting up towards him as
he proceeds up the steps.
This time he is on the other
side of the spider-web, but
the web has not been dis-
turbed by his progress.

A-41   INT. CLOSE SHOT RENFIELD

Halted before the web, unable
to go on. He takes his stick
and slashes out, tearing
it out of the way.

A-42   INT. CLOSEUP WALL
       QUICK PAN SHOT

Showing a big spider, disturbed by the destruction
of his web, scurrying up the
side of the moonlit wall.

A-43   INT. MED. SHOT

Matching action as Renfield
steps gingerly past the
broken web and continues on
up the stairs. CAMERA FOLLOW-
ING. Dracula pauses and turns
to Renfield, saying, as points
to broken web

                    DRACULA

                    The eternal struggle for
                    life - each living creature
                    must have blood to live.
                    The spider, spinning his
                    web for the unwary fly -
                    the blood is the life,
                    Mr. Renfield!

       CONTINUED

A-43   CONTINUED

    Renfield murmurs something
    unintelligible, as we
    CUT TO:

A-44   INT. UPPER HALLWAY
       REVERSE ANGLE - MED. SHOT

    Shooting across wall of the
    staircase. Through broken
    crevices in the wall the
    moonlight filters. Dracula
    and Renfield cross hall to
    a door. As Dracula opens
    door and stands aside for
    Renfield to pass on into the
    chamber before him, CAMERA
    MOVES UP TO THEM AND SHOOTS
    THROUGH DOOR past them into
    a luxuriously appointed, com-
    fortable room. An open fire
    is burning in a big stone
    fireplace. Renfield enters
    slowly, and CAMERA FOLLOWS
    DRACULA through - they stand
    with backs to camera. Renfield
    reacting to room's comfort,
    turns with a half-shy smile -
    Dracula closes door and says,

                                DRACULA

                  I'm sure you will find
                  this part of my castle
                  more inviting -

A-45   INT. CHAMBER REVERSE
       ANGLE

    Matching angle as Dracula
    completes speech. Renfield
    says, with an air of relief

                                RENFIELD

                                Rather!

    Dracula guides him to
    table in center of room at
    which are two huge carved
    chairs. CAMERA FOLLOWS TO
    CLOSE SHOT and we see that
    the table is laid for supper -
    silver and crystal gleam
    against the fresh snowiness
    of the cloth. Dracula indi-
    cates table - says,   CONTINUED

ES

A-45   CONTINUED

                    DRACULA
                    I didn't know but that
                    you might be hungry -

Renfield replies, diffidently -

                    RENFIELD
                    That's very kind of you,
                    Count Dracula -

He sinks into chair which
Dracula indicates. Dracula
stands staring down at
him. Renfield looks up
at him, gives a little
apprehensive smile - returns
to his wine, sipping again
to cover his confusion.

A-46   INT. CLOSEUP DRACULA

Regarding Renfield intently -
says - after a breif pause,

                    DRACULA
                    I trust you've kept your
                    coming here a secret -

A-47   INT. CLOSEUP RENFIELD

glancing up quickly - replies

                    RENFIELD
                    Oh, yes, indeed - just as
                    you requested.

A-48   INT. CLOSE SHOT DRACULA
        AND RENFIELD

Dracula nods soberly -
continues, with a searching
gaze

                    DRACULA
                    And you've destroyed all
                    our correspondence - ?

            CONTINUED

A-48 CONTINUED

RENFIELD

I've followed your instructions implicitly.

DRACULA

Excellent, Mr. Renfield, excellent! And now, if you're not too fatigued I'd like to discuss the lease on Carfax Abbey.

(exits from scene)

RENFIELD

But all the papers are in my portfolio. -

A-49 INT. WIDER ANGLE.

matching action as Dracula crosses to bed upon which portfolio is lying. Picks it up and starts back to Renfield, saying,

DRACULA

I took the liberty of having your luggage brought up -,

Renfield in fore., matching action as Dracula exits towards him - lays portfolio on table. Renfield starts to take papers from the portfolio, saying,

RENFIELD

Everything is in order, awaiting your signature -

Hands Dracula some papers, Dracula takes them and runs through them quickly, satidfied that what he says is true. Renfield waits for him to speak - then as he notes the look of careless approval on Dracula's face, he turns to his portfolio and takes out a handful of baggage labels, saying

(CONTINUED)

A-49   (CONTINUED)

                              RENFIELD
                                  I hope I brought enough -
                                  labels for your luggage.

                              DRACULA
                                      (Glancing at labels)
                                  I am taking with me
                                  only three - boxes -

Renfield looks sur-
prised - Dracula lays
the papers aside and
moves out of scene,
saying,

                              DRACULA
                                  We will be leaving
                                  tomorrow evening
                                      (Exits from scene)

                              RENFIELD
                                  Everything will be ready.

A-50   INT. CLOSE SHOT AT BED

     Dracula stands beside
     bed, indicating the
     drawn-down covers,
     says,

                              DRACULA
                                  I hope you'll find this
                                  comfortable -

A-51   INT. CLOSE SHOT
        RENFIELD AT TABLE

     He bows in acknowledge-
     ment says, gratefully,

                              RENFIELD
                                  Thanks - it looks
                                  very inviting -

     Starts to stuff papers
     back into his portfolio
     and pricks his finger.

                                              (CONTINUED)

A-51   (CONTINUED)

                    RENFIELD

                        Ouch - !

    Drops papers with
    clip that has pricked
    him and starts to suck
    the wounded finger.

A-52   INT. FLASH CLOSEUP DRACULA

    making a quick move
    towards Renfield, his
    eyes gleaming at sight
    of the blood.

A-53   INT. FLASH CLOSEUP RENFIELD

    Still sucking finger -
    takes out handkerchief
    to wipe finger on - his
    back is half-turned to
    Dracula and he is unaware
    of the reaction this slight
    misadventure has had upon
    him.

A-54   INT. FLASH MOVING
        CLOSEUP DRACULA

    Approaching Renfield
    with swift stealthiness.

A-55   INT. MED. CLOSE SHOT

    Matching action as Dracula
    comes quickly up to Renfield,
    who is still absorbed in his
    finger. Dracula's long
    prehensile fingers reach
    out convulsively for
    Renfield's throat when
    suddenly the Cross which
    has been hanging by its
    chain around Renfield's
    neck swings forward at a
    forward movement of
    Renfield's body. Dracula
    recoils, Renfield, feeling

                            (CONTINUED)

A-55 (CONTINUED)

his presence, turns sharply, and sees the expression on Dracula's face - misunderstands, thinking it one of concern - says lightly -

> RENFIELD
>
> That paper clip - it's just a small cut.

Attention is attracted to Cross, swinging free - he stuffs it back into his pocket as Dracula, moving quickly away to table, takes up the decanter and pours another glass of wine, saying,

> DRACULA
>
> This is very old wine - I trust you will like it.

Dracula sets bottle down. Renfield takes glass - waits for Dracula to pour himself one - then says,

> RENFIELD
>
> Aren't you drinking?
>
> DRACULA
>
> I never drink - wine -

Turns one of his keen, penetrating looks upon Renfield, who uncomfortable under it, conceals his uneasiness by sipping the drink. Dracula nods as if pleased with the way things are going, and turning toward door, says,

> DRACULA
>
> And now, I'll leave you -

CAMERA PANS WITH HIM TO DOOR. Here, he pauses with one hand on the latch - says, as if as an afterthought.

> DRACULA
>
> I may be detained elsewhere most of the day tomorrow - in which case we will meet here - at - sundown.

A-56   INT. FLASH CLOSEUP RENFIELD

Watching - his attitude
one of unconscious defense.

A-57   INT. WIDE ANGLE

Renfield in fore., looking
across at Dracula, who
stands at door, Dracula
opens door, and lingers
just long enought to
say -

                    DRACULA

          Goodnight, Mr. Renfield.

With a peculiarly
diabolical inflection
which is not lost upon
Renfield. Then, Dracula,
with a low, sweeping
bow exits, closing the
door behind him.

Renfield stands in-
decisively by the table
for a moment, pondering
these strange happenings
and his weird host - then,
hiw brow furrowed by un-
easy thoughts, exits slowly
towards bed, removing his
coat. CAMERA PANS WITH
HIM TO BED. He lays coat
on a chair and removes his
tie. As he does so his
hand comes in contact with
the Cross - he holds it
for a moment - looks around
the room with a quick nervous
movement - and then, as if
mentally shaking off what
he considers a foolish
state of nerves, smiles and
unloops the Cross from
about his neck. He is
about to toss it careless-
ly on a nearby small table -
then changes his mind, and
with a little shamefaced
air, lifts up the edge of
his pillow and places the
Cross under it. Then,
sitting down upon the
edge of the bed, he
starts to unlace his
shoes. He removes
his shoes and kicks
them loose upon the floor.
Then he sits for a moment
on the edge of the bed,

(CONTINUED)

A-57 (CONTINUED)

        as if something intuitive has warned him of his danger. With a little shiver, he rises and Xes to window, CAMERA PANNING TO FOLLOW HIM. The casement is closed - he leans forward and tries to pry it open, but it is sealed with the dust and disuse of generations. For a moment he struggles with it - the dancing shadows cast by the firelight flickering across his strained face. CAMERA SWINGS AROUND TO SEMI CLOSE SHOT - of door - a little to one side of the bed. Very slowly, very quietly, this door starts to open - it does so, CAMERA MOVES SWIFTLY FORWARD, to CLOSE SHOT. The door continues to open, as yet by an unseen hand, and as it slowly swings wide we see into the chamber beyond. It is a large room, somewhat similar to the one in which Renfield is occupying, but in complete ruin. Hardly a wall stands. Above we see the night and the stars - the pale shafts of moonlight coming down through the great rents in the ceiling and the crumbling apertures of the olden walls - the floor is deep in broken masonry. CAMERA CONTINUES MOVING FORWARD, more slowly now, to LARGE CLOSEUP DOOR. Around the edge of it there come the faces of three women, watching Renfield.

        Women who have once been beautiful. Their skins are dead white - their lips full and scarlet. Their eyes are wild and blazing with blood-lust. Yet withal, there is something still beautiful, still arresting about them - they are faces that, once seen, should leave an indelible impression of weird decadence.

(CONTINUED)

A-57   (CONTINUED- 2)

>   CAMERA MOVES BACK TO
>   MED. SHOT of Renfield
>   at window. He finally
>   succeeds in flinging it
>   open - looks down into court-
>   yard below.

A-58   EXT. COURTYARD   MED SHOT

>   A Ricketty looking
>   dray is standing in the
>   courtyard, which is
>   bounded on one side by
>   a wall about eight
>   feet high and on the
>   other by the castle.
>   This is not the court-
>   yard seen at the entrance
>   door, but a smaller one,
>   about twenty feet wide.
>   At the wall side of the
>   courtyard is a sheer
>   drop of hundreds of feet
>   to a dark chasm below.
>   This is shot from
>   Renfield's angle --
>   on the dray are two
>   coffin-like boxes.

A-59   INT. CLOSE SHOT RENFIELD
       AT WINDOW

>   As he looks down a mist
>   comes rushing in, and
>   with it a gigantic bat.
>   Renfield, dizzy from the
>   blow, recoils and in
>   doing so, strikes his
>   head against the window
>   and collapses, uncon-
>   scious, upon the floor.
>   CAMERA MOVES BACK TO
>   LONG SHOT.

A-60   LONG SHOT

>   The three women who had
>   been watching all this
>   enter - go to Renfield
>   with a curious, measured
>   cat-like tread.

                    FADE OUT.

SEQUENCE B

(SOUNDS OF A TERRIFIC
STORM AT SEA - SHRIEKING
OF THE GALE - BOOM OF
CRASHING SEAS)

(THESE EFFECTS CONTINUE
UNBROKEN THROUGHOUT EN-
TIRE SEQUENCE)

B-1 FADE INTO:
     EXT. LONG SHOT
     STORM SEA - NIGHT

   Miniature shot of a
   ship at sea in the
   teeth of the gale -
   a schooner, battling
   its way through
   incredible seas.

   Over this L.S. a great
   wall of roaring water
   crashes, blotting out
   everything in the hiss
   of its swirling fury.

                              DISSOLVE THROUGH TO:

B-2 EXT. DECK OF SHIP
     LARGE CLOSEUP CAPTAIN

   Lashed to his wheel, a
   crucifix gripped tightly
   in his hands. His face
   is contorted with terror.
   A wave almost engulfs him,
   but he stands firm at the
   wheel.

                              DISSOLVE THROUGH TO:

B-3 INT. HOLD.FLASH
     CLOSEUP THREE BOXES

   A ship's lantern swings
   madly above them, casting swift shadows.

B-4   INT. HOLD. FLASH LARGE
       CLOSEUP BOX

       With label on it: "Count
       Dracula, Carfax Abbey,
       Whitby, England."

B-5   INT. HOLD. LARGE
       CLOSEUP CORNER OF BOX

       The lid has been pried
       open and Dracula's bony
       fingers are creeping
       over the side.

       DISSOLVE TO:

B-6   EXT. DECK. FLASH LARGE
       CLOSEUP TWO SAILORS

       Their faces filling
       entire screen. One is
       yelling something into
       the other's ear - storm
       makes words unintelligi-
       ble, but faces of both
       men are masks of terror.

       DISSOLVE TO:

B-7   INT. COMPANIONWAY FLASH
       CLOSEUP DRACULA

       Coming slowly up towards
       camera, his eyes bestial
       and predatory - comes up
       into huge closeup, as we -

       DISSOLVE TO:

B-8   EXT. CLOSE SHOT IN
       RIGGING

       A sailor clings there,
       half mad, staring down
       at deck with insane eyes -
       sees Dracula appear, and
       throwing back his head in
       a burst of maniacal laughter,
       drops out of sight into the   (CONTINUED)

OH

B-8   CONTINUED

surging seas. Over
this SUPERIMPOSE SHOT
OF FOAMING WATERS, and

DISSOLVE TO:

B-9   EXT. DECK. FLASH SERIES
        OF IMPRESSIONISTIC SHOTS

All these shots are briefest
of flashes, some dissolving
into others; some quick cuts,
but giving effect of furiously
increasing tempo towards a
crescendo of both action and
sound, somewhat as follows:

CLOSEUP CAPTAIN AT WHEEL,
screaming....SUPERIMPOSE
FACES OF SAILORS, five or
six, dissolving in and out -
all wild with fear - screaming, staring - driven beyond
the bounds of human endurance
....
LARGE CLOSEUP DRACULA, fangs bared.

MED. SHOT SAILOR, vaulting over
the rail into the sea...CLOSEUPS
ad lib, to be worked out in detail
later - ending with huge and
impressive shot of Dracula, arms
upraised, dark cloak billowing in
the gale, about to close in upon a
screaming, helpless wretch he has
cornered. As he does so,

DISSOLVE THROUGH TO:

B-10   EXT. DECK. FLASH CLOSEUP
        CABIN WINDOW

Renfield's face is staring out,
his hands flattened against the
storm-swept pane - he is moving
from side to side, like an animal
in a cage - his shirt is open at
the throat, his hair disheveled,
and he is screaming and laughing
and gesticulating, a stark, raving maniac.

Over this, as in the beginning
of the sequence, the great wall
of water crashes, bloting out
everything but its foaming eddies,
and we
                DISSOLVE TO:

B-11   EXT. WHARF AT WHITBY,
       DAY; LARGE CLOSEUP PILE

About which a ship's hawser is looped. A low buzz of excited conversation comes over the Closeup, and CAMERA STARTS MOVING BACK TO MED. SHOT, revealing a throng of villagers, clustered at the edge of the wharf by side of which the storm-battered schooner is moored. The hull shows signs of a titanic battle with the elements.

B-12   EXT. DECK. LARGE CLOSEUP
       WHEEL

Against the wheel is the dead body of the captain, slumped down to one side, supported only by the rope which is knotted about his wrists. His face is stamped with the ghastly look of a man who has seen Hell. OVER CLOSEUP comes the sound of voices.

                    VOICES

                    - Look, how his fingers
                    grip the wheel - as if
                    they were frozen to it!

                    - He must have died of
                    fright -

                    - Horrible tragedy -

B-13   EXT. CLOSEUP BROKEN
       SPAR

A few shreds of canvas hanging from it - ropes hanging loose. Voices continue over scene,

                    VOICES

                    - Not a stitch of canvas
                    left.

                    - They must have gone
                    through a terrible storm.

OH

B-14   INT. HOLD. MED.
        SHOT RENFIELD

        He is seated on the
        floor. One arm is flung
        over Dracula's box - he
        leans closer to lid of
        box and says in confiden-
        tial tones,

                        RENFIELD

                    Master - Master - we're
                    here! Can you hear what
                    I'm saying, Master - can
                    you -

B-15   EXT. DECK. MED. CLOSE

        Battered cabin door, panels
        splintered - door half hang-
        ing from its hinges. CAMERA
        MOVES EAST, and we hear foot-
        steps as of several men. Voices
        continue,

                        VOICES

                    - The crew gone - what
                    could have happened to
                    them?
                            (Sharply)
                    - What was that?

                    - It seems to come from
                    that hatchway there -

        CAMERA MOVES ALONG DECK
        TO COVERED HATCHWAY -
        in this shot we see feet
        of several men walking.
        CAMERA STOPS AT HATCHWAY,
        as several hands come into
        scene and start to lift up
        hatch.

B-16   INT. HOLD. MED. SHOT
        RENFIELD

        The scraping noise caused by
        the raising of the hatch
        directs his attention, and he
        looks up just as the cover of
        the hatch is thrown back, and
        a great blinding shaft of sun-
        light streams down upon him.
        He shrinks back against the
        box, looking up at them as he
        starts to laugh in a low, crazy
        way.
                            FADE OUT.

SEQUENCE "C"

C-1 FADE INTO: (SOUND OF TRAFFIC NOISES)
EXT. LONDON STREET.
NITE AND FOG

    The scene is enveloped in a typical dense London fog. CAMERA MOVING SLOWLY ALONG - picks up a pedestrian or two, groping hazily along and almost immediately lost in the fog again. Back of the almost opaque fog wall we are conscious of many moving shapes, passersby going to and fro - we hear taxi horns - clatter of night traffic - we see a dim light burning feebly from a lamp-post - and then the cloaked figure of Dracula passing slowly by with a peculiar gliding walk. As his figure becomes clear enough to distinguish, the fog thickens and everything is completely obliterated as we DISSOLVE THROUGH TO:

C-2 EXT. TRAFALGAR SQUARE
MED. SHOT NEAR NELSON
MONUMENT

    The fog is not quite as dense at this point, CAMERA STILL MOVING, approaches a flower-girl with her tray of boutonnieres standing at base of monument. People passing by without paying any heed to her constantly reiterated cry:

                    FLOWER-GIRL

            Vi'lets - flowers, sir -
            flowers, miss? - 'ere's
            your boutonniere, sir -

    Dracula appears out of the fog, looming up into fore, hesitates for a moment and then glides forward towards flower-girl. Girl sees him and chirps, like a wet sparrow,

                    (CONTINUED)

C-2   (CONTINUED)

        FLOWER-GIRL
         (To Dracula)

       Flower for your
       button'ole, sir?

Dracula moves closer to her - CAMERA FOLLOWING INTO A CLOSE SHOT. He leans over her, staring down into her up-turned eyes with a strange, fixed stare. Then he nods slowly, indicating that he'll take a flower, and makes a sign that she is to place it in his button-hole. She selects a flower, and with a half-timid, half-coquettish air, starts to obey. CAMERA MOVES FORWARD TO LARGE CLOSEUP OF HER FACE, as her eyes start to move around and around in a dizzy, circular movement under the spell of Dracula's hypnotic stare. As we see her eyelids flutter wildly, CUT TO:

C-3   EXT. LARGE CLOSEUP
   DRACULA

Staring intently at girl, his eyes following hers in their curious motion. CAMERA MOVES BACK, including flower-girl, her back to camera - we see her hands drop limply from his lapel, her body suddenly slack. She seems about to collapse, but Dracula catches her in his arms, and as his lips part, disclosing the fang-like teeth, and his face bends closer to the side of her neck, the fog thickens, blotting out the scene, and we DISSOLVE THROUGH TO:

C-4   EXT. MED. SHOT ANOTHER
      PART OF STREET

   A moving shot, showing
   Dracula gliding along
   through crowds as before -
   there are more dark shapes
   now, indicating a more
   populous thoroughfare -
   and as he walks, the fog
   seems to lift even more
   than before, revealing
   the dim light from store
   fronts - perhaps some
   familiar place, like
   Scott's Fish Bar, etc.
   Then the mist comes down
   over the scene again,
   and over it we hear the
   sudden excited shrilling
   of a bobby's whistle.

                                        (BOBBY'S WHISTLE,
                                        FOUR OR FIVE TIMES)

C-5   EXT. MED. SHOT NEAR
      NELSON MONUMENT

   Fog not as heavy as
   before, enabling us to
   see with more clarity
   what is going on.
   Prostrate figure of the
   flower-girl lying on the
   pavement - a bobby is
   kneeling beside her.
   He blows his whistle
   again - and this time is
   answered by two or three
   other whisltes, as if
   from different points.
   As he starts to pick the
   girl up in his arms, the   (BOBBY'S WHISTLE)
   mist again sweeps in,
   blanketing the scene.
   DISSOLVE THROUGH TO:

C-6   EXT. WIDE ANGLE NEAR PICCADILY CIRCUS.
      CAMERA STILL MOVING ALONG

   Through dense fog, which
   starts slowly to clear.
   Brilliant lights appear,
   and the crowd becomes
   denser - we see men in
   top hats and the gleam of
   white shoulders, the rich-
   ness of furs.

                                        (CONTINUED)

C-6   (CONTINUED)

Flanking either side of the theatre entrance are huge posters announcing the appearance of some famous symphony orchestra. There is the usual busy scene at the curb as we pass by - cars arriging - starter in uniform - taxis, sleek limousines, etc. moving up and discharging passengers. Into the midst of the gay, chattering throng the sinister figure of Dracula moves as before. He pauses for a moment and then moves into lobby, where he is lost in the crowd. DISSOLVE THROUGH TO:

C-7   INT. THEATRE WIDE ANGLE

On house, lights dim - a flash of a vast audience as they listen to the number which is being played on the stage in front of them. The music is impressive in quality, something rather impressive, perhaps almost Wagnerian, to sustain atmosphere of the scene's dramatic movement.

(MUSIC OVER THESE SCENES)

C-8   INT. CLOSE SHOT BACK OF HOUSE.

Lighting dim. Dracula and usherette, who flashes light on ticket stub and says in low voice,

                    USHERETTE

          Right this way, sir -

They start off in direction of side aisle. CAMERA DROPS DOWN TO CLOSE MOVING SHOT OF FLOOR as we see the ray of the usherette's flashlight moving down along the floor. Follow for a few feet and CUT TO:

C-9   INT. MED. SHOT BOX

    In which Doctor Seward, Mina, Harker and Lucy Weston are seated. Harker and Mina are seated very close to each other, his arm draped over the back of her chair. She turns and smiles at him, her hand stealing to his - he smiles back, taking it - their attitude indicating that they are very much in love with each other.   (MUSIC OVER SCENE)

    CAMERA PANS AROUND, over the heads of those seated in pit near box to side aisle, as Dracula and the usherette come down towards boxes. As usherette pulls curtain aside for Dracula to continue on into passage behind boxes, CUT TO:

C-10   INT. PASSAGE BACK OF BOX

    Curtains shut off front of box - a single light is burning dimly near a wall-rack for coats. Dracula and usherette have come in - he is handing her his hat - as she looks up at him -

C-11   INT. FLASH CLOSEUP USHERETTE

    Looking up at Dracula - her eyes become suddenly fixed - then her arms, raised to receive his cloak, fall slowly to her sides.   (MUSIC CONTINUES OVER THESE SCENES)

C-12   INT. FLASH BOX

    The party listening to music, which is reaching a crescendo.

C-13   INT. PASSAGE

> Dracula has moved closer to usherette, and is now removing his cloak, his eyes still on hers, as he says, as if in completion of something he has been telling her,

DRACULA

> - and the message delivered, you will remember nothing -

> Usherette nods slowly - Dracula goes on removing his cloak - usherette turns to box.

C-14   INT. BOX

> shooting from fore., towards curtains in back. Music comes to a close - there is the sound of applause, and the house lights start to go on. As the applause dies away, the curtains part and the usherette addresses Doctor Seward.

USHERETTE

> Doctor Seward -
>   (Seward turns)
> - you're wanted on the telephone -

> Doctor Seward nods - rises - starts to leave box, pushing back the curtains. There is a low hum of conversation over the house. Lights are now full on. As Doctor Seward pushes back curtains, we see Dracula hanging his cloak on wall-rack.

C-15   INT. PASSAGE REVERSE ANGLE

> matching action as Doctor Seward comes out of box - we see Mina and the others watching, their heads turned. As Doctor Seward steps out into passage, Dracula says, softly,

CONTINUED.

C-15   CONTINUED

> DRACULA
>
>> Pardon me -
>>> (Seward turns, nodding, with an air of enquiry)
>
> DOCTOR SEWARD
>
>> Yes - ?
>
> DRACULA
>
>> I could not help overhearing your name -
>>> (Seward waits politely)
>> Might I enquire if you are the Doctor Seward whose sanitarium is at Whitby?
>
> DOCTOR SEWARD
>
>> Why, yes -
>
> DRACULA
>
>> I'm Count Dracula - I've just leased Carfax Abbey, I understand it adjoins your grounds -
>
> DOCTOR SEWARD
>
>> Why, yes - it does -
>>> (more cordially)
>> I'm very happy to make your acquaintance, sir -

Hesitates for a moment -then indicating those in box, says

>> Allow me to present my daughter, Mina - Miss Weston - and Mr. Harker -

The trio nods politely - Harker rises and remains standing for a moment. Dracula bows in his most ingratiating manner, his eyes mostly for Lucy. Doctor Sewards say to them by way of explanation,

> DOCTOR SEWARD
>
>> Count Dracula has just taken over Carfax Abbey.
>
> MINA   (with gracious air)
>
>> It'll be a relief to see lights burning in those dismal old windows -

CONTINUED.

MBK

C-15   CONTINUED...2

>   DOCTOR SEWARD
>   (Remembering his phone
>   call)
>   You'll excuse me - I'm
>   wanted on the phone -
>   meanwhile - (indicates
>   vacant chair)
>   - won't you join us?
>
>   DRACULA
>
>   Thank you!

Doctor Seward briefly smiles and exits. Dracula turns to the others.

>   HARKER
>
>   I should think the Abbey
>   could be made quite attrac-
>   tive - but it's going to
>   need rather extensive
>   repairs -
>
>   DRACULA   (Quietly)
>
>   I shall do little repairing -
>   it remindsme of the broken
>   embattlements of my own
>   castle in Transylvania.

Lucy, under the spell of Dracula's eerie fascination, says with reminiscent eyes -

>   LUCY
>
>   The Abbey always reminds
>   me of that old toast
>   about -

C-16   INT. CLOSE SHOT
         LUCY AND DRACULA.

as she looks up at him, as if almost unable to avoid his searching gaze. Her voice continues unbroken:

>   LUCY
>
>   " - lofty timbers - the
>   walls around are bare -
>   echoing to our laughter ..
>   as though the dead were there - "

Over shot there is the sound of Harker's grunt

MBK

C-17   INT. MED. SHOT REVERSE
        ANGLE.

        shooting into box.
        Match action as Harker
        continues -   HARKER

                                            Nice little sentiment!

                                       LUCY   (with a laugh)

                                            Oh, but wait - there's
                                            more - even nicer -
                                                (Teasing him with
                                                mockingly dramatic
                                                gestures)
                                            "Quaff a cup to the dead
                                            already! Hurrah for the
                                            next who dies! "

                                       MINA   (with a shiver)

                                            Never mind the rest, dear!

        At this, the house
        lights start to dim -
        the hum of conversation
        from the rest of the
        house dies slowly away. -

C-18   INT. CLOSEUP DRACULA.

        as he says, half-dreamily,
        a deeply tragic note
        underlying his words.

                                       DRACULA

                                            To die - to be really dead -
                                            that must be glorious.

C-19   INT. MED. SHOT. GROUP

        matching action as Dracula
        finishes speech. Every-
        body looks at everybody
        else - a sudden feeling
        of constraint falls over
        them - no one speaks for
        a moment; then Mina exclaims
        with a nervous little laugh -

                                       MINA

                                            Why, Count Dracula - !

                                       CONTINUED

C-19   CONTINUED

> Dracula turns swiftly to her - his face suddenly stern, his eyes dark and brooding. House lights almost out - CAMERA MOVES QUICKLY TO LARGE C.U. OF HIS FACE, as he says somberly.

                    DRACULA
> There are far worse things awaiting man - than death,-

As he finishes speech, the box is in deep shadow- lights from stage casting dim, weird lighting on his face. The sound of music from stage starts to come over scene - a low prelude of woodwinds and strings, adding to the macabre quality of scene as we

FADE OUT.

SEQUENCE "D"

D-1 FADE INTO:
INT. LUCY'S BEDROOM
NIGHT. LARGE CLOSEUP
VIENNESE PERFUME BOTTLE

stand of which contains   (TINKLE OF MUSIC BOX
a tiny music box which   AT FADE)
plays when bottle is
removed. Lucy's hand into
CU, replacing perfume bottle-
the music stops abruptly and
Mina's voice is heard laughing.

CAMERA STARTS MOVING BACK
TO REVEAL LUCY, in negligee,
seated before a dressing table
which contains a long mirror
reaching to floor, with
drawers and compartments on
either side. In b.g., seen
through mirror, Mina is
perched on one end of a
chaise longue.

CAMERA STOPS ON MED. CLOSE
SHOT LUCY BEFORE DRESSING
TABLE.

          LUCY

          Laugh all you want to - I
          thought he was fascinating-
             (picks up a comb and
             starts to run it
             through her hair)

          MINA

          Lucy - the romantic -!
             (teasingly)
          I know what it was - it
          was those broken battle-
          ments of his -
             (Rises with a shrug)
          Oh, well - give me someone
          a little more - normal -

          LUCY   (smiling)

          Like John.

          MINA

             (Xing slowly into
             scene)

          Yes, dear - like John -

Comes into scene -
bending over Lucy,
kisses her lightly.

          Well, Countess, I'm sleepy.

Starts out of scene
towards door.

          (CONTINUED)

RS

D-1   (CONTINUED)

        MINA
         (continues)
      I'll leave you to your
      Count and his ruined
      abbeys -

In mirror we see her X to door in b.g. CAMERA SWINGS AROUND TO MED. CLOSE SHOT NEAR DOOR, as Mina pauses, her hand on door-knob, and says playfully,

        MINA
      -- and I hope you'll have
      very pleasant dreams -

Exits, waving a flippant goodnight to Lucy.

D-2   INT. WIDE ANGLE

  Lucy in fore, at dressing-table - as door closes behind Mina, she lays aside her comb, and rises, her negligee falling over the back of the chair. She Xes to window, and starts to open it.

D-3   EXT. STREET. BERKELEY SQUARE
    NIGHT AND FOG.

  The fog has lifted slightly. Under street lamp in fore., strolls a bobby. Dracula, muffled in his cloak, enters scene, walking slowly. Bobby greets him:

        BOBBY
      Looks like the fog is
      closing down again,
      sir!

Dracula nods curtly - Bobby gazes curiously at him as he moves off down street. CAMERA FOLLOWS Dracula a few steps - he steps and looks up towards house.

RS

D-4   EXT. WESTON HOME
        MED. CLOSE OF WINDOW

        Shooting up at angle from
        street below, from Dracula's
        point of view, Lucy appears
        at window - pushes back
        the curtains and flings wide
        the casement - stands there
        for a moment, head thrown
        back - then turns back
        into room.

D-5   INT. LUCY'S BEDROOM
        WIDE ANGLE

        matching action as Lucy
        crosses from window towards
        bed, snapping out the
        lights as she goes. Only
        one light remains, that of
        a lamp on bedside table.
        Lucy takes up book from
        bedside table, climbs into
        bed, and arranging herself
        comfortably, starts to read.

D-6   INT. CLOSE SHOT AT WINDOW

        The fog outside the window
        comes to have grown denser-
        it is creeping slowly into
        the room. A large bat
        suddenly appears, circling
        near the window outside.
        It emerges from the fog
        briefly and then flies
        back into fog again - then
        once more comes into sight,
        flying past window.

D-7   INT. CLOSE SHOT LUCY IN
        BED

        She lays the book aside,
        feeling drowsy-lays the
        book on covers, face down,
        fighting impulse to sleep.

D-8   INT. CLOSE SHOT AT WINDOW

Bat re-appears, cicling closer, almost coming into room.

D-9   INT. CLOSE SHOT LUCY

She has given up the idea of reading and is lying back, her eyes slowly closing. They close completely and she relaxes - breathing evenly. One arm is thrown behind her head - as she lies there, a faint smile hovering about her lips. CAMERA MOVES SLOWLY BACK DOWN BED, and at the foot we see Dracula standing, looking intently down at her. Slowly he advances towards head of bed, nearer, nearer, moving with infinite stealth. As he approaches her, CAMERA MOVES INTO CLOSE SHOT. Dracula's hands reach out, his lips part in a wolfish snarl and as he lowers his head slowly towards Lucy's white, exposed throat, we

DISSOLVE TO:

D-10 INT. OPERATING ROOM HOSPITAL
      WIDE ANGLE

This operating room is in a modern, thoroughly up-to-date London hospital. Through a glass skylight overhead, daylight streams. At one side is a student's gallery, separated from the room by a glass partition. The gallery is crowded with onlookers, whose attention is centered upon the operating table in the center. Around table are two doctors, Seward and a French surgeon. The doctor in charge, an Englishman, is bending over the shrouded form of Lucy. A couple of nurses are in attendance, hovering at his elbow for instructions.

(CONTINUED)

D-10   CONTINUED

CAMERA MOVES SWIFTLY FORWARD TO CLOSE SHOT GROUP. The Englishman, who is the senior doctor, straightens up after his examination of Lucy's neck and turns to the others with a puzzled air...

          SENIOR DOCTOR
            (grimly)

      Another death -
        (turns to Seward)
      When did Miss Weston have the last tranfusion?

          DR. SEWARD

      About four hours before she died.

          SENIOR DOCTOR

      Every case has revealed the same symptoms -- an unnatural loss of blood which we've been powerless to check -

Pauses, shaking his head - then turns his attention to Lucy again - takes a large magnifying glass from the nurse and studies Lucy's neck with it.

D-11   INT. LARGE CLOSEUP LUCY'S NECK

Two marks on her neck, like swollen pin-pricks, can be plainly seen through the glass. Over CU we hear the doctor's voice,

          SENIOR DOCTOR

      - and these same two marks were found on the throat of the victim -

DISSOLVE THROUGH TO:

RS

D-12   INT. VAN HELSING'S LABORATORY
       LARGE CLOSEUP VAN HELSING'S EYES

seen through the heavy, thick lenses of his glasses which magnify the eyes so that they almost fill the screen. The eyes are staring directly at an object beyond the camera.

CAMERA MOVES BACK VERY SLOWLY until we see the head and shoulders of Professor Van Helsing. Eyes keep staring fixedly at object beyond camera.

CAMERA MOVES BACK TO reveal table upon which is a test-tube, filled with what is presumably blood, in a rack over a small burner. Van Helsing is studying the chemical reactions in this tube with complete absorption.

CAMERA CONTINUES MOVING BACK TO INCLUDE Van Helsing's assistant, who is reading from an enormous, ancient volume which lies spread out on the table before him. As CAMERA CONTINUES MOVING BACK, we include three doctors, who are sitting with their backs to camera, literally hanging breathlessly upon the result of Van Helsing's delicate experiment. These doctors prove to be Doctor Seward, the English Senior doctor of the preceding shot, and a little hunchback Austrian, who sits straddling stool like a mis-shapen frog.

Van Helsing, with a pair of wire tweezers, lifts the test-tube from the burner and tilting it carefully, starts to apply a chemical from another tube which he picks up from table.

D-13   INT. FLASH LARGE CLOSEUP
       TEST-TUBE

as chemical is added. It changes from its dark, vicious composition to one of milky whiteness. There is the hissing intake of breath over closeup.

RS

D-14   INT. CLOSE SHOT AT TABLE

Van Helsing whirls upon
his assistant - snaps:

> VAN HELSING
>
> Read - dumkopf! Where
> I marked -!

Assistant, a scraggly
little old fellow, bald-
headed, also with thick
glasses, ducks his head
to book and starts reading
aloud in Latin, tracing
words with his fore-
finger.

D-15   INT. LARGE INSERT BOOK

The leaves are almost
falling apart with age -
it is printed in black
Gothic type and written
in Latin. As the bony
finger of the assistant
traces out the words, we
hear his voice, reading
laboriously:

> ASSISTANT (reads in Latin
> to be filled in
> later)

D-16   INT. LABORATORY WIDE ANGLE

showing laboratory in
full for the first time.
It is a huge room with a
high arched ceiling -
foreign in feeling -
littered with racks of
bottles, test-tubes,
scientific apparatus -
retors, etc., - veritable
modern magician's retract.
Dominating one whole side
of the room is a huge square
window through which we
catch a glimpse of dark,
distant mountains - of the
steady drip-drip-drip of
rain on the pane - of the
bare branches of trees
waving starkly in the
unheard gale without.

(CONTINUED)

D-16   (CONTINUED)

    The group around the table show dark against the dim glow of the light between them and camera - a weird effect, their shadows looming in gargantuan proportion upon the vaulted dome of the ceiling.. The voice of the assistant finishes reading.

(VOICE OF ASSISTANT READING OVER SCENE)

D-17   INT. CLOSEUP VAN HELSING

    He now pours a single drop of blood on the glass slide - over this he drops a tiny square of glass and thrusts the whole under the lens of a powerful looking microscope.

D-18   INT. CLOSE SHOT DOCTORS

    their faces in half light, leaning forward with rapt attention to watch result of final test.

D-19   INT. MED. SHOT GROUP

    as Van Helsing, after peering carefully through microscope, straightens up and faces them grimly.

              VAN HELSING

        Gentlemen, we are dealing with - the undead.

D-20   INT. CLOSE SHOT DOCTORS

    They exchange bewildered, horrified glances. The little Austrian, his eyes nearly popping out of his head, leans forward so far that he almost falls off his stool, hissing:

(CONTINUED)

RS

D-20 (CONTINUED)

        AUSTRIAN DOCTOR

        Nosferatu!

D-21 INT. MED. CLOSE SHOT

  matching action as Van
  Helsing nods gravely and
  replies:

        VAN HELSING

        Yes - nosferatu - the
        undead - the Vampire!
         (to the others)
        The vampire attacks the
        throat - he leaves two
        little wounds, white with
        red centres!

  There is a momentary silence.
  Then the English Senior doctor
  frowns and says in mildly
  impatient tones of disbelief:

        SENIOR DOCTOR

        But, Professor Van Helsing,
        modern medical science
        doesn't admit of such a
        creature! The Vampire is
        pure myth - superstition-!

  Van Helsing shakes his
  head patiently - indicating
  Doctor Seward, says:

        VAN HELSING

        Doctor Seward's patient
        Renfield, whose blood I
        have just analyzed, is a
        man obsessed with the
        idea that he must devour
        living things to sustain
        his own life!..I'm return-
        ing to England with Doc-
        tor Seward to study
        Renfield -
         (pauses impressively)
        - and I may be able to
        furnish you with proof
        that the superstition of
        yesterday can become the
        scientific reality of
        today!

  As he looks around upon
  their amazed faces, we

  FADE OUT.

HN

SEQUENCE "E"

E-1   FADE IN TO:
        EXT. SEWARD SANITARIUM
        LATE AFTERNOON. CLOSE
        SHOT ORNAMENTAL IRON GATES

> Gates swing open as CAMERA MOVES SWFITLY THROUGH and up, past flowering shrubs and bushes, around a semi-circular driveway towards house. This is seen to be a rambling, Georgian affair, the main part of which is used as living quarters for Dr. Seward and his immediate household; while on both sides of the main building, two wings extend, in which patients are quartered.
>
> CAMERA CONTINUES ON PAST FRONT ENTRANCE TOWARDS RIGHT WING. A sudden series of screams are heard. CAMERA CRANES SWIFTLY TO CLOSE SHOT WINDOW ON SECOND FLOOR OF WING - a barred window, open. Through this window, we see Martin, a keeper, and Renfield, engaged in some sort of minor struggle, Renfield is screaming.

                        RENFIELD

                            Oh, Martin - please -
                            good Martin! Don't take
                            him away from me! Don't -
                            don't -

        DISSOLVE THROUGH TO:

E-2   INT. RENFIELD'S ROOM

> This is rather severely furnished room, probably in white, with a plain white bed of hospital type - a single white chair - a dresser, etc. The only sinister note is the bars at the window. Martin, a husky Cockney, has forced Renfield to his knees. He has just wrenched a spider from Renfield's hand and throws it on the floor, grinding it disgustedly under his heel.

                                            CONTINUED.

E-2   CONTINUED

      MARTIN

       Ain't you ashymed - now,
       ain't you! Spiders, now,
       is it? Flies ain't good
       enough for you!

Glares at Renfield,
flinging him away from
him. Renfield gets to
his feet, his cries
ceasing - draws himself
up with a superior air
and looking Martin up and
down with cold dignity,
says,

      RENFIELD

       Flies - flies! Poor,
       puny things! Who wants
       to eat flies?

      MARTIN

       You do, you looney!

      RENFIELD   (with relish)

       Not when I can get nice,
       fat spiders -

Martin shakes his head
hopelessly - takes
Renfield by the arm and
starts to steer him, more
gently, towards door
leading to hall, saying,

      MARTIN

       Orl right - 'ave it your
       own wye. Now, come - the
       professor's waitin' to
       tork to you again -

As they exit, we CUT TO:

E-3 INT. DOCTOR SEWARD'S
    LABORATORY

A typical doctor's
laboratory, with office
combined. Everything
spick-and-span - white -
up-to-the minute. Dr.
Seward's desk occupies
a relatively unimportant
position near window.

      CONTINUED.

HN

E-3   CONTINUED

Van Helsing and Dr. Seward
are seated at desk in
earnest consultation, as
CAMERA MOVES TO UP CLOSE
SHOT. Some sort of a
discussion has evidently
been in progress.

                    DR. SEWARD

            But Renfield's cravings
            have only been for small
            living things - nothing
            human -

                    VAN HELSING

            As far as we know, doctor.
            But you tell me he escapes
            from his room - is gone for
            hours -
                (keenly)
            Where does he go?

There is the sound of a
door opening - they turn-

E-4   INT. LABORATORY
      WIDE ANGLE

matching action as men
turn and Martin enters
with Renfield. In
appearance, Renfield is
quite normal and sane,
now. He comes forward
quietly, nodding to the
two men at the desk.
Van Helsing rises and
greets him, extending his
hand in the friendliest
manner possible

                    VAN HELSING

            Well, Mr. Renfield, you
            look much better than you
            did this morning when I
            arrived.

Martin takes up a position
a little to one side;
watchful, alert, gloomily
suspicious of anything
Renfield says or does.

E-5   INT. CLOSEUP RENFIELD

nodding politely - replies,

                RENFIELD

            Thanks, Professor Van
            Helsing; I'm feeling
            much better.

Seats himself in chair.

E-6   INT. CLOSE SHOT AT DESK

Van Helsing leaning back
easily in his chair, his
manner chatty, casual.
Doctor Seward lounges
against windowsill, his
attitude also disarming.
Renfield seems quite normal,
ready to assist them.

                VAN HELSING   (amiably)

            I understand you're an
            Oxford man -

                RENFIELD   (modestly)

            Why, yes; I received my
            degree in '27 and was
            admitted to the Bar a
            year later. Then I -

Pauses, following some-
thing with his eyes - half
turns - then says quietly,

                RENFIELD

            Pardon me -

Rises from chair and Xes
towards back wall, CAMERA
MOVING BACK TO WIDER ANGLE.
Van Helsing and Dr. Seward
stare quizzically at him,
not knowing what he may be
after.

E-7   INT. CLOSE SHOT AT WALL

Renfield enters, stealthily,
walking on tip-toe - we see
his objective is a fly
crawling on the white wall.
He leans forward and swoops
it up in his hand - brings it
close to his face and is just   CONTINUED.

E-7   CONTINUED

        about to raise it to his
        mouth when he looks across
        at Van Helsing and Dr.
        Seward, pausing.

E-8   INT. FLASH CLOSE SHOT
        DR. SEWARD AND VAN HELSING

        They are watching him narrowly.

E-9   INT. MED. SHOT

        including group - matching
        action as Renfield pauses
        in the act of transferring
        the fly to his mouth.
        Seeing how closely the
        others are watching, he
        suddenly opens his fingers
        and lets the fly escape-
        says with an air of
        indifference

                        RENFIELD (watching fly buzz
                                    away)
                            A low form of life -
                            beneath my notice -

        Walks back to his chair
        in the most nonchalant manner,
        as if this procedure were
        the most natural thing in the
        world.

E-10   INT. CLOSE SHOT
        VAN HELSING AND SEWARD

        They exchange quick glances -
        then Val Helsing, without
        changing his position, regards
        Renfield with a tolerant
        smile, asking in calmly
        conversational tones,

                        VAN HELSING
                            What would you have done
                            with that fly if we hadn't
                            been here?

E-11　INT. FLASH CLOSEUP
RENFIELD

    hesitating, as if a
    bit embarassed.

E-12　INT. FLASH CLOSEUP
MARTIN

    his face clouding
    darkly as he growls

                MARTIN

            'E'd of _et it!_

E-13　INT. MED. SHOT

    Renfield in fore., he
    turns and favors Martin
    with a look of mild
    annoyance. Van Helsing
    leans forward, studying
    Renfield closely now -
    asks,

                VAN HELSING

            Tell me, Mr. Renfield,
            what makes you want to
            eat - flies?

    Renfield smiles airily
    and replies,

                RENFIELD

            The wings of the fly,
            my dear sir, typify the
            aerial powers of the
            psychic faculties -

    Van Helsing darts him
    a shrewd glance - Martin
    shakes his head in
    grudging admiration -
    says to Doctor Seward,

                MARTIN

            'E's a cute one, aint
            'e, doctor?
              (to Van Helsing)
            Always got an answer!

                CONTINUED.

E-13   CONTINUED

> Van Helsing looks back over his shoulder at Doctor Seward, who shrugs- then addresses himself to Renfield, dropping his casual manner and becoming more incisive.

                    VAN HELSING

> Come, come, now, Renfield!
> I want to talk seriously
> to you -

E-14   EXT. MED. SHOT TERRACE
        SUNSET

> This terrace is at one side of the sanitarium, opening off the library by means of low French windows. It faces Carfax Abbey, which can be faintly seen across a wide stretch of wooded lawn, beyond a wall. At one side can be seen the sea- a vague suggestion of Whitby Harbor. (All this can be done with process shot or backing) Harker is standing near rail, his arm about Mina. She wears a light frock, and a long chiffon scarf, somewhat incongruously wound once about her throat. She is in a strange mood, and he is frankly ill at ease as he tries to discover the cause.

                    HARKER

> Mina, I've never seen you
> like this before! What is
> it? Have I done anything?
> Is something worrying you,
> or what?

> Mina avoids his sober eyes, as she gazes off towards sunset.

E-15   EXT. LONG SHOT. SUNSET.
        THROUGH TREES

>   Wall and Carfax Abbey in
>   background. A very soft,
>   hazy shot of the sun dipping
>   behind the grove of trees
>   which surround the Abbey.

E-16   EXT. TERRACE
        CLOSE SHOT HARKER AND MINA

>   as she stares into the
>   sunset with a faraway look
>   in her eyes, says,

                    MINA

            It isn't anything you've
            done, dear - and you
            mustn't worry -

                    HARKER

            But -

>   She turns impulsively
>   to him - says,

                    MINA   (clinging to him
                               nervously)

            I don't know what it is -
            I've been afraid lately -
            when night comes on,
            I feel as if - something
            were closing in around me -

>   Harker looks down into
>   her harried eyes with
>   genuine concern.

E-17   INT. ROOM IN CARFAX
        ABBEY. SUNSET. WIDE ANGLE

>   The room, ecclesiastical
>   in motif, shows signs of
>   abandonment and utter
>   decay - cob-webs, dust,
>   tumbled bits of stone
>   columns and architrave.
>   The last rays of light
>   are coming through a
>   ragged oriel window, and
>   falling upon a stone wall
>   opposite. As we hold
>   camera, the light fades, the
>   last glimmer of daylight goes,
>   and the whole scene is almost
>   obscured in a grey, dim light.   CONTINUED.

E-17   CONTINUED

In fore., are three boxes, previously established on shipboard. CAMERA MOVES DOWN TO LARGE CLOSEUP END OF BOX, as it starts to show signs of containing life. The lid is pushed slowly upward, and Dracula's long fingers appear over the side.

CAMERA MOVES DOWN TO LARGE CLOSEUP LABEL ON BOX, showing it to be addressed to "Count Dracula, Carfax Abbey, Whitny, England." HOLD CAMERA ON THIS FOR A MOMENT as there is the sound of the lid being laid aside - then MOVE CAMERA QUICKLY BACK TO MED. SHOT and pick up Dracula, standing beside box from which he has just emerged. His attitude is one of a heavy sleeper aroused from a restful dream. Lethargic at first, his expression becomes singularly alive - his eyes light up in anticipation of the period of freedom before him. He starts to move slowly towards door, with the curious, gliding movement so characteristic of him, as we CUT TO:

E-18   EXT. TERRACE CLOSE SHOT
HARKER AND MINA

Mina shivers slightly, as if already aware of Dracula's awakening. Harker studies her critically - then, with an attempt to be matter-of-fact banishing her strange mood, he says,

     HARKER

    It's my fault. I should
    have made you come up to
    London while your father was
    away instead of leaving you
    down here with nothing to
    think about but Lucy.

    MINA (after a moment's
       hesitation)
    It isn't only that - but
    I can't sleep at night
    without having the most
    awful dreams -

HN

E-19   EXT. SANITARIUM GROUNDS.
       EVENING. FLASH CLOSE SHOT
       BREAK IN WALL

   a high, crumbling wall -
   through broken place we
   see a wild tangle of
   underbrush and woods on
   Abbey grounds. Dracula steps
   through break and starts
   walking slowly towards
   sanitarium.

E-20   EXT. TERRACE CLOSE SHOT
       HARKER AND MINA

   Mina, her nervous tension
   apparently increasing,
   shivers. Harker says,

                HARKER

           You're cold, dear -

                MINA

           No, but - let's go inside.

   Turns to go into house
   through French window.
   Harker follws her, saying
   with an air of grim
   determination.

                HARKER

           I'll tell you what we're
           goin to do - we're not
           going to wait - we're going
           to get married right away
           and go away from here -

E-21   INT. LABORATORY
       MED SHOT

   Renfield is to all
   appearances himself
   again. Van Helsing has
   risen and is standing
   before him, and is
   saying, gently,

                VAN HELSING

           I'm here to help you. You
           understand that, don't you?

                    CONTINUED.

E-21   CONTINUED

        He holds out his hand
        to Renfield. Renfield
        takes it in a friendly
        fashion, replying,

                      RENFIELD

              Why, of course - I'm really
              very grateful -

As he speaks, Van Helsing
slides his thumb over
Renfield's finger tips.
Renfield's manner changes
quickly - he jerks his
hand away, snarling angrily:

                      RENFIELD

              Keep your filthy hands to
              yourself!

He backs away, his face
contorted with fury.
Dr. Seward comes forward
hastily, interposing -
Martin also steps towards
him, as if to prevent any
possible attack upon Van
Helsing.

                      DOCTOR SEWARD

              Here, here, Renfield -!

The sound of his voice
cause Renfield to whirl
saying,

                      RENFIELD

              I want you to send me away
              from this place -

E-22   INT. FLASH CLOSEUP VAN
       HELSING

        interested in this sudden
        outburst on Renfield's
        part, asks quietly,

                      VAN HELSING

              Why are you so anxious to
              get away?

E-23   INT. MED SHOT GROUP

Renfield turns to
Van Helsing, in answer,
says,

> RENFIELD
>
> My cries at night - they
> might disturb Miss Mina -
> they might give her bad
> dreams -

Turns to Van Helsing,
significantly,

> - bad dreams, Professor -
> bad dreams!

As he says this, there
is the sudden howl of a
wolf outside. As they
all indicate that they
have heard it, Renfield
takes a step away from the
window, his face suddenly
filled with fear.

E-24   EXT. SANITARIUM GROUNDS
        EVENING. MED. SHOT NOT
        FAR FROM HOUSE

Dracula walking slowly
along towards house.

E-25   INT. LABORATORY
        FLASH CLOSEUP
        VAN HELSING

as he says slowly, his
head slightly turned in
a listening attitude,

> VAN HELSING
>
> That sounded like a wolf -

RS

E-26 INT. WIDE ANGLE

matching action as
Seward nods.

      DOCTOR SEWARD

   Yes, it did -
    (smiles politely)
   - but I hardly think there
   are wolves this close to
   London!.

Martin points to Renfield
who is still huddled
fearfully near the wall,
listening, waiting - says:

      MARTIN (sarcastically)

   'E thinks they're wolves.
   Me, I've 'eard 'em 'owl
   at night before. 'E says
   they're talking to him.
   'E 'owls an' 'owls back
   at them!
    (by way of explana-
    tion)
   'E's crazy.

Van Helsing Xes to desk
and leans against it, his
face grave, his eyes
deeply thoughtful, Ren-
field, uneasy before this
scrutiny, turns away.
Van Helsing says, half to
himself:

      VAN HELSING

   I might have known - I
   might have known -

Xes towards Renfield,
slipping one hand into
the pocket of his coat
as he does so.

      VAN HELSING
    (to Renfield, purringly)
   You know why the wolves
   talk, don't you, Mr.
   Renfield.

E-27 INT. CLOSE SHOT
   RENFIELD AND VAN HELSING

matching action as Van
Helsing approaches him
slowly - his speech
continuing unbroken
over the sound-track

      (CONTINUED)

E-27   (CONTINUED

                                    VAN HELSING

                                        -- and you know how we can
                                        stop them--?

As he says this, he
suddenly brings his
hand out of his pocket
and thrusts a small
sprig of wolfbane right
under Renfield's nose.
Renfield, with a scream
of rage and loathing,
springs back. Van Helsing
follows him out of scene.

E-28   INT. WIDE ANGLE

    matching action as
    Renfield in a rage,
    glares at Van Helsing.

                                    RENFIELD

                                        You know too much to live,
                                        Van Helsing!

Van Helsing, with an
air of satisfaction, Xes
to desk in fore., where
he takes the two parts of
a small black box from
his pocket and replaces
the sprig of wolfbane,
saying to Doctor Seward,
who joins him:

                                    VAN HELSING

                                        We won't get any more out
                                        of him now, for awhile --

Doctor Seward nods --
turns to Martin with a
sigh.

                                    DOCTOR SEWARD

                                        Take him away, Martin.

                                    MARTIN   (giving Renfield a
                                                yank)
                                        On yer way, fly-eater--

As they start towards
door, we CUT TO:

E-29   INT. CLOSE SHOT AT DOOR

matching action as Martin and Renfield enter - Renfield, much quieter and somewhat cowed by Martin, wrenches around to deliver one last ultimatum at Dr. Seward - his tone more pleading than threatening.

          RENFIELD

I'm warning you, Doctor Seward! If you don't send me away, you must answer for what will happen to Miss Mina!

Martin yanks him out into the corridor before he has a chance to say anything else.

E-30   INT. LABORATORY
        CLOSE SHOT AT DESK

Van Helsing replacing wolfbane in box as Dr. Seward enters scene. Seward indicates wolfbane, saying:

          DR. SEWARD

What's that herb that excited him so?

          VAN HELSING

Wolfbane -
   (as Seward looks blank)
It's a plant that grows in Central Europe. The natives there use it to protect themselves against vampires.

          DR. SEWARD (frowning)

Renfield reacted very violently to its scent -

          VAN HELSING (nodding gravely)

He must be watched day and night - especially at night!

E-31   INT. DR. SEWARD LIBRARY
       NIGHT. WIDE ANGLE

>   This is a well-appointed room with a large fireplace flanked by low French windows leading to the terrace, from which Harker and Mina have just entered. The windows are hung with heavy brocaded portieres with a deep box valance, so that a person might conceal himself behind them without being too noticeable. There is a davenport before fireplace - a table behind it, with periodicals, etc. The only important prop for table is a large cigarette box, which contains a mirror on its inside cover.
>
>   Mina is lying on the sofa, with Harker seated beside her. She is still highly nervous, and looks as if she were terribly fatigued. The scarf is still wound about her neck.
>
>   CAMERA STARTS MOVING IN TO CLOSE SHOT as we hear her voice, apparently continuing an account of the dream she has been describing to Harker.

                              MINA
                  - I lay in bed for quite a-
                  while, reading; and just
                  as I was commencing to feel
                  drowsy, the dogs started
                  barking - and when the
                  dream came, it seemed as
                  if the room were filled
                  with mist --

>   While she has been saying this, CAMERA HAS SWUNG AROUND TO CLOSE SHOT, shooting past sofa towards library door. As she gets to this point, Van Helsing and Dr. Seward appear in doorway, unseen by Mina and Harker, and pause, listening.

                              MINA
                  It seemed so thick that I
                  could just see the lamp by
                  the bed - a tiny spark in
                  the fog -
                              (CONTINUED)

E-31   (CONTINUED)

CAMERA MOVES PAST HER TO
DOOR, moving into CU Van
Helsing and Dr. Seward,
listening - Mina's voice
continuing over scene:

                    MINA

                            - and then I saw two red
                            eyes staring at me -
                                (Van Helsing's eyes
                                narrow)
                            -and a livid white face
                            looking down at me out of
                            this mist -

Van Helsing and Dr.
Seward exchange quick
glances and start down
into room. CAMERA MOVES
QUICKLY BACK TO INCLUDE
MINA AND HARKER ON SOFA
IN IMMEDIATE FORE.,
Mina still talking without
interruption:

                    MINA

                            It came closer and closer-
                            and then I felt its breath
                            on my face, and its lips-
                                (Breaks off with
                                shudder)
                            Oh -!

Covers her face with
her hands. As she says,
"closer and closer",
Van Helsing and Dr.
Seward have been approaching into fore. Harker
looks up and sees them,
and is about to speak, but
Van Helsing signals for him
to remain quiet and let Mina
go on with her recital. Harker,
with an uneasy frown, turns
to Mina and takes one of her hands
in his - murmurs:

                    HARKER

                            But, dear - it was only a
                            dream - you mustn't -

                    MINA

                            The next morning I felt so
                            weak - it seemed as if all
                            the life had been drained
                            out of me -

Van Helsing's jaw sets
grimly.

                                        (CONTINUED)

E-31   CONTINUED 2

VAN HELSING (interrupting
               quietly)
When did you have this
dream, Miss Mina?

Mina turns and faces him.

MINA

Why, I - it was the night
Father left for Switzer-
land - the night after
Lucy's funeral -

A shadow passes over her face as she says this. Harker rises with another perturbed glance at Van Helsing, indicating more strongly than before that he'd rather have them change the subject. With an annoyed look at Van Helsing, he pats Mina's hand and says:

HARKER

Darling, we're going to
forget-
     (at Van Helsing)
all about these dreams-
and - think of something
more cheerful - aren't we?

Mina looks up at him with a vague smile - presses his hand to her cheek and releases it. Harker, with a heavy sigh as if glad to have settled the matter for the time being. Xes to end of sofa and Xes around to where Dr. Seward is standing, at end of table behind sofa. Van Helsing, who has been regarding Mina thoughtfully, Xes around fore., and drops down beside Mina.

E-32   INT. CLOSE SHOT ON SOFA

matching action as Van Helsing
seats himself beside Mina,
saying,

(CONTINUED)

E-32   CONTINUED

          VAN HELSING

          Think for a moment - is there anything that might have brought this dream on?

          MINA   (Thinking briefly)

          No -

E-33   INT. CLOSE SHOT
      HARKER AND DR. SEWARD

    Harker looks back towards Mina - says in a worried undertone to Dr. Seward:

          HARKER

          There's something worrying Mina - something she doesn't want to tell us -

          DR. SEWARD (puzzled)

          I don't understand -

    Both look off towards Mina and Van Helsing, Dr. Seward frowning mildly.

E-34   INT. CLOSE SHOT MINA
      AND VAN HELSING

    Van Helsing has just finished exploring Mina's pulse with his deft, expert fingers - she has submitted quietly, her eyes fixed inquiringly on his grave face. He releases her wrist.

          VAN HELSING

          - and the face in this dream - you say it seemed to come closer and closer?

          (Mina nods, her eyes on his)

          The lips touched you -

          (CONTINUED)

E-34   (CONTINUED)

>   (Mina nods again, shiver-
>   ing)
>
>   Where?

As he says this, he leans forward suddenly and one hand seems to reach up towards her scarf. Immediately her own hand flies toward her neck with an instinctive gesture of concealment, and she shrinks back, exclaiming:

>   MINA
>
>   No, no - please -!

CAMERA MOVES BACK as Harker and Dr. Seward enter scene, alarmed by her unexpected action.

>   VAN HELSING
>
>   Is there anything the
>   matter with your throat?
>
>   MINA
>
>   Please - I -

Van Helsing smiles gently and lays his fingers upon the scarf, as he says soothingly:

>   VAN HELSING
>
>   Permit me -

CAMERA MOVES INTO LARGE CLOSEUP VAN HELSING AND MINA, as he removes her scarf - she stares into his keen, penetrating eyes, frightened, trapped. As Van Helsing sees the marks on her neck, his face becomes grim.

>   VAN HELSING
>
>   Hm-m-m!

Reaches into his pocket and takes out a small magnifying glass.

RS

E-35   INT. MED. CLOSE GROUP

   matching action as Van Helsing
   lowers glass to Mina's neck -
   Harker and Dr. Seward watch,
   tense, worried.

E-36   INT. LARGE CLOSEUP
   MINA'S NECK

   a portion of which is
   magnified by the glass.
   Through the circle of the
   lens can be seen the two
   little red marks with white
   centers. Van Helsing's voice
   over CU:

                    VAN HELSING'S VOICE

                    How long have you had
                    those little marks on
                    your throat?

E-37   INT. MED. CLOSE GROUP

   Matching action as Van
   Helsing completes speech,
   Harker exclaims:

                    HARKER

                    Marks -!

   and turns swiftly to
   Dr. Seward, who meets his
   gaze with equal alram. Mina
   says, falteringly:

                    MINA

                    Since the morning after
                    the dream -

   Harker, with an air of
   great concern, makes a
   move towards her.

                    HARKER

                    Mina, why didn't you let
                    us know?
                         (Turns to Van Helsing)
                    What could have caused
                    them?

RS

E-38   INT. CLOSE SHOT
       LIBRARY DOOR

   as maid, standing
   there, announces:

                        MAID

                           Count Dracula!

   Dracula appears behind
   her.

E-39   INT. CLOSE SHOT GROUP

   As they turn, as of one
   accord, and look towards
   doorway.

E-40   INT. WIDE ANGLE

   Group around sofa in fore.,
   Dracula bows to them with
   extreme politeness - maid
   gives him a look and exits.
   Dracula comes down towards
   group, as Doctor Seward says,
   without too much cordiality:

                        DR. SEWARD

                           Good evening -

   Van Helsing rises, annoyed
   at the interruption. Dracula
   advancing, says:

                        DRACULA

                           It's good to see you back
                           again, Doctor - I heard
                           you'd just returned -

                              (Turning to Mina)

                           And you, Miss Mina - you're
                           looking exceptionally -

   Breaks off, noticing for
   the first time the feeling
   of constraint which seems
   centered about her - his
   voice takes on a mildly
   solicitous note:

                                          (CONTINUED)

E-40   (CONTINUED)

> DRACULA
>
> Oh - I'm sorry - are you ill?
>
> VAN HELSING
>
> You'll pardon me, Doctor, but I think Miss Seward should go to her room at once -

E-41   INT. CLOSEUP DRACULA

Darting a swift look at Van Helsing, struck by the peremptoriness of his tone. He shrugs commiseratingly.

> DRACULA
>
> In that event, I shan't remain -
>
> (to Mina)
>
> Nothing serious, I hope-?

E-42   INT. MED. SHOT

As Mina raises a restraining hand.

> MINA
>
> Oh, please don't go -
>
> (Smiling at Van Helsing)
>
> I'm sure it's not as important as you seem to think.

Dracula regards Van Helsing with an air of polite detachment - Dr. Seward, remembering they are not acquainted, says hastily, taking a step towards them,-

> DR. SEWARD
>
> Pardon me - Count Dracula - Professor Van Helsing -

(CONTINUED)

E-42   (CONTINUED)

> Van Helsing bows stiffly.
> Dracula does the same.

DRACULA

> Van Helsing - a distinguished scientist - whose name we know even in the wilds of Transylvania -

> He takes a step towards Van Helsing, which brings him nearer to sofa. Mina looks up at him with a smile and says, by way of explanation:

MINA

> I had a frightful dream a night or so ago that I haven't been able to get out of my mind -

> Van Helsing Xes up towards end of sofa away from Dracula, working casually around to end of table where cigarette box is lying. His manner indicates very plainly that he resents Dracula's presence and is anxious to get on with his examination of Mina's symptoms.

DRACULA   (Reprovingly)

> I hope you haven't been taking my stories too seriously -

E-43   INT. FLASH CLOSEUP HARKER

> echoing sharply,

HARKER

> Stories?

E-44   INT. WIDE ANGLE

> Dracula and Mina in fore. Dracula turns at the rather challenging quality of Harker's exclamation and replies, deprecatingly,

(CONTINUED)

E-44   (CONTINUED)

                        DRACULA

                            In my humble effort to
                            amuse your fiancee, Mr.
                            Harker, I've been telling
                            her some rather grim
                            tales of my far-off
                            country -

                        HARKER   (darkly)

                            I can imagine -!

Xes towards Van Helsing.

                        MINA

                            (reprovingly)

                            Why, John -

E-45   INT. CLOSE SHOT TABLE

        Harker reconsiders -
        says somewhat grudgingly:

                        HARKER

                            Sorry - I didn't mean to
                            be rude -

E-46   INT. CLOSE SHOT
        DRACULA AND MINA

        Dracula smiles courteously.

                        DRACULA

                            Of course not -

                            (turns back to Mina)

E-47   INT. CLOSE SHOT AT TABLE

        TAKING IN BOTH HARKER
        AND VAN HELSING. Van Helsing
        snaps lid of cigarette box open
        and takes out a cigarette,
        still watching Dracula,
        whose voice comes unbroken
        over scene.
                                        (CONTINUED)

E-47   (CONTINUED)

> DRACULA'S VOICE
>
> I can quite understand Mr. Harker's concern.

As he is saying this, Van Helsing's gaze is attracted to mirror which is in lid of cigarette box. He leans forward attentively, glancing from mirror back to sofas, and back to mirror again - reaches forth his hand to adjust mirror at slightly different angle.

> DR. SEWARD'S VOICE
>
> I'm afraid it's quite serious.

CAMERA MOVES FORWARD TO CLOSE SHOT MIRROR - it shows reflection of Mina on sofa, Dr. Seward crossing into area of reflection as he says these words, but no reflection of Dracula, who is obstensibly standing between Dr. Seward and Mina.

E-48 INT. FLASH CLOSEUP
      VAN HELSING

   Looking up from mirror
   toward group.

E-49 INT. GROUP

   as seen from Van Helsing's
   angle. Dr. Seward says,

                    DR. SEWARD

                         My dear, I'm sure Count
                         Dracula will excuse you -
                         you must go to your room,
                         as Professor Van Helsing
                         suggests -

E-50 INT. CLOSEUP VAN HELSING

   studying mirror with a
   furtive air - starts to
   maneuver it quietly, not
   wanting to attract attention
   to what he is doing.
   Voices over closeup ...

                    MINA'S VOICE

                         But, father, I'm feeling
                         quite all right now -

E-51 INT. MED. SHOT

   Van Helsing in fore.,
   with mirror - his manner
   tense, watchful. Dracula
   is staring fixedly down
   at Mina, whose eyes seem
   drawn to his.

                    DRACULA

                         You had better do as your
                         father advises -

   Mina hesitstes, then
   starts to rise slowly,
   her eyes still on his -
   says in a curiously
   dead tone,

                    CONTINUED.

E-51   CONTINUED

                    MINA

                        Very well - -

    Starts around end of
    sofa towards door leading
    to hall.

E-52   INT. FLASH CLOSEUP
        VAN HELSING

    jockeying mirror quickly.

E-53   INT. FULL SHOT ROOM

    matching action - Mina
    half-way across to door.
    Harker makes a move
    towards her, but Van
    Helsing, without looking
    at him, puts forth a quiet
    hand, restraining him.
    Harker glances at him,
    puzzled.

                    MINA   (to Dracula; turning)

                        Good night.

    Her voice still has the
    same evenness. She Xes
    slowly towards door,
    Dracula bowing and coming
    around so that he is
    between Van Helsing and
    door. Van Helsing quickly
    closes lid.

                    DRACULA

                        I'll be going.
                            (to Van Helsing)
                        Professor, I hope to have
                        the pleasure of seeing
                        you again.
                            (Van Helsing inclines
                            his head slowly)
                        Mr. Harker -

    Bows slightly to Harker,
    who returns his bow
    stiffly. Then Dracula
    Xes after Mina, in
    direction of hall, saying,

                        CONTINUED.

E-53   CONTINUED

                            DRACULA

                                Miss Mina -

Mina, in door near bottom
of stairs outside, turns
slowly, waiting. As
Dracula Xes to her,
CAMERA MOVES UP TO CLOSE
SHOT DRACULA AND MINA.
He bends over her hand.

                            DRACULA

                                I shall call again, later,
                                and inquire how you are
                                feeling -

He looks deep into her
eyes - she stares at
him - says,

                            MINA

                                Thank you -

E-54   INT. FLASH CLOSEUP
        VAN HELSING

        opening lid of cigarette
        box and adjusting mirror
        to catch their reflection
        across room.

E-55   INT. FLASH CLOSEUP MIRROR

        As Van Helsing's hand
        holds it - we see
        reflection of Mina -
        alone.

E-56   INT. FULL SHOT ROOM

        Van Helsing in fore., -
        We show his grim reaction to
        what the mirror has revealed.
        Mina turns to the others in
        the room and with a vague
        smile in their general
        direction, turns and exits
        up the stairs out of sight.
        Dracula, now ready to leave,
        turns to group, facing room,
        saying,   CONTINUED.

E-56   CONTINUED

                    DRACULA

                         Good night - I'm sorry my
                         visit was so ill - timed -

          DR. SEWARD

                         Not in the least -

Van Helsing closes the
lid of cigarette box - says
hastily, seeking to detain
Dracula.

                    VAN HELSING

                         On the contrary, it may
                         prove to be most enlighten-
                         ing - in fact, before you
                         go, you can be of definite
                         service -

Dr. Seward and Harker
look at him, surprised.
Dracula comes forward
politely.

                    DRACULA

                         Anything I can do - gladly.

E-57   INT. SEMI CLOSEUP
       VAN HELSING

       as he picks up the
       cigarette box, turning it
       over in his hands, the lid
       closed. As he speaks the
       following lines, musingly,
       Dracula slowly enters
       scene . . .

                    VAN HELSING

                         A moment ago, I stumbled
                         upon an amazing phenomenon -
                         something so incredible that
                         I distrust my own
                         judgement.
                              (holding up cigarette
                               box)
                         I want you to help me
                         prove something -

MBK

E-58   INT. CLOSEUP VAN HELSING

as he flips back the lid
of the box, revealing the
mirror, which he thrusts
challengingly at Dracula,
snapping,

> VAN HELSING
>
> Look! ......

In the mirror there is
no reflection of Dracula

E-59   INT. LARGE CLOSEUP DRACULA

as he stares into the mirror -
We show there is no reflection there.
Dracula's face is contorted
by a livid snarl of rage
and he raises his hand to
strike the mirror from Van
Helsing's hand.

E-60   INT. CLOSE SHOT DRACULA
       AND VAN HELSING

matching action as Dracula
strikes the box from Van
Helsing's hand and leaps
back.

E-61   INT. FLASH CLOSEUP
       CIGARETTE BOX.

strking floor - glass
breaks - cigarettes spill
out upon carpet.

E-62   INT. MED. SHOT GROUP

as they all stare speechless -
Dracula quivering with rage -
he regains control of himself
with a terrific effort -
turns to Dr. Seward and says
with a little apologetic bow -

CONTINUED

MBK

E-62   CONTINUED

        DRACULA

      Doctor Seward - my humble
      apologies - it was una -
      voidable -

E-63   INT. FLASH CLOSEUP
   VAN HELSING.

  Watching Dracula with
  a quiet smile of
  satisfaction.

E-64   INT. CLOSE SHOT DRACULA

  He turns to Van Helsing
  and says with cold menace -

        DRACULA

      For one who has not lived
      even a single lifetime,
      you're a wise man, Van
      Helsing!

E-65   INT. MED SHOT

   matching actions as
   Dracula completes speech,
  turns and exits through
  window. Harker and Dr. Seward
  stand non-plussed - Van Helsing,
  his eyes agleam, quivering with
  excitement and triumph. Harker
  turns from one to the other -
  says blankly -

        HARKER   (with an exclamation)

      Phew! What caused that?
      Did you see the look on
      his face? Like a wild
      animal --

  Xes toward windows,
  still wondering - looks
  out into the night. Then
  suddenly points, exclaiming -

        CONTINUED

,, MBK

E-65 CONTINUED

>   HARKER
>
>   What's that - running
>   across the lawn? It
>   looks like a huge dog!

Doctor Seward joins
him at window - they
both look out. Van Helsing,
who has not moved, smiles
acridly and says -

>   VAN HELSING
>
>   Or a wolf - ?
>
>   HARKER (turning and looking
>   back into room)
>
>   A wolf - ?
>   (starts toward
>   Van Helsing)

E-66 INT. MED. SHOT REVERSE
      ANGLE.

as Harker and Dr. Seward
rejoin Van Helsing. Van
Helsing points out to
lawn - says,

>   VAN HELSING
>
>   He was afraid we might
>   follow -

Harker and Doctor
Seward exchange bewildered
glances.

>   HARKER
>
>   I'm afraid I don't under-
>   stand -
>
>   VAN HELSING (Musingly)
>
>   Sometimes they take the
>   form of wolves.

Harker just looks at
him - Van Helsing continues
in his musing tone -

>   But generally - bats -
>
>   HARKER
>
>   What are you talking
>   about?
>
>   VAN HELSING
>
>   Dracula

CONTINUED

MBK

E-66   CONTINUED

> HARKER   (impatiently)
>
> But what's Dracula to do with wolves and bats?
>
> VAN HELSING   (firmly, with authority)
>
> Dracula is our vampire!

E-67   INT. FLASH CLOSEUP
       HARKER

looking now as if he believed Van Helsing to be utterly mad. With his incredulity is mingled considerable disgust at what he looks upon as a completely irrational remark.

E-68   INT. MED. SHOT GROUP

Even Dr. Seward seems a bit aghast.

> DR. SEWARD
>
> But, surely, Professor --!
>
> VAN HELSING   (Pounding the point home)
>
> A vampire casts no shadow - no reflection in a glass! That's why Dracula smashed the mirror!

Points to the shattered glass on the floor. Harker shakes his head - looks at Dr. Seward with a bewildered air.

> HARKER
>
> But - I say, Professor, that doesn't seem to make sense - !
>
> VAN HELSING   (interrupting swiftly)
>
> Dracula's responsible for Lucy Weston's death - for those marks on Miss Mina's neck!

CONTINUED

MBK

E-68   CONTINUED

Harker studies him for a
moment - then turns towards
table, restraining the im-
pulse to call Van Helsing
a damned fool - but his
irritation is too strong
for him to let it pass
completely - he blurts
out doggedly,

                    HARKER

                Well, really, I don't mean
                to be rude - but that's
                the sort of thing I'd
                expect one of the patients
                here to say!

            VAN HELSING (Bitterly)

                Yes - and that's what
                your English doctors would
                say - your police!
                        (impressively)
                <u>The strength of the vampire
                is that people will not
                believe in him.</u>

E-69   EXT. SANITARIUM. NIGHT
        MED. SHOT SIDE ENTRANCE.

        Mina, walking as if in a
        trance, emerges from house
        and starts walking slowly
        across lawn in direction
        of the Abbey.

E-70   EXT. GROUNDS. CLOSE SHOT
        BENEATH LARGE TREE.

        Dracula is waiting in the
        shadows, his dark cloak
        wrapped around him - only
        his white face seems to
        stand out against the dark
        background. His whole
        figure is rigid with
        command - his eyes burning.

MBK

E-71   EXT. GROUNDS.
        LONG SHOT.

   Mina walking towards
   tree where Dracula awaits
   her - passing beneath
   other smaller trees - now
   lost in their shadow - now
   appearing, a white figure
   in the moonlight.

E-72   EXT. GROUNDS. MED. SHOT

   Dracula, his back to camera,
   stands beneath tree in fore.,
   a menacing silhouette. He
   faces the wide lawn, across
   which Mina is seen approaching
   as camera shoots past him, over
   his shoulder. As she nears him,
   he extends his arms, full length,
   like a gigantic bat, his cloak
   almost blotting out the scene.
   Mina approaches - advances into
   his arms, her face upraised -
   her eyes perfectly blank and
   staring into space. His arms
   sweep down around her, muffling
   her white-clad figure completely
   in the folds of the cloak. As
   he pulls her back into the dark,
   their action is lost in a hazy
   blur of dark cloak and shadows.

E-73   INT. LIBRARY. FULL SHOT.

   Doctor Seward, at his wit's
   end, is facing Van Helsing in
   fore. Harker stands somewhat
   apart, his whole attitude
   reflecting a healthy contempt
   for what has been going on
   between Van Helsing and Seward.

                    DR. SEWARD (as if trying to
                                find a loophole
                                of sanity)

                    But according to your own
                    theory, vampires must
                    return to their graves
                    before sunrise - to their
                    native soil, where they
                    were buried! And Count
                    Dracula's native soil
                    would be Transylvania!
                                    CONTINUED

MBK

E-73   CONTINUED

Van Helsing starts to pace
up and down, trying to solve
this. Dr. Seward meets
Harker's disbelieving eye -
Harker makes a derogatory
gesture as if to say, "The
man's out of his mind!"
Dr. Seward shakes his head
worriedly and looks back
to Van Helsing for an answer.

E-74   INT. CLOSE VAN HELSING

matching action as he
exclaims.

                VAN HELSING

                Then he brought his
                native soil with him!
                Boxes of it! Boxes of
                earth large enough for
                him to rest in!

E-75   INT. FULL SHOT.

matching action as
Van Helsing completes
speech, tremendously
excited over the possi-
bility that he had solved
one angle of the puzzle.
At this there comes a
peal of maniacal laughter
from the direction of the
windows. They all stiffen -
then Seward, recognizing
Renfield's laughter, calls
out sharply.

                DOCTOR SEWARD

                Renfield! What are you
                doing there?

E-76   INT. CLOSE SHOT AT WINDOW

matching action as Renfield
appears from behind portieres.
Dr. Seward regards him angrily.

                DR. SEWARD

                Did you hear what we
    CONTINUED   were saying?

MBK

E-76 CONTINUED

      RENFIELD (craftily)

      Yes, I heard - something - enough -

E-77 INT. MED.SHOT.

As Dr. Seward starts to bring Renfield forward into the room. Renfield wrests himself loose, and pointing a quivering finger at Van Helsing, cries,

      RENFIELD

      Be guided by what he says! It is your only hope! (Exits toward Harker, saying) It is her only hope!

Stands looking into Harker's suspicious eyes for a moment - then Xes to Van Helsing and falls to his knees before him, pleading,

      RENFIELD

      Save me! Save my soul!

E-78 INT. CLOSE SHOT RENFIELD AND VAN HELSING.

matching action - Renfield's voice unbroken.

      RENFIELD

      I am weak and you are strong - I am crazy - but you are sane -

      VAN HELSING (with compassion)

      I'll save you, Renfield - but you must tell us what you know - everything!

MBK

E-79   INT. WIDER ANGLE.

   Renfield looks up at
   Van Helsing - then gets
   to his feet - crying.-

                    RENFIELD

            Fool, fool - and I
            thought you were wise!
                (shrewdly, his mood
                 changing)
            What have I to gain by
            telling you anything?
            The doctor here keeps me
            shut up all day - and if
            I'm good he gives me a
            little sugar to catch
            flies with -
                (with rising note of
                 exultation)
            but, if I serve the
            Master -
                (points towards
                 window)
            A wise madman will obey
            him who can give him life!
                (laughs crazily)

                    VAN HELSING

            Him? Who do you mean?

E-80   INT. CLOSE SHOT RENFIELD
         AND VAN HELSING.

   Renfield smiles a little
   wildly into Van Helsing's
   stern, determined face.

                    RENFIELD

            Need we mention names
            among friends, Professor-?

                    VAN HELSING   (Relentlessly)

            What have you to do with
            Dracula?

MBK

E-81　INT. FLASH LARGE
　　　CLOSEUP RENFIELD.

Shrinking back -
convulsed with terror.

     RENFIELD

      Dracula!

Then he gains control of
himself, and drawing
himself up defiantly,
says through his teeth,

     RENFIELD

      I've never even heard
      the name before!

Van Helsing's voice
comes over closeup savagely.

     VAN HELSING

      You're lying!

     RENFIELD (with lofty dignity)

      Madmen, Professor, lack
      the power to discriminate
      between truth and false-
      hood - therefore, I take
      no offense -

E-82   INT. MED. SHOT ANOTHER ANGLE

> matching action as Renfield completes speech - Van Helsing releases Renfield with a baffled air. Renfield, undergoing one of his abrupt transitions, now turns to Doctor Seward and says, in pleading tones:

> > RENFIELD
> >
> > I begged you to send me away - but you wouldn't! Now it's too late - it's happened -
> >
> > HARKER (Stepping forward, sharply)
> >
> > What's happened?
> >
> > RENFIELD (Trembling)
> >
> > I daren't tell you - I daren't! I'd die in torment if I betrayed him-

E-83   INT. FLASH CLOSEUP
VAN HELSING

> Saying with grim ruthlessness:

> > VAN HELSING
> >
> > You'll die in torment if you die with innocent blood on your soul!

E-84   INT. CLOSEUP RENFIELD

> Turning to Van Helsing - stares at him for a moment - then tears well up into his eyes as he says in heart-breaking tones:

> > RENFIELD
> >
> > God will not damn a poor lunatic's soul - He knows that the powers of evil are too great for those with weak minds -

RS

E-85   INT. MED. SHOT

At this, Van Helsing steps
forward again, quick to seize
upon the opportunity afforded
by the moment.

> VAN HELSING
>
> Then have faith in me, Renfield! Tell me what I want to know!

Renfield hesitates -
glances around fearsomely - then moves slowly towards Van Helsing, and
speaking in lowered tones,
says:

> RENFIELD
>
> What do you want to know?

> VAN HELSING
>
> The name of the man who destroyed your mind - the man whom you call - Master!

E-86   INT. FLASH CLOSEUP
        RENFIELD

His eyes wide with fear -
says, shaking his head:

> RENFIELD
>
> No, no, no - don't ask me that!

E-87   INT. MED. SHOT

Matching action as Renfield cowers against table.
Van Helsing Xes toward him
from one side - Dr. Seward
from the other, exclaiming:

> DR. SEWARD
>
> You must! You must!

Renfield shrinks away from
them, as they close in on him -
Van Helsing's face white and
drawn in its grim-lipped intensity. Renfield puts up his hands -
says to Dr. Seward:

(CONTINUED)

RS

E-87   CONTINUED

>   RENFIELD
>
>   Go away - go away -

>   VAN HELSING
>
>   Tell us, Renfield - before
>   it's too late - before your
>   soul is damned forever!

Renfield wilts completely-
the situation is too much
for his harried brain to cope
with. He buries his face in
his hands for a moment, shud-
dering, then looks up at Van
Helsing, haggard-eyed, and
stammers:

>   RENFIELD
>
>   I'll tell you! I'll tell
>   you!

Then, chancing to look off-
scene, he gives a sudden
scream, pointing.

E-88   INT. FLASH CLOSEUP
       HUGE BAT

       As it sweeps in through
       the open window. Renfield's
       scream over closeup.

E-89   INT. WIDE ANGLE ROOM

       Matching action as bat
       wings its way swiftly about
       the room, almost grazing
       Renfield's head - he ducks -
       they all start back, to avoid
       coming in contact with it.

>   RENFIELD
>
>   Master! Master! I wasn't
>   going to say anything!

E-90   INT. FLASH CLOSEUP BAT

    Swooping out through window
    into darkness beyond.

E-91   INT. WIDE ANGLE

    Matching action as Renfield
    dashes across the room after
    it, his arms flung wide in
    frenzied supplication as he
    screams wildly.

                    RENFIELD

        I told them nothing! I'm
        loyal to you, Master - I'm
        loyal!

    Sinks to his knees at window
    and buries his face in his
    hands, sobbing with hysterical
    fear. The others stand as if
    turned to stone, speechless with
    surprise. Before anyone has a
    chance to make any sort of a move,
    there comes from out on the lawn,
    another scream - this time a woman's
    voice - faint, but coming nearer.
    As they start forward, the scream
    is heard again, coming nearer, and
    in through the French window rushes
    the maid. She makes for Dr. Seward,
    almost in a state of complete collapse.

                    MAID

        Doctor Seward-Doctor
        Seward!

            (Pointing outside)

        Miss Mina - out there -
        dead!

    There is a concerted rush
    for the window, and they
    exit, leaving the maid alone
    with Renfield. Renfield
    stares after them - then
    turns to the maid and starts
    to laugh in a low tone. The
    maid takes one look at him -
    gasps - and collapses to the
    floor, unconscious. Renfield
    stands looking down at her for
    a moment. Then as he surveys
    her prostrate figure, his eyes
    become greedy, his face starts
    to twitch, and he sinks to his
    hands and knees and starts
    crawling slowly toward her.

                            (CONTINUED)

E-91   CONTINUED

CAMERA DROPS TO ANGLE ON FLOOR, with Renfield crawling towards it. As he comes into a LARGE CU, CAMERA PULLS BACK A LITTLE TO INCLUDE MAID, lying in immediate fore. Renfield approaches her with catlike stealth and pauses, hovering directly above her - one hand upraised as if to descend and fasten about her throat- then he pauses, looking down at her, with the most satanic light imaginable in his eyes.

E-92   INT. FLASH LARGE CLOSEUP
       MAID

as seen from Renfield's angle. A fly is crawling across her cheek.

E-93   INT. CLOSE SHOT ON FLOOR

Maid in fore., as Renfield reaches out slowly, with infinite caution, and then with a swift swoop, makes a grab for the fly, which gets away. Renfield watches it fly off - then sits back upon his haunches with a frustrated air and starts to snivel.

E-94   EXT. GROUNDS SANITARIUM

A very picturesque, moonlit view of the grounds - a soft composition of dark trees - patches of white moonlight - dappled shadows. From b.g. comes Harker, bearing the limp form of Mina in his arms. Van Helsing and Dr. Seward bring up the rear, talking excitedly. We do not hear their exact words until they come abreast of the camera, which starts to PAN AROUND following their progress back towards the house. Harker exits past camera, grim-jawed and silent. This to him is the last straw - we see by his air that he has made up his mind to take matters into his own hands without any more nonsense - the incident has shaken him completely.

(CONTINUED)

E-94   (CONTINUED)

CAMERA REMAINS WITH VAN HELSING AND DR. SEWARD, PANNING AS THEY WALK. Dr. Seward is almost a wreck - his nerves shot to pieces - his hands flutter tremblingly as he makes helpless, ineffective gestures with them. He is mumbling over and over again.

DR. SEWARD

Thank Heaven she's alive - I can't stand much more of this - I can't -

VAN HELSING.

Alive - but in greater danger she's already under his influence!

DR. SEWARD

It's horrible - horrible - incredible -

VAN HELSING

Incredible, perhaps, but the truth! We've got to face it - we've got to cope with it -

CAMERA SWINGS AROUND TO CLOSE SHOT large tree at one side of the path - one with a huge, gnarled trunk. Van Helsing and the trembling Seward pass by tree and exit from scene. Dracula appears quietly from behind, looking after them with an evil sneer - he wraps his cloak about him as we hear the voice of Van Helsing as he walks away:

VAN HELSING

- for if these attacks continue, she'll come more and more under his spell, and then -

FADE OUT

(CG)

SEQUENCE "F"

F-1 FADE INTO:
INT. MINA'S BEDROOM
NITE. LARGE CLOSEUP
BESIDE LAMP.

With dimming arrangement. Hand of nurse into closeup and lowers light as WE MOVE CAMERA BACK TO CLOSE SHOT BED, showing nurse leaning solicitously over Mina, who is asleep. The nurse fusses about with the coverlet and very carefully places a small sprig of wolfbane in a protective position. Then she wheels, startled, as we hear a sharp "sss-s-st!" out of scene.

F-2 INT. BEDROOM CLOSE SHOT BEDROOM DOOR.

Which opens inward from boudoir adjoining. Harker's head is thrust discreetly through - he asks in a low, guarded tone:

HARKER

How is she now?

F-3 INT. FLASH CLOSEUP NURSE

Placing finger to lips - glances back at Mina and exits from scene.

(CG)

F-4 INT. BOUDOIR CLOSE SHOT AT DOOR

Shooting in through to where Mina is lying in background. Nurse Xes into fore., where Harker is waiting, closing door softly behind her. Harker is anxious and worried, but her tone is reassuring as she says with an understanding smile:

NURSE

She's resting quietly. You'd better go get some sleep, Mr. Harker.

HARKER (Shaking his head with a frown)

No -- I'll wait until Doctor Seward gets back -

They both turn sharply as another "Ss-s-s-st!" attracts their attention, this time coming from direction of door leading to corridor.

F-5 INT. CLOSE SHOT DOORWAY

Leading to corridor. Martin stands there asking with a desperate, forehead-furrowed air:

MARTIN

Is Doctor Seward abaht?

Starts into room --

F-6 INT. BOUDOIR WIDER ANGLE

Matching action as Martin approaches Harker and nurse - Harker shakes his head:

HARKER

No - what do you want?

(CONTINUED)

(CG)

F-6 (CONTINUED)

        MARTIN (Helplessly)

         Old fly-eater's on the
         loose again - 'e's li'ble
         to do anythink -

Harker and nurse ex-
change nervous glance.

F-7 INT. MINA'S BEDROOM
   FLASH CLOSEUP MINA.

   Stirring restlessly
   in her sleep - her
   arm brushes wolfbane
   off bed to floor as
   she turns.

F-8 INT. BOUDOIR MED.
   CLOSE SHOT GROUP

   As Harker explains
   with biting sarcasm:

         HARKER

          Doctor Seward and his
          previous professor are over
          in the Abbey - looking for
          Vampires!

        MARTIN (Wagging his head
           sadly)

          Vampires - fly-eaters - look
          here, Mr. 'Arker, anyone
          wot wants my job 'ere can
          'ave it!

           (Starts toward door,
           muttering)

          I'm goink to find a plyce
          with some nice, normal
          loonies - Napoleons an'
          Josephines an' such-like -

(CG)

F-9   INT. MAIN HALL ABBEY
      NITE. MED. SHOT STAIRS

   Van Helsing and Dr. Seard, bearing lanterns are coming slowly down the stairs. Their attidues indicate that they have been searching fruitlessly for hours. Dr. Seward's nerves are in bad shape - Van Helsing filled with a sense of defeat and self-reproach. CAMERA PANS DOWN AS THEY DESCEND, talking.

   VAN HELSING   (Discouraged)

   We've failed -- and all because of my own stupidity--

   DR. SEWARD

   You shouldn't blame yourself entirely -

   VAN HELSING

   But I do. This creature is more than mortal - his cunning is the growth of ages. I shouldn't have let him know I suspected -- that mirror warned him-

   This brings them to the bottom of the stairs, where they pause for a moment, Van Helsing crestfallen and weary. They exit into room to left of stairs.

F-10 INT. SMALL ROOM OFF HALL

   One of Dracula's boxes lies undisturbed in fore. Van Helsing and Dr. Seward enter and X into fore., towards it. Van Helsing is musing aloud.

   VAN HELSING

   One box - there are two more hidden somewhere in the Abbey

   (CONTINUED)

(CG)

F-10 (CONTINUED)

DR. SEWARD

Could the shipping office at Whitby Harbor have been wrong?

Van Helsing shakes his head - by light of lantern takes bill from his pocket and studies it - Dr. Seward looks over his shoulder.

VAN HELSING

Here's the bill of lading itself.
(Reading)
"Three large boxes - Count Dracula, Carfax Abbey, consignee. Earth for experimental purposes."
(With a bitter laugh)
Experimental purposes!

F-11 INT. LOWER CRYPT IN ABBEY

Very dimly lighted. Dracula stands in silhouetted in fore., back to camera, tall and forbidding, looking down at Renfield, who grovels at his feet in an attitude of supplication. Beyond Renfield we see the two missing boxes

RENFIELD

Master, Master, you will be be merciful with me - you will not be angry with me? They tried to make me talk, but I told them nothing - nothing! Then I learned that they were coming here, to find the boxes.. You will reward me, as you promised, Master - with lives - not little lives any longer-

CAMERA STARTS MOVING SLOWLY PAST HIM to boxes as they lie in the filthy decay of the floor of the crypt.

(CG)

F-12   EXT. COUNTRY ROAD. NIGHT

  A country constable is wheeling along his bicycle. As he comes into fore., there is a wail of a child crying off to L. He stops and listens - the crying is repeated - a wailing, frightened cry. He dismounts and leans his bicycle against a wall or tree - starts to take out his flashlight.

            (SOUND OF CHILD CRYING)

F-13   EXT. CHURCHYARD. NIGHT

  A weird, unearthly shot, with a low ground-mist curling about the white headstones. Lucy Weston, walking slowly, staring straight ahead with unseeing eyes, passes by camera between the headstones. CAMERA PANS BRIEFLY TO follow as we CUT TO:

F-14   EXT. ROAD. MED. SHOT

  At side of road. Constable Xes into fore., from other side of the road, flashing his light - exits into bushes.

            (CRYING BECOMES LOUDER)

            FADE OUT.

SEQUENCE "G".

G-1 FADE IN.
     CLOSEUP INSERT NEWSPAPER
     ITEM.

English type of local paper with a single streamer, "THE WHITBY HORROR".

Martin's voice sounds over insert as he reads -

                    MARTIN
               " - further attacks on
               small children committed
               after dark by the mysteri-
               ous woman in white, took
               place last night. Narra-
               tives of two small girls -"

DISSOLVE THROUGH TO:

G-2 MED. SHOT IN UPPER HALL
     OF SANITARIUM

Martin is seated in a chair beside a nurse's small desk, upon which are charts, a small white lamp and several bottles of medicine. A trim-looking nurse sits behind the table, listening to Martin as he reads. Another nurse, a buxom country type, stand nearby also listening - the maid is peering over Martin's shoulder, following the newspaper account as he reads it.

                    MARTIN
               " - each child, describ-
               ing a beautiful lady in
               white who promised her
               chocolates, enticed her to
               a secluded spot, and there
               bit her slightly in the
               throat - "

They all look up at each other in horror, as we cut to;

BR

G-3   INT. MINA'S BOUDOIR
      MED. SHOT.

    Mina is reclining in
chaise-longue, with
Van Helsing seated in
a chair in front of her.
Harker is pacing up and
down, a newspaper in his
hand, very angry and ex-
cited - he comes to a
halt and exclaims ex-
asperatedly -

          HARKER

      What does she know about
      the woman in white? How
      could she know <u>anything</u>?

        (indicates paper)
      Isn't it bad enough for
      her to read about it,
      without

G-4   CLOSEUP VAN HELSING.

    He looks across at
Harker and says with
weary patience,

          VAN HELSING

      Please, please, Mr.
      Harker

G-5   MED. SHOT

    matching action, as Van Hel-
sing exits to Mina, and says -

          VAN HELSING
      And when was the next time
      you saw Miss Lucy, after
      she was buried - ?

    Mina looks up at him with
a little frightened look
on her face - it's evident
that what she has been saying
has made her very nervous and
apprehensive - she says, as
if continuing a narrative,

          CONTINUED

MBK

G-5   CONTINUED

                    MINA

                         I was on the terrace -
                         she came out of the
                         shadows and stood looking
                         at me, I started to
                         speak to her -
                              (hesitates and
                              concludes in low
                              voice)
                         then I remembered she
                         was dead -

G-6   CLOSEUP MINA

      She stares straight ahead
      of her and continues -

                    MINA

                         The most horrible ex-
                         pression came over her
                         face - she looked like
                         a hungry animal - a wolf!
                         Then she turned and ran
                         back into the dark. -

G-7   MED.SHOT

         matching action, as Mina
         concludes her recital,
      Harker is staring down at
      her with an expression of
      deep concern. Van Helsing
      and Dr. Seward exchange
      glances, and then Van
      Helsing says gently -

                    VAN HELSING

                         Then the woman in white -

      Mina looks up at him and
      averts her eyes for a
      moment without speaking.
      Finally manages to say in
      low, strained tones -

                    MINA

                         Lucy -
                              (Buries her face in
                              her hands)

                    CONTINUED

MBK

G-7 CONTINUED

Harker utters an incredulous exclamation and turns away, harried, bewildered. Dr. Seward rises and crosses around behind chaise-longue, his head bowed, his hands clasped tightly behind him, struggling in the grip of a horror which leaves him speechless. Van Helsing looks down into Mina's pitiful eyes, and says gravely -

VAN HELSING

Miss Mina, I promise you - that after tonight she will remain at rest - her soul released from this horror.

Mina gets to her feet and says pleadingly

MINA

If you can save Lucy's soul after death, then promise you'll save mine!

This brings Harker quickly to her side - he takes her in his arms, exclaiming savagely -

HARKER

But, you're not going to die, darling! You're going to live!

Mina shakes her head, avoiding his eyes, and pushes him away with a little shudder, saying -

MINA

No, No, John - you mustn't touch me - you mustn't kiss me - ever again!

HARKER

What are you trying to say?

Mina turns pleadingly to Van Helsing.

MINA

Oh, make him understand, tell him - I can't!

CONTINUED

MBK

G-7 CONTINUED 2

Van Helsing gazes at her with an air of infinite, but helpless compassion - then turns and exits slowly from the scene. Mina turns back to Harker, her voice rising on a sob of despair -

MINA

John - it's all over - our love - our life together -
(as he stares at her uncomprehendingly)
Oh, don't look at me that way! I love you, John - I love you more than life itself - but this horror - he wills it and I must obey -
(breaks down, sinking upon chaise-longue)

HARKER

Doctor, do you know what you two are doing? You're driving her crazy!

G-8 INT. CLOSE SHOT VAN HELSING

He is standing by a large, bay window, overlooking the lawn, a sprig of wolfbane in his hand. He turns quickly and looks at Harker with a sigh - says with admirable forbearance -

VAN HELSING

Mr. Harker
(points out of window)
- that's what you should be worrying about -

G-9 MED. SHOT ANOTHER ANGLE;

matching action as he speaks. Harker and Dr. Seward turn as Van Helsing continues to point - his speech continues unbroken -

CONTINUED.

MBK

G-9   CONTINUED.

VAN HELSING

The last rays of the day's sun are gone - a nother night is upon us -

He lets the curtain drop and comes forward toward group, crossing to Mina and laying one hand on her shoulder, says,

VAN HELSING

Both this room and your bedroom are prepared with wolfbane, so you will be safe from Dracula if he returns -

HARKER
(with air of finality)

She's going to be safe: because she's leaving with me for London at once - or I'm going to call in the police!

G-10   CLOSEUP VAN HELSING

as he stiffens, eyes becoming hard, his jaw firm as he says, with an air of authority, addressing himself to Dr. Seward.

VAN HELSING

Seward, I must be master here or I can do nothing!

G-11   INT. WIDE ANGLE ON ROOM

matching action as Van Helsing finishes speech. At this, the nurse enters from bedroom - Van Helsing turns to her and says, controlling his anger as he indicates a wreath of wolfbane on adjacent table.

CONTINUED

MBK

G-11 CONTINUED

                    VAN HELSING

                         Miss Mina is to wear this
                         wreath of wolfbane when
                         she goes to bed - watch
                         her closely and see that
                         she does not remove it
                         in her sleep.
                              (Nurse nods, taking
                              wreath)

Harker, who has been
standing to one side,
more furious than ever
at Van Helsing's authori-
tative manner, glares
first at him and then at
Seward, and then, Xing
brusquely to Mina, says,

                    HARKER

                         Mina - get your bags
                         packed - I'll be waiting
                         for you in the library!

Mina looks up at the
sound of his voice - as
he completes speech, he
turns and exits from room,
slamming the door behind
him. For a moment no one
speaks - Mina looks with
agonized helplessness
from her father to Van
Helsing, who turns to
nurse again, quite as
if nothing had happened,
his self control reasserting
itself, says,

                    VAN HELSING

                         And under no circumstances
                         must these windows be
                         opened tonight -

                    NURSE

                         I understand, Professor.

G-12 INT. RENFIELD'S ROOM.

     Renfield is seated on
the bed, his head buried
in his hands, softly sobbing.
Suddenly he raises his head
with a listening attitude,
and then rises slowly,
whispering,   CONTINUED

G-12   CONTINUED

                    RENFIELD

                        Yes, Master -

Exits slowly across
room toward window, as
though drawn by some
irresistible force over
which he has no control.
CAMERA FOLLOWS HIM TO
WINDOW. As he leans for-
ward and peers out, we
CUT TO:

G-13   EXT. LAWN CLOSE SHOT DRACULA

As he stands in the shadow
of a tree, looking up to-
wards Renfield's window.

G-14   EXT. CLOSE SHOT. RENFIELD'S
        WINDOW.

Shooting from the outside in
through iron bars. Renfield's
face is transfigured with
mingled fear and exultation at
the presence of Dracula. The
knuckles of his hand stand out
white as he clutches the
bars and whispers tensely.

                    RENFIELD

                        Master, you've come back -
                        You're not angry with me?

G-15   EXT. CLOSEUP DRACULA

He is staring up at Renfield -
eyes commanding, his whole
attitude one of domination,
as if he were sending an
intense mysterious message
to Renfield.

(CG)

G-16   EXT. CLOSEUP WINDOW

Shooting into room. Renfield sinks back a little into the room and exclaims in low, horrified tones.

                    RENFIELD

                        No, no, master - please -!
                        Not her - not again -

G-17   EXT. VERY LARGE
        CLOSEUP DRACULA

As he draws himself up, silent anger - his eyes threatening - his whole attitude indicating that he is projecting a terrific mental force towards Renfield.

G-18   INT. RENFIELD'S ROOM
        CLOSE SHOT RENFIELD

His hands are gripping the bars of the window more fiercely then ever. His head lowered as if he were trying to avoid contact with Dracula, his eyes roving restlessly about the floor, like a trapped animal as he whispers feverishly:

                    RENFIELD

                        Please - please - Master!
                        Please don't!

(CG)

G-19   INT. WIDE ANGLE OF
       LIBRARY

Shooting towards hall.
Harker is pacing up
and down, angry, im-
patient, in fore...
Just as Doctor Seward
and Van Helsing come
down stairs, talking
quietly. As they are
about to enter the
room, the maid enters
from hall and says:

                    MAID

                         Mr. 'Arker,-

Harker turns and is
about to speak to her,
when Doctor Seward
interrupts.

                    DOCTOR SEWARD
                         (To Maid)

                         What is it?

                    MAID

                         Mr. 'Arker's car is outside.

She looks back at
Harker, who nods
curtly and crosses
toward door leading
to hall, saying crisply.

                    HARKER

                         Thanks! Please go up
                         and see if Miss Mina's
                         bags are ready -

G-20   INT. LIBRARY MED. CLOSE

Dr. Seward and maid,
as Dr. Seward checks
her with a gesture,
saying

                    DR. SEWARD

                         I hardly think that will
                         be necessary -

Maid looks from Dr.
Seward toward Harker.

(CG)

G-21 CLOSEUP HARKER

As he frowns and says sharply.

HARKER

Please do as I ask -!

G-22 INT. MED. SHOT

Matching action, as maid looks from Harker to Dr. Seward, then back again, not knowing what to do.

DR. SEWARD
(To Maid)

You may go -

Maid glances back at Harker, a little puzzled, and then exits. Dr. Seard turns to Harker with an air of determination, and says:

DR. SEWARD

Mina's not going to leave her room -

He and Van Helsing start forward into library as if the matter were settled. Harker stands quite still for a moment, his fists clenched - with a slightly baffled air, and then pulls himself together and says violently,

HARKER

She's going with me!

Flinging this ultimatum at them, he starts to exit to hallway. Dr. Seward and Van Helsing turns. Van Helsing exclaims:

VAN HELSING

If you take her from under our protection, you'll kill her!

(CG)

G-23 CLOSEUP HARKER

    Stopping suddenly and turning, getting over his reaction to this speech - he glances from one to the other.

G-24 MED. SHOT.

    Matching action as John stands uncertain what to do, impressed against his will by the sincerity of Van Helsing's warning. Dr. Seward crosses to him and says:

                         DR. SEWARD
)Pleadingly)

                        Please, John, be patient!

    Harker shrugs - comes down from steps into room. The three men move toward sofa near fireplace. Dr. Seward sinks into sofa - Van Helsing stands studying Harker for a moment in silence - Harker lights a cigarette and says curtly:

                          HARKER

                        Well -?

                        VAN HELSING
                        (Back to fireplace)

                    Mr. Harker, I've devoted my lifetime to the study of many strange things - little known facts which the world, with its placid acceptance of the commonplace, is perhaps off for not knowing.

(CG)

G-25   CLOSEUP VAN HELSING

    As his voice continues
    unbroken on sound track.

                VAN HELSING

            The name Dracula has been
            connected with a legend
            still current among the
            natives of Dracula's own
            country - a legend of an
            old family, extinct for
            five hundred years, said
            to have been vampires.

G-26   CLOSEUP HARKER

    Listening with a half-
    tolerant, half- impatient
    air. Van Helsing's voice
    continues unbroken:

                VAN HELSING

            When I accidently dis-
            covered that Dracula cast
            no reflection in the mirror-
            then, that three boxes of
            earth had been delivered
            to him at Carfax Abbey -

G-27   CLOSEUP VAN HELSING

    Contining, with con-
    siderable impressiveness:

                VAN HELSING

            - and knowing that a vampire
            must rest by day in his
            native soil, I realized
            that this Dracula must be
            he whom Renfield calls the
            Master an undead creature
            whose life has been un-
            naturally prolonged by
            feeding upon the blood of
            living!

(CG)

G-28   MED. SHOT GROUP

Matching action as
Van Helsing continues:

> VAN HELSING
>
> Our only chance to save
> Miss Mina is to find the
> resting place of his living
> corpse and drive a stake
> through its heart.

He brings this speech
to a conclusion with
great impressiveness.
As Van Helsing says
the last couple of
words, Harker suddenly
leaps up from the sofa
and darts across to
the portiere. CAMERA
PANS SWIFTLY to follow
in a CLOSEUP as Harker
yanks aside the
portiere and pulls Ren-
field into sight.

G-29   MED. SHOT.

Matching action as
Harker pulls Renfield
into room. Dr. Seward
and Van Helsing turn.
Renfield glares at
them all defiantly
for a moment, and then
shaking himself loose
from Harker, says craftily

(CONTINUED)

MBK

G-29   CONTINUED

              RENFIELD

                  Isn't this a strange conversation for men who aren't crazy?

              DR. SEWARD (Coming forward impatiently)

                  Renfield, you're compelling me to put you in a strait-jacket!

He picks up hand phone from desk, presses a little buzzer on the phone.

              RENFIELD

                  I'm afraid it will do no good now, doctor -

G-30   INT. UPPER HALL
       SANITARIUM

Martin in chair, tilted against the wall, next to Renfield's door, calm and peaceful. Nurse at her desk making out her reports, when the telephone tinkles. Martin reaches over the nurse's desk and picks up phone.

              MARTIN   (Into phone)

                  What? - What, again?... Yes, sir, at once, sir... right away, sir.

He hangs up phone, turning to the nurse, and says,

                  The Doctor's pet looney is loose again!

Exit out of scene.

G-31   LARGE CLOSEUP WINDOW

As seen from Martin's point of view - the iron bars are twisted and bent completely out of shape.
CUT BACK TO -

MBK

G-32 INT. HALL

Getting over
Martin's reaction.

     MARTIN

     Strike me pink - 'e's
     turned into a blinkin'
     'Ercules!

     NURSE

     What's he done now?

     MARTIN

     Look an' see for yourself.

As nurse gets up from
desk, Martin exits.

G-33 INT. MINA'S BOUDOIR
   LARGE CLOSEUP NURSE.

Staring into camera.
Dracula's voice comes
over CLOSEUP:

     DRACULA'S VOICE

     From now on, you will
     carry out any suggestion
     that reaches you through
     my brain. When I will you
     to do a thing, it shall
     be done!

CAMERA STARTS MOVING
BACK - Bedroom door in
b.g. CAMERA MOVES BACK
TO INCLUDE DRACULA
standing with his back
to camera.

     NURSE (In dead, monotonous
        tone)

     It shall be done.

     DRACULA

     When you awake you will
     not remember what I say.
     Do you hear me?

     NURSE (As before)

     I hear you

     DRACULA

     You have received your
     orders. Obey!

     CONTINUED

G-33   CONTINUED

    Nurse mechancially turns, exiting thru door into bedroom. Dracula follows her thru door, CAMERA FOLLOWING. Dracula halts just inside doorway - shooting past him we see nurse cross to the bed. Dracula raises his arm and muffles his face in his cloak.

G-34   INT. BEDROOM   CLOSEUP BED

    As nurse bends over and removes the wolfbane from about Mina's neck. Mina stirs restlessly, but does not open her eyes. SWING CAMERA REVERSE SHOT - Bed in f.g. as nurse leaves bed, crosses to Dracula - he still stands with his cloak shielding his face and directs her with silent gesture to the boudoir. Nurse exits, closing door behind her. Dracula starts into f.g. towards Mina.

G-35   INT. LIBRARY

    Van Helsing is saying to Renfield,

> VAN HELSING
>
> You know where those boxes are, Renfield! Tell us -- and we'll protect you -
>
> RENFIELD (smiling triumphantly)
>
> But I don't need your protection! The Master isn't angry with me - he's pleased. He came and stood below my window in the moonlight, and he promised me things - not in words, but by doing them-
>
> VAN HELSING
>
> Doing them -?

              CONTINUED.

G-35   CONTINUED

        RENFIELD

          By making them happen --

He starts to explain with
crazy enthusiasm.

         a red mist spread over
         the lawn, coming on like
         a flame of fire - and then
         he parted it an I could
         see that there were
         thousands of rats, with
         their eyes blazing red like
         this, only smaller! He
         hold up his hand and they
         all stopped; and I thought
         he seemed to be saying,
         !Rats - rats - rats -
         thousands, million of
         them - and every one a life-
         all red blood - years of
         life in it! All these will
         I give you - aye, and many
         more and greater, through
         countless ages, if you
         will obey me!

        VAN HELSING (Quickly stepping
            forward)

         What did he want you to do?

        RENFIELD

         That which has already
         been done -

At this, Martin enters
hurriedly, stops and
says to Dr. Seward

        MARTIN

         Strike me down dead,
         Doctor, 'e's got me going!
         Now 'e's twisted and
         broken them iron bars as
         if they was match sticks!

        VAN HELSING (Grimly)

         Dracula is in the house!

G-36 CLOSE UP HARKER

   Showing his startled
   reaction. He exits
   out of scene towards
   stairs.

HN

G-37 MED. SHOT

Renfield says, drawing
himself up proudly,

      RENFIELD

      Where else would he be?

Harker exits upstairs
before anybody can stop
him. Dr. Seward makes
a gesture to restrain
him, but Van Helsing cuts
in with -

      VAN HELSING

      This time he can do no
      harm. We were ready for
      him!

Renfield's only reply is
a laugh. Dr. Seward
turns to Martin and
says,

      DR. SEWARD

      Come, Martin, I'll show
      you where we'll put Mr.
      Renfield, so that he
      can't escape again!

Martin takes Renfield by
the arm. He and Renfield
follow Dr. Seward out of
the library, Martin
shaking his head dubiously
as they go.

      MARTIN

      Maybe you're right, but I
      'aves me doubts -

Van Helsing is left alone
in the library. He turns
back toward the fireplace
in an attitude of deep
thought. CAMERA MOVES
FORWARDS TO CLOSE SHOT
as he stands beside fire-
place, thinking suddenly an
alarming thought occurs to
him, and with a muttered
exclamation, he turns
quickly, to exit. As
he does so, Dracula's
voice comes over scene, suave,
ironical..

      DRACULA

      Van Helsing -

As Van Helsing turns
quickly, CUT TO -

G-38   INT. MED. SHOT

    Dracula has entered thru
    window and is coming
    forward slowly, with
    measured steps. He pauses
    a few feet away, facing
    Van Helsing, and continues,

                  DRACULA

          Now that you have learned
          what you have learned, it
          would be well for you to
          return to your own
          country!

                  VAN HELSING

          I intend to remain and
          protect those whom you
          would destroy!

G-39   CLOSEUP DRACULA

    His lips parted in a
    smile of evil triumph,
    as he replies with some
    emphasis.

                  DRACULA

          You are too late -- the
          blood of Dracula now flows
          through her veins! She
          will live through all
          Eternity, as I have lived!

G-40   INT. MED. SHOT

    matching action as Van
    Helsing stares at
    Dracula for a moment in
    horrified silence - then,
    rousing with a gesture of
    grim determination, says,

                  VAN HELSING

          Should you escape us,
          Dracula, we know how to
          save Miss Seward's soul -
          if not her life!

                  DRACULA   (sneering)

          Ah - the stake - yes!
          But only if she dies by
          day! I shall see that she
          dies by night -!

HN

G-41   INT. MINA'S BOUDOIR

Harker is there with
Mina, his attitude one
of surprised relief. The
door of Mina's bedroom is
open, and through it we
see her bed, with the bed
covers tumbled about, as
if they had been thrown
back hastily. Mina is
wearing a charming
peignoir and has undergone
a complete and startling
change. Her eyes are bright.
She is radiant, vital, her
manner vivacious and gay -
altogether a complete
transformation from the
girl we have seen in
previous action. She is
moving restlessly about
the room while Harker
looks at her in amazement,
scarcely able to believe
his eyes. She turns and
faces him laughingly,
saying,

     MINA (gaily)
      Of course I'm all right!
      I never felt better in
      my life!

She pauses and smiles
across the room at him,
struck by his wondering
attitude

      But why are you looking
      at me that way?

Harker shakes his head
in bewilderment and sits
down upon the end of the
chaise-longue, saying

     HARKER
      Darling, you look so -
      (pauses)
      I can't believe it -
      you're like a different
      girl -

Mina goes to him with a
little laugh and holds
out her hand - he takes
it, looking up into her
eyes, stammering -

     HARKER
      - you look gorgeous -!

    CONTINUED.

G-41   CONTINUED

                    MINA   (patting his hand)

                    And I feel gorgeous.
                        (drops his hand and
                        moves restlessly away
                        from him)
                    But It's close in here
                        (looks around vaguely)
                    - that odour -
                        (sees wreath on table)
                    - oh, it's the wreath the
                    Professor wanted me to -
                        (turns and calls into
                        bedroom)
                    Briggs!

G-42   CLOSE SHOT BEDROOM DOOR

    as Briggs enters quickly -
    her attitude is one of
    grave misgiving - she
    doesn't like this sudden
    change in Mina, and is
    suspicious without knowing
    why, and without knowing
    what to do about it.

                    BRIGGS

                    Yes, Miss Mina - ?

G-43   INT. BOUDOIR. MED SHOT.
         ANOTHER ANGLE.

    matching action as Mina
    turns to Briggs, indicating
    wreath on table, and says,
    with a little gesture of
    distress.

                    MINA

                    Throw this awful wreath
                    away, will you, Briggs?
                    And please open the window-
                    let's have some fresh
                    air.

                    BRIGGS   (coming forward
                              slowly)

                    But the Professor won't
                    like it, Miss Mina -

                    HARKER   (rising)

                    Never mind about him now!

                    CONTINUED.

G-43   CONTINUED

He crosses to Mina -
nurse looks at them both,
tight-lipped, shaking her
head - she doesn't like all
this - picks up the wreath
from the table and crosses
to French windows leading to
balcony, which she opens,
removing the wolfbane.
During this action, Harker
says,

                    HARKER

                        It's good to see you this
                        way - you certainly had
                        me worried -

At this point, nurse opens
French doors. Mina draws
a deep breath of relief,
and says -

                    MINA

                        Ah- h! That's better!
                            (turns to Harker)
                        What's been wrong with me,
                        dear? It's all been like
                        a nightmare -

Leaves Harker side-
crosses toward balcony -
Briggs crosses into
foreground with wreath,
crosses and exits out of
scene. Mina, with her
back to camera, stretches
forth her arms, drawing
in a deep breath of fresh
night air, her had turned
back exultantly, as she
exclaims

                    MINA

                        What a heavenly night!

G-44   CLOSE SHOT. NURSE AND HARKER

Harker is staring at Mina -
still a little puzzled -
nurse comes into scene
and says in undertone,

                    NURSE

                        I think you're doing
                        wrong, Mr. Harker, - it's
                        liable to be dangerous.

                    CONTINUED.

G-44   CONTINUED

Harker turns to her with
a placating smile and
says,

> HARKER (very confidently)
>
> It's all right, Briggs,
> as long as I'm here.

Nurse looks at him and
shakes her head -
Harker exits out of
scene toward window.

G-45   INT. CLOSE SHOT AT WINDOW

Mina is still standing,
looking out into the
night, as Harker comes
into scene. She smiles
at him over shoulder and
says -

> MINA
>
> Isn't it lovely, John -
> the moonlight -

G-46   INT. CLOSE SHOT DOOR.
        LEADING INTO HALL.

FLASH CLOSEUP NURSE
as she stands there,
one hand on the door
knob, looking across
the room at them.

G-47   INT. MED. CLOSE SHOT
        WINDOW

Mina, takes Harker's
hand, and, pointing up
into the sky, exclaims-

> MINA
>
> Look - have you ever seen
> so many stars? Millions
> of them!

CONTINUED.

G-47   CONTINUED

Harker follows direction of her hand - as he is looking up into the sky with in indulgent smile, she turns and looks at him - the rapt expression on her face alters imperceptibly as her eyes drop and she stares at his throat.

G-48   LARGER CLOSE UP MINA.

as she stares at Harker's throat, her eyes slightly dilated, a startling look of animalism flashing over her face. Harker's voice continues over Close-up

HARKER'S VOICE

My, they look close - as if you could almost reach out and touch them -

G-49   MED. CLOSE SHOT
        MINA AND HARKER

He hesitates and looks at her - smiling as he completes speech -

HARKER

How would you like me to reach up and get you a handful?

The predatory expression on her face gives way to a more natural look as she smiles back at him and, taking his hand, says nervously, hastily,

MINA

Yes - aren't they beautiful? - and the night-
    (starts to pull him
    out to balcony)
Let's go out here on the balcony -

As she leads him out of scene to balcony, we CUT TO:

G-50   INT. FLASH CLOSEUP AT
        DOOR

>   Nurse staring across
>   the room at Mina, a look
>   of alarm on her face.
>   She turns and exits quickly.

G-51   INT. LIBRARY MED. SHOT

>   Van Helsing is facing
>   Dracula across table -
>   has worked himself up
>   to a dramatic pitch, as
>   he levels his finger at
>   Dracula and cries,

                    VAN HELSING

                        - and I'll have Carfax
                        Abbey torn down, stone
                        by stone - excavated for
                        a mile around!

G-52   INT. FLASH CLOSEUP
        VAN HELSING

>   His voice rising and
>   continuing through
>   closeup..

                    VAN HELSING

                        - I'll find your hiding
                        place and in the bright
                        glare of sunlight you
                        dread, I'll rip the cover
                        from your earth-box and
                        drive that stake through
                        your heart!

G-53   FLASH CLOSEUP DRACULA

>   Reacting to this threat -
>   his eyes narrow ominously.
>   He does not speak for a
>   moment and directs a pierc-
>   ing gaze toward Van Helsing -
>   he seems about to burst forth
>   in fierce speech - then, con-
>   trolling himself with a mighty
>   effort, and his voice taking
>   on a smooth, silky quality,
>   he purrs,

                                        (CONTINUED)

G-53 (CONTINUED)

DRACULA

In the past five hundred years, Van Helsing, those who have crossed my path have all died -

G-54   INT. MED. SHOT
       VAN HELSING & DRACULA

Dracula in f.g., his back to camera; Van Helsing facing him.

DRACULA
(completing speech)

- and some not pleasantly.

We see Van Helsing's shoulders stiffen and he braces himself against this threat. Dracula continues looking at him with fierce intensity - then slowly lifts his arm and says, with terrible emphasis and force,

DRACULA

Come - here - !

G-55   INT. FLASH CLOSEUP
       VAN HELSING

Standing very straight and rigid - all his mental faculties whipped into play to combat this sudden danger.

G-56   INT. FLASH CLOSEUP
       DRACULA

Matching action as he completes speech and concentrates his entire willpower on Van Helsing, his eyes growing large.

G-57   INT. MED. SHOT ANOTHER ANGLE

>Both men hold their positions for a moment, unbending - Van Helsing, fighting to maintain his defensive position. Then he takes an involuntary step toward Dracula, which is followed by a slight pause as he attempts to gain control of himself. Dracula tightens up, baffled for a moment, then says,

>>DRACULA

>>>Your will is strong - then I must come to you -

>He takes a couple of slow steps toward Van Helsing, never once removing his eyes from Van Helsing's.

G-58   LARGER CLOSEUP
        VAN HELSING

>His hand flies quickly to his vest pocket - this move is instantly checked by Dracula's voice sounding authoritatively over Closeup.

>>DRACULA'S VOICE

>>>Stop!

>Van Helsing's hand stops.

G-59   FLASH CLOSEUP DRACULA

>Bringing all his will to bear on Van Helsing, as he says,

>>DRACULA

>>>You cannot move your hand - until I will it.

G-60 FLASH CLOSEUP VAN HELSING

As he tries to move his hands closer to his pocket and finds he cannot - it remains rigid, shaking a little with his effort to move it.

G-61 INT. MED. SHOT

Matching action as Dracula notes with satisfaction that he is apparently overcoming Van Helsing - stretches forth his hand and says,

>   DRACULA
>
> Remove what you have there and place it in the drawer in that table -

G-62 INT. CLOSEUP VAN HELSING

Regaining the use of his hand - it goes slowly into his upper vest pocket and starts to remove the cross - as the tip of the cross appears from beneath the edge of coat lap - CUT -

G-63 INT. FLASH CLOSEUP DRACULA

Swiftly muffling his face behind his cloak as he cries,

>   DRACULA
>
> Quickly!

G-64   CLOSEUP VAN HELSING

>   As he takes out the cross, his other hand reaching toward table drawer. He is staring at Dracula now, with a slightly different expression on his face.

G-65   CLOSEUP DRACULA

>   As he stands hidden in his cloak. There is a brief pause and we hear the sound of a drawer closing sharply.

DRACULA

You have obeyed me?

Van Helsing's voice coming over Closeup:

VAN HELSING'S VOICE

Yes.

>   Dracula slowly lowers his cloak, then springs back with a snarl.

G-66   INT. FLASH CLOSEUP VAN HELSING

>   Completely in control of himself, the contact having been broken by Dracula's hiding his eyes behind the cloak. Van Helsing stands with the cross presented squarely before Dracula's face, his eyes gleaming with fierce triumph. Over the Closeup is heard Dracula's snarl of rage.

G-67   MEDIUM SHOT

>   Matching action as Van Helsing comes slowly around corner of table, advancing toward Dracula, the cross held aloft. As Van Helsing advance, Dracula

(CONTINUED)

G-67   (CONTINUED)

retreats toward windows - his cloak held between his face and the cross as a shield -- then suddenly with a final snarl of frustated fury, Dracula whirls and dashes through the window into the night. It is only after he has left that we see the terrific toll this incident has exacted from Van Helsing. He almost collapses against a chair, back to camera - leans weakly against arm of chair, fighting to regain his strength. Then, pulling himself together, with a mighty effort, he turns and starts towards door leading to hall.

G-68   MINA'S BOUDOIR. MED. CLOSE SHOT.

Harker is lounging easily on a long, low settee, heaped with gay colored cushions, looking up fondly at Mina, who is leaning against the rail, facing him, her head thrown back as she laughs, a little self-consciously, and says, as if in answer to some statement he has just made,

                    MINA

          But, John, I never could
          have said anything so
          silly. You're making it up!

                    HARKER   (doggedly)

          No - you said you were
          afraid of the night --

                    MINA

          What's there to be afraid
          of? I love the night. Its
          the only time I really
          feel alive.

At this her eyes travel to a point beyond John's head, and we see the shadow of a bat flying across scene, reflected on the white wall opposite. Her laughter dies - Harker, noticing that something is attracting her attention, looks around and sees the bat.

G-69   EXT. BALCONY FLASH
        CLOSEUP SHADOW OF BAT

   Flitting by.

G-70   EXT. BALCONY MED.
        SHOT ANOTHER ANGLE

   Matching action as
   Harker sees bat and
   springs up, saying,

                        HARKER
                  There's a bat -- it'll get
                  in your hair -

   He crosses balcony in
   front of Mina and starts
   striking out into the
   air, at the bat, following
   its progress in pantomime
   as it apparently flits
   around just out of Harker's
   reach.

G-71   EXT. CLOSEUP MINA

   A strange expression on
   her face - an expression
   of awe - she speaks in
   a whisper.

                        MINA
                  Yes - yes -

G-72   EXT. MED. SHOT

   Harker chasing bat.
   Follows it to balcony
   rail, where it ap-
   parently flies away,
   making one last circling
   whirl towards Mina in
   f.g. - we hear Mina say,
   in the same odd tone,

                        MINA
                  I will.

   Harker hears this and
   turns quickly, asking,

                        HARKER
                  You will what?

                              (CONTINUED)

G-72 (CONTINUED)

      MINA

       I didn't say anything –

She drops onto the
settee, curling her
foot under her, holding
out her hand invitingly
to Harker.

      HARKER (as he comes over to
            her)

       I <u>thought</u> you did –

        (looks of in direction
        bat has flown)

       My, that was a big bat!

He sits down – she
snuggles up a little
to him.

G-73 INT. BOUDOIR MED.
   SHOT VAN HELSING.

Van Helsing is walking
across room, looking
around quickly as he
sees that Mina and the
nurse are not there. As
he crosses towards open
door leading to balcony,
Mina's voice comes over
scene, stopping him just
within the door.

      MINA

       John, I want you to make
       me a promise --

      HARKER

       Anything, darling -- any-
       thing at all--

Van Helsing peers
around corner of door
cautiously.

BRL

G-74   EXT. BALCONY. CLOSEUP
       MINA AND HARKER

   She is cuddling up to
   him with a wheedling
   air - says;

                                    MINA

                                         That funny little old
                                         professor and those herbs
                                         of his - I can't stand
                                         them - I want to get them
                                         away from him --

   As she says this last,
   a cunning look comes
   into her eyes. She
   watches Harker narrow-
   ly to note the effect
   of her words.

G-75   INT. BOUDOIR CLOSEUP
       VAN HELSING

   As he listens to Mina
   and Harker outside.
   Mina's next speech
   comes over closeup.

                                    MINA

                                         And his crucifix - get
                                         that, too --

   Van Helsing reacts
   to this.

G-76   EXT. BALCONY. MED. CLOSE
       HARKER AND MINA

   on settee. Mina's voice
   continues unbroken,

                                    MINA

                                         He'll be wanting to pro-
                                         tect me again -
                                              (her voice takes on
                                              a mocking tinge)
                                         from the night - Count
                                         Dracula - or whatever it
                                         is -

                                                   CONTINUED

BRL

G-76   CONTINUED

                                    HARKER
                                        (suddenly serious)
                                    I don't know - maybe he's
                                    right. He's been telling
                                    me some terrible things
                                    about Count Dracula -

    She starts to laugh,
    a little hysterically.

G-77   INT. BOUDOIR
        FLASH CLOSEUP VAN
        HELSING

    shooting from balcony
    into room, getting
    over his alarmed re-
    action. As laugh sounds
    over scene, CUT TO

G-78   EXT. MED. SHOT

    matching action as
    Mina's laughter dies
    down on an unnatural
    note. She eyes him
    with a recurrence of her
    previous attitude of con-
    straint - very nervous -
    wanting only one thing -
    to kiss him. He notices
    this - says with a little
    frown of concern,

                                    HARKER

                                    What is it? What's the
                                    matter?

    She stares at him with
    the odd light in her
    eyes, says, quickly,

                                    MINA

                                    Why?

                                    HARKER

                                    Your eyes - they're looking
                                    at me so strangely -

BRL

G-79   EXT. BOUDOIR WINDOW

leading to balcony, shooting into room. In background, Doctor Seward is slowly coming up, attracted by Van Helsing's watchful attitude. Doctor Seward comes into fore to Van Helsing - says, in a low voice,

                    DOCTOR SEWARD
                What is it, Van Helsing-?

Van Helsing turns quickly, and placing his finger to his lips, - Doctor Seward comes forward a little more, his voice lowered to almost a whisper, as he continues,

                    DOCTOR SEWARD
                What's happened?

CAMERA MOVES FORWARD TO CLOSE SHOT DOCTOR SEWARD AND VAN HELSING, as Van Helsing replies in a tragic whisper,

                    VAN HELSING
                What we've feared from
                the beginning -

Doctor Seward looks startled, follows direction of Van Helsing's eyes, and we CUT TO

G-80   EXT. BALCONY. MED. CLOSE SHOT HARKER AND MINA

matching action of previous scene as Mina draws closer and closer to Harker - her eyes filled with a savage hunger. Harker is staring at her as if too amazed to move - he finally manages to falter,

                                                CONTINUED

G-80 CONTINUED

        HARKER

         Mina -

As he says this, CAMERA MOVES FORWARD PAST HIM TO LARGE CLOSEUP MINA'S FACE Coming slowly forward - it passes right by the camera and out of scene.

G-81 EXT. BALCONY. CLOSE SHOT AT DOOR LEADING FROM BOUDOIR.

Harker's voice comes sharply over scene,

        HARKER'S VOICE

         Mina! You're -

The faces of Doctor Seward and Van Helsing are suddenly alive with horror, as Doctor Seward cries,

        DOCTOR SEWARD

         No - ! Mina - !

Van Helsing dashes forward into scene - Doctor Seward shrinks back against the door, hiding his face - over scene comes a snarl, the sound of a chair being overturned, the sound of scuffling feet.

G-82 MED. SHOT BALCONY REVERSE ANGLE

Mina has leaped up and stands crouching with her back against the wall - Harker has also gotten up to his feet - Van Helsing stands between them with his cross upraised.

           CONTINUED

G-82 CONTINUED

HARKER (furiously)
What's the matter with you -- have you gone crazy?
(wrenches the cross from him)
Are you trying to frighten her to death?

He stands facing Van Helsing.

VAN HELSING
No, I was trying to save her!

Harker turns to Mina.

HARKER
Darling, it's all right - I -

Mina gives a little cry - recoils .. covers her face with her arm as she sees the cross in Harker's hand.

G-83 EXT. CLOSEUP MINA

her face hidden in the crook of her arm.

MINA
The Cross - John - !
After what's happened, I can't look at it!

her strength seems to give way and she starts to slither to the floor from sheer weakness and reaction from the shock.

G-84 EXT. CLOSE SHOT
HARKER & VAN HELSING

Harker looks dazedly from Mina to Van Helsing, not understanding -

CONTINUED

G-84   (CONTINUED)

    Van Helsing stretches
    forth his hand to receive
    the Cross. Harker hands
    it to him mechanically,
    as he exclaims,

                  HARKER

              But <u>what's</u> happened - ?

G-85   EXT. CLOSEUP MINA

    in a huddled heap on the
    floor. She looks up at
    them with tears in her eyes -
    her expression one of deep
    horror as she says,

                  MINA   (Falteringly)

              I can't tell you -
              I can't - !

G-86   EXT. MED. SHOT GROUP

    matching action as she
    breaks off with a shudder
    and starts to sob violently.
    Van Helsing and Dr. Seward
    in fore., backs to camera -
    Harker sinks to his knees
    beside Mina. He tries to take
    her in his arms as he says,

                  HARKER

              You must - I've a right
              to know!

    Mina draws away from him,
    trying to control herself,
    but too shaken by her
    experience. Her words come
    hurriedly, almost incoher-
    ently,

                  MINA

              It's the truth - every-
              thing! Dracula - he came
              to me - opened a vein in
              his arm - he made me -
              drink -
                  (She collapses in
                  faint)

                  (CONTINUED)

G-86   CONTINUED.

At this, the sound of two
quick shots from the yard
below interrupt. They all
turn, startled - Van Helsing
indicates that Dr. Seward
and Harker are to confine
their attention to Mina -
he exits towards rail,
out of scene. Dr. Seward
drops to his knees on the
other side of Mina and
starts to locate her pulse.
Harker, his arm resting
under Mina's head, starts
ad libbing.

                      HARKER

        Darling - it's going to
        be all right - we'll
        save you - we'll save you -

G-87   EXT. CLOSE SHOT RAIL

as Van Helsing leans over,
calling down into the darkness below.

                      VAN HELSING

        What is it? Who is it?
        Martin - ?

G-88   EXT. TERRACE BELOW
        MED.SHOT FROM VAN
        HELSING'S ANGLE.

as Martin stands there in
the moonlight, a shot-gun
in his hand. Behind him,
leaning against the side
of the house, in an attitude
of terror, is the maid.
Martin looks up toward balcony
rail and calls,

                      MARTIN

        A bat, sir - a large black
        one -

Van Helsing's voice comes
from above..

                      VAN HELSING

        There's no use wasting
        your bullets, Martin -
        they can't harm <u>that</u> bat!

MBK

G-89   EXT. TERRACE. CLOSE SHOT.

Martin looks up at him
with a peculiar look in
his face, hesitates for a
moment and then says,

MARTIN

Yes, sir.

He turns away and en-
counters the maid staring
at him. Maid points up
toward balcony and says in
a low whisper,

MAID

'e's crazy.

MARTIN

(Confidentially in
her ear)

They're all crazy - all
but you and me -

(He hesitates, look-
ing her over criti-
cally, then adds)

And sometimes, I 'aves
me doubts about you.

FADE OUT.

SEQUENCE H

H-1   FADE INTO:
       EXT. LONG SHOT
       CHURCHARD. NITE

> An eerie, awesome view of
> the churchyard at Whitby,
> as it lies beneath the wan
> light of a cloud-flecked moon.
> Gound mists curl, wraithlike,
> about the ancient and moss-
> covered tombstones, and in
> immediate fore., a melancholy
> willow droops sweepingly over
> a headstone. In b.g., and dotting
> the churchyard here and there are
> the more pretentious mausoleums
> and family vaults. The Weston
> vaults, one which looks as if
> it had served as the final
> resting-place of the Westons
> for generations, is prominently
> established.
>
> In the background, slowly approach-
> ing, is the figure of a woman in
> white. - Lucy Weston. As Lucy
> draws closer to the door of the
> vault, we see it stands partly open,
> Lucy comes walking slowly, as if in
> a trance, eyes staring straight ahead,
> and enters the vault. As the door
> of the vault closes slowly, with a
> faint creaking sound, behind Lucy,
> and from somewhere near at hand, an
> owl hoots, CAMERA SWINGS AROUND
> TO MED. CLOSE SHOT HARKER AND VAN
> HELSING, crouched behind a nearby
> tombstone, and we get over Harker's
> reaction to Lucy's appearance, which
> has left him speechless and shaken.
> He stares at the closed door of the
> vault with an expression of complete
> stupefaction - can't credit his
> senses - there is a faintly pitiful
> look in his eyes as if he almost
> suspected his own sanity. Van Helsing
> does not speak. He studies Harker
> gravely, narrowly, watching to see
> the effect this will have upon him,
> his manner paternal. One hand goes
> out, steadying, to Harker's trembling
> shoulder. For the first time, we
> see that Van Helsing is carrying an
> oblong, paper-wrapped parcel. He
> indicates parcel - pointing
> to vault, says gtavely

                    VAN HELSING

>   I would have spared you
>   this, but I wanted you to
>   see for yourself.

                              (CONTINUED)

H-1   (CONTINUED)

    Harker hesitates for
a moment, the horror
of the situation almost
overcoming him. Then
he braces himself and says
through his teeth,

                HARKER

                Come on!

H-2   INT. MINA'S BEDROOM - NITE

    The room is dim and quiet.
Mina lies in bed, wuiet
under the effects of an
opiate. Dr. Seward sits
beside the bed, the
night-light tilted slightly away from her face,
its ray directed to a book
he is half-heartedly reading.
He shows evidence of hies
nervous, harried state of
mind.

    CAMERA MOVES SLOWLY FORWARD
TO MED. CLOSE SHOT as we
see Mina commence to come
out of her stupor and
move slightly with a
restless air. Dr. Seward
lays aside his book and
glances at her solicitously.

H-3   INT. FLASH CLOSEUP
        MINA IN BED

    Stirring faintly. One
arm, which has been under
her head, moves slowly
towards sprig of wolfbane
which rests on the cover-
let, and displaces it
accidentally.

H-4   INT. MED SHOT
        DOCTOR SEWARD

    Watching her closely.
He leans over and restores
the wolfbane to its original
position. Then he draws his
chair a little closer to the
bed and sits there, studying her attentively.

H-5 INT. MINA'S BOUDOIR

>Briggs, the nurse stands talking to a night nurse who has just come in. The night nurse has a half dozen charts in her hand. Their voices are low as they glance towards Mina's bedroom, Briggs saying,

>>BRIGGS
>>
>>>We've had to keep her under opiates all night - the minute she smells that wolfbane, she goes out of her head and starts to fight us.
>>
>>NIGHT NURSE
>>
>>>I don't blame her. The whole house rocks with it.
>>
>>BRIGGS (Nodding)
>>
>>>I'll tell the doctor you're here -

Exits towards bedroom.

H-6 INT. BEDROOM - WIDE ANGLE

>Matching action as Briggs comes from B.G. and approaches Dr. Seward in fore. He looks up inquiringly.

>>BRIGGS
>>
>>>Lynch would like to speak to you, Doctor -

NS

H-6   CONTINUED

                    DR. SEWARD (Rising)
                    Thank you -
                        (Starts to exit - then
                        turns and indicates Mina
                        who seems more rest-
                        less than before)
                    We may have to give her
                    another injection before
                    daylight. -

Dr. Seward exits across
room into boudoir. Briggs
stands looking down at
Mina - picks up book Dr.
Seward has been reading and
straightens lampshade.

H-7   INT. BOUDOIR

    matching action as Dr. Seward
    enters from bedroom - comes into
    fore., where night nurse is stand-
    ing at small table.

                    DR. SEWARD
                        What is it, Lynch?

She hands him the charts,
saying -

                    NIGHT NURSE
                    I'm a little worried
                    over the patient in No.11.

                    DR. SEWARD (dropping into chair
                            at table.)

                    Let me see.

She hands him the chart -
he starts to check over it
as she starts to explain.

H-8   EXT. BALCONY.

    Bedroom window, curtains
    parted, in b.g. - through
    it we see Briggs moving
    about.

    Dracula appears in immediate
    fore., silhouette. - stands for
    a moment watching Briggs whose
    back is for the time being
    toward the window..

H-9   EXT. FLASH LRGE
        CLOSEUP DRACULA

    Staring at Briggs -
    his eyes commanding.

H-10   EXT. MED. SHOT BALCONY

    Dracula in fore., as in
    previous shot - through
    window we see Briggs
    turn slowly, as if impelled
    by some force she knows
    nothing of for the moment -
    she slowly approaches
    window and stands looking
    out.

    CAMERA MOVES FORWARD TO
    LARGE CU BRIGGS AT WINDOW,
    staring out through pane.

H-11   EXT. VERY LARGE
        CLOSEUP DRACULA

    Regarding her fixedly.

H-12   EXT. MED. SHOT WINDOW

    Shooting in from balcony.
    Briggs slowly reaches up
    and removes wolfbane
    from over the catch -
    unlocks the windows and
    opens them - then stands
    aside as Dracula enters
    and stands before her.

    CAMERA MOVES IN THROUGH WINDOW,
    pausing for a moment as
    Dracula stares down at Briggs
    - she stands as if awaiting
    his silent command, then
    exits from scene as if in
    obedience; Dracula con-
    tinues on into room,
    starting for bed -
    CAMERA FOLLOWS HIM OVER
    TO BED - he stands looking
    down at Mina, who has now
    almost reached complete
    consciousness.

H-13   INT. BOUDOIR   MED SHOT

Dr. Seward glancing over charts - suddenly looks up, as a sound from the next room reaches his ears - he rises quickly and crosses to door, looking in.

H-14   INT. BOUDOIR. MED. LONG SHOT THROUGH DOOR

Looking into bedroom from Dr. Seward's point of view. Briggs comes into scene, book in hand, and seating herself in a low rocker, starts to read. Her manner appears in every way normal and disarming.

H-15   INT. BOUDOIR. MED. SHOT ANOTHER ANGLE

Matching action as Dr. Seward turns back from bedroom door, satisfied that everything is all right. He crosses back to his charts, his air one of nervous tension. Night nurse looks down at him sympathetically.

H-16   EXT. CHURCHYARD. MED LONG SHOT

Vault in fore. Through the open door there comes the sound of a heavy blow being struck - followed by a piercing, unearthly scream. An owl, disturbed by the sound, flutters across scene. For a moment there is absolute silence, then slowly the figure of Harker appears, a ghastly, stricken look on his face - he emerges and leans limply against door of vault, head bowed, body sagging. Van Helsing follows after a moment, backing out, his eyes looking back into the darkness of the vault.

(CONTINUED)

H-16   (CONTINUED)

> VAN HELSING
>
> Driving that stake in her heart was an act of mercy - may her sould rest in peace!

Crosses himself and starts to draw door of vault shut - Harker watches him in silence - then we see his horror give place to cold fury of destruction, and he says harshly,

> HARKER
>
> Let's go to the abbey!

As they start off -
CUT TO:

H-17   EXT. FLASH LONG SHOT
        GROUNDS - MOONLIGHT

A very picturesque angle, possibly down shot from elevation, showing moonlit lawn and deep shadows, as Dracula, in b.g., walks slowly with Mina at his side.

H-18   EXT. CHURCHYARD
        MED. CLOSE SHOT GATE

Leading to road - shooting through gate, with tombstones and mist-hung churchyard in b.g.

Harker and Van Helsing approach gate, walking swiftly, but in silence - as they come into fore., and are about to pass through the gate, Van Helsing stops and points grimly off, saying,

> VAN HELSING
> (Musingly)
>
> Carfax Abbey -

LG

H-19 EXT. VERY LONG SHOT
      CARFAX ABBEY (Glass)

   Looming grim and desolate
   on cliffs overlooking the
   sea, which can be seen
   beyond.

H-20 EXT. MED. SHOT HARKER
      AND VAN HELSING

   Van Helsing's speech
   continues,

                    VAN HELSING
                Somewhere in there we
                must find the two
                remaining boxes -

H-21 EXT. MED. CLOSE
      SHOT AT GATE

   As Van Helsing finishes
   speech. Harker follows
   direction of his arm -
   suddenly strains his
   eyes, leaning a little
   forward - points off,
   exclaiming,

                    HARKER
                Look! Who's that?

H-22 EXT. VERY LONG
      SHOT ABBEY

   The figure of a man is
   seen scrambling down over
   rocks leading down around
   cliff. He carries a
   lantern.

H-23 EXT. MED. CLOSE OF GATE

   Matching action as Van
   Helsing, also looking, says,

                    VAN HELSING
                Renfield - !
                    (Turns to Harker,
                    the light of triumph
                    in his eyes)
                - Come - !

   They start hurriedly
   out of scene.

H-24   INT. MAIN HALL ABBEY
       LONG SHOT

   As Dracula and Mina come
   in from fore. - she is walking
   at his side now, slowly, mechanically, like a sleep-
   walker. As they advance
   across main hall towards
   corridor leading to steps
   below, CAMERA FOLLOWS.
   Dracula halts for a moment
   at side of hall, where
   there is an ancient wall
   sconce with a solitary
   candle, covered with the
   grease drippings of years.
   This he takes down.

H-25   EXT. ROCKS BELOW ABBEY
       MED. SHOT

   as Renfield comes down
   into fore., and proceeding
   cautiously and with some
   difficulty through a
   tangled mass of scrub
   and weeds, approaches a
   small iron-bound door
   at the very lower part
   of the abbey wall.
   CAMERA MOVES FORWARD INTO
   CLOSER SHOT as he fumbles
   with the door, finally
   opening it and letting
   himself in.

H-26   INT. LOWER CRYPT
       MED. SHOT

   Shooting towards door
   leading out as Renfield
   enters and closes door
   behind him - raises his
   lantern and looks around,
   panting a little. His
   eyes are wild, his hair
   in disorder, his clothing
   torn from his passage over
   the sharp rocks. As he
   leans agains the door,
   getting his breath, he
   looks up.

H-27   INT. LONG SHOT CRYPT

Shooting across and up, as seen from Renfield's point of view. This is the first time we see the crypt in its entirety. A narrow stone stairway curves up and around to an apparently great height. Far up near the top, just entering from the Abbey above, comes Dracula, carrying Mina. He starts to come slowly down the steps.

H-28   EXT. ROCKS MED. SHOT

As Harker and Van Helsing come slowly down, climbing carefully over rocks, Van Helsing with lantern raised.

    VAN HELSING

    We must have come
    down this way --

Harker points, exclaiming,

    HARKER

    Look -- an opening
    in the wall - !

He starts toward wall, Van Helsing right behind him.

H-29   EXT. ABBEY WALL
    CLOSE SHOT AT OPENING

This is a small opening not large enought for a men to crawl through, where the masonry or stone work has fallen away - perhaps an air hole, with iron bars - it permits a limited view into the crypt from outside. Harker and Van Helsing into scene - raising the langern, they peer through.

H-30 INT. CRYPT...LONG SHOT
      OF STAIRWAY

　　　　As seen from viewpoint
　　　　of Harker and Van Helsing.
　　　　On far side of the crypt -
　　　　Dracula just coming into
　　　　view, carrying Mina -
　　　　Renfield running up to-
　　　　wards Dracula, lantern in
　　　　hand crying,

                    RENFIELD

                        Master! Master!
                        I'm here!

H-31 INT. CRYPT...LARGE CLOSEUP
      AT OPENING

　　　　Showing the faces of
　　　　Harker and Van Helsing,
　　　　lit by the flickering
　　　　lights of the lantern,
　　　　staring across in
　　　　horror.

NS

H-32   INT. MED. CLOSE
        SHOT ON STAIRS

Just as Renfield draws closer to Dracula, his face wildly radiant with his greeting. Harker's voice cries out across scene,

               HARKER

                   Mina!...Mina!

Instantly, Dracula comes to a dead halt - turns his head, looking towards opening - Renfield seems frozen in his tracks.

H-33   INT. FLASH CLOSE
        SHOT OPENING

showing Harker and Van Helsing peering in.

H-34   MED. SHOT

Dracula turns his head from direction of opening to look down at Renfield - his face a mask of concentrated venom. Renfield looks up at Dracula and sees Dracula's accusing eyes - he backs down a step or two, crying,

               RENFIELD

                   I didn't lead them here, Master! I swear - I didn't know - Master - Master - !

        CONTINUED

NS

H-34 CONTINUED

Dracula, without a word but his whole attitude pregnant with terrific ominousness, lowers Mina to a standing position on the stairs and starts down after Renfield, with the same unhurried, deliberate pace. Renfield starts backing down the steps in a frenzy of fear - Dracula raises his hand briefly and commands.

> DRACULA
>
> Wait!

Renfield obeys - turns and looks up, sinking to his knees in an agony of supplication - starts to scream.

> RENFIELD
>
> Master, I've been loyal! I'm your slave! Didn't betray you - !

Dracula keeps bearing relentlessly down upon him as he crouches fearfully on the steps. Then, Dracula pauses a step or two above him and stands looking down at him with murderous eyes.

H-35 INT. CLOSEUP RENFIELD ON STAIRS

shooting down from Dracula's angle as Renfield screams,

> RENFIELD
>
> Master, don't kill me. Let me live - punish me - torture me - but let me live. I can't face God with all those lives on my conscience, all that blood on my hands.

EC

H-36 INT. MED. SHOT STAIRS

    Dracula, comes down to Renfield, and stretching forth his hands, grips him about the throat. Renfield gives a shriek of terror.

H-37 INT. FLASH CLOSE SHOT OPENING

    As Renfield's screams, one after the other, come across scene. There is the sound of rending, of tearing - the thump of a body - the thud of blows - Renfield gives one final cry and then there is a significant silence. Harker closes his eyes to shut out the horrible sight - Van Helsing exits from window, pulling Harker after him.

H-38 INT. LONG SHOT STAIRS

    As Renfield's limp body comes slithering and rolling to the bottom, where it lies a broken, twisted heap. Dracula turns to Mina - she starts to follow him down.

H-39 EXT. ROCKS. ANOTHER ANGLE

    Shooting up - small iron-bound door in immediate fore., concealed by weeds. Harker and Van Helsing in background, clambering down hastily, risking their necks on the rocks, which are slippery with early morning mist. As they come into fore., they are searching every foot of the stone walls - suddenly Harker spots the door and makes for it with a cry ...

                       HARKER

            Here's how he got in -!

    crosses to it, stumbling in his eagerness - Van Helsing after him - they start to work at the door, meeting with resistance.

EC

H-40 INT. LOWER PART OF CRYPT

Dracula has come down the stairs, Mina following - they are crossing around towards entrance to catacombs, door of which stands open, revealing nothing but the darkness beyond.

H-41 EXT. MED. SHOT IRON-BOUND DOOR

Harker and Van Helsing straining and pulling to get it to open. The door quivers under their combined on-slaughts - bursts open - Harker and Van Helsing rush into crypt. Shooting past them towards background, we see the door leading to the catacombs, with Dracula and Mina just passing through it. As Harker and Van Helsing rush forward, Harker crying,

                HARKER

            Mina - Mina -!

The door swings shut just as they reach it.

CAMERA MOVES SWIFTLY FORWARD TO CLOSE SHOT DOOR, as they frantically try to push it open. As they continue to push, the door starts slowly to give way, a little shower of dust dislodged - door creaks open an inch or two - Harker cries in triumph,

                HARKER

            It's giving way - it's opening - !

As he says this, from inside comes a terrible scream - they stop and stare at each other in horror. Then as the scream dies away into a hollow silence, Harker cries:

                (CONTINUED)

H-41 (CONTINUED)

> HARKER
>
> Mina! Mina! We're here!

Starts to kick and hammer at the door with almost maniacal frenzy, Van Helsing assisting with a certain grim resignation.
As they use all their combined strength, start to push it open - it swings back with almost maddening slowness - finally stands wide - just as the first ray of morning sunlight illumines the crypt and the door -

H-42   INT. CATACOMBS. MED. SHOT

Harker and Van Helsing enter from camera -. Harker stands for a moment, lantern upraised, looking around - calls,

> HARKER
>
> Mina! Where are you?

Then Harker starts off in one direction and Van Helsing in another.

H-43   INT. CATACOMBS. ANOTHER ANGLE.

The faint gleam of oncoming daylight is creeping in, revealing the character of the place - a low broad, tunnel-like room, with low arches leading off to various sections. From somewhere above

(CONTINUED)

H-43 (CONTINUED)

and from a break in
the masonry, a little
light is streaming
through - barely
enough to distinguish
the moving figures of
Van Helsing and Harker.
Van Helsing is seen
moving about in back-
ground, the ray of his
lantern, raised aloft,
casting mammoth, weird
shadows as he advances.
Throughout balance of
scene, interior becomes
slowly lighter with
the advancing down ...
Their voices are heard
calling, ad lib,

H-44 INT. FLASH CLOSEUP HARKER.

Passing by camera
under an arch, calling

HARKER

Mina! Mina!

H-45 INT. CLOSE SHOT VAN HELSING

Coming towards camera
lantern held high --
suddenly stops, peering
dimly ahead.

H-46 INT. CATACOMBS FAIRLY LONG SHOT

In fore., are the tow
earth boxes. Van Helsing
starts forward, calling
at the top of his voice,

VAN HELSING

Harker! Harker!
I've found them!

EC

H-47   INT. FLASH CLOSEUP
         HARKER

        About to start into a
        dark section of the
        catacombs - turns, his
        face lighting up -
        yet his eyes filled with
        dread at the thought of
        what may be awaiting him -
        dashes out of scene.

H-48   INT. CATACOMBS
         MED. SHOT

        Harker comes running
        into scene, fore.,
        Van Helsing standing
        in fore., back to camera-
        looking down at the two
        boxes - camera shooting
        past.

                        HARKER   (as he comes in)

                        Where is she?

        Van Helsing grips his
        arm, pointing to boxes.

                        VAN HELSING

                        Look!

        They start slowly
        forward - as they
        reach boxes, Van Helsing
        (back to camera) - leans
        over and slowly starts to
        raise the lid of the
        first box - Dracula's.

H-49   INT. CLOSE SHOT
         REVERSE ANGLE

        matching action as
        Van Helsing lifts up
        the cofer. Harker
        just behind him - as
        Van Helsing straightens
        up, a look of savage
        satisfaction on his
        face, we see Harker's
        eyes glisten with
        horror as he looks down
        into box. Van Helsing
        stands studying Dracula
        (out of scene) for
        a moment in grim
        silence - then he says,

                                      'CONTINUED.

H-49   CONTINUED

                  VAN HELSING

                      His life in death will
                      soon be at an end!

                HARKER   (in agonized tones)

                      And - Mina -

He looks past Dracula's
box to where the second
box is lying. All the
life seems to have been
drained out of him - his
eyes are lifeless, stricken.
Van Helsing lays his hand on
his shoulder, steadying -
says,

                  VAN HELSING

                      You must be strong -

Sees that he must do
something to rouse
Harker from his
momentary stupor,
induced by the swift-
ness of his grief -
says,

                  VAN HELSING

                      Get a large rock -
                      anything - to help me
                      drive the stake through
                      his heart -

Harker does not move,
but remains staring
dully at Mina's box,
Van Helsing takes him
by the shoulders, and
literally turns him
around, almost pushing
him away. Harker goes,
stumbling, hardly conscious
of what he is doing. As
he exits from scene, Van
Helsing's eyes follow him
with pity - then he turns
and crosses toward Mina's
box - stands staring down
at it with a heavy sigh.

H-50   INT. CLOSE SHOT HARKER

groping his way blindly
across scene - leans
against one of the
arches, trying to get a   (CONTINUED)

H-50   (CONTINUED)

grip on himself - then he turns his head, listening. From off-scene, comes the sound of ripping and tearing of the wooden lid - Harker's whole body quivers with horror - it seems as if he can bear no more - he exits slowly, brokenly, from the scene.

H-51   INT. CATACOMBS MED. SHOT VAN HELSING

He has turned away from Lucy's box and has been splitting up lid of Dracula's box - the piece he is now holding in his hand, regarding with grim satisfaction, is about three or four feet long, tapering to a sharp point at one end.

H-52   INT. MED. SHOT HARKER

As he comes into scene from behind an arch, looking around for something to use to drive the stake into Dracula's heart. In fore., is an old bit of iron, quite large, with a broad flat surface - possibly an old hinge of some sort. He picks it up and turns back towards Van Helsing.

H-53   INT. MED. SHOT

Fairly wide angle, Van Helsing in fore., stake in hand. He has just crossed and has raised the lid of Mina's box - is staring down into it as Harker comes forward out of the shadows, and crossing to him, falters,

(CONTINUED)

H-53 (CONTINUED)

                                  HARKER

                              Mina - how does she - is she -?

Van Helsing turns to him, a baffled look on his face. He points to box - Harker looks down into it.

                              VAN HELSING

                              She's not here --

Harker rouses, his eyes lighting up with renewed hope - he wheels, as if to dash off in search, exclaiming,

                              HARKER

                              Then she may be alive!

He rushes out of scene, dropping the piece of iron, leaving Van Helsing alone with Dracula.

Van Helsing makes a move as if to restrain him - then, with a pitying shake of his head, permits him to go. He turns and looks over at Dracula - then slowly reaching down, picks up the piece of iron and crosses to Dracula's box, where he stands gazing down into box with a look of grim determination to delay no further.

H-54   INT. MED. SHOT

Harker comes running into scene, calling,

                              HARKER

                              Mina! Mina!

                                (CONTINUED)

H-54 (CONTINUED)

> Stops to listen for an answer. As he does so, over scene comes the sound of iron striking heavily against wood - then a loud and shuddering groan. Harker covers his face with his hand, leaning weakly against pillar.

H-55 INT. CATACOMBS CLOSE SHOT MINA

> As she leans back in a huddled heap against an arch, her eyes staring unseeingly straight ahead of her, not moving, a look of agony on her face. She is so still that we might almost believe her to be dead. Over scene comes the last agonized groan of Dracula - then silence. Mina stirs faintly - slowly the look of agony leaves her face, which becomes peaceful. As a look of sanity is restored to her eyes and she commences to look around bewilderedly, as if remembering what has happened, she springs to her feet in sudden panicky realization, and is about to cry out when Harker's voice is heard calling:

HARKER'S VOICE

Mina! Where are you?

> She calls back, her voice vibrant with hysterical relief.

MINA

John! John! Here I am!

> She rushes out of scene towards sound of his voice.

H-56   INT. MED. SHOT CATACOMBS

> Boxes in background. Van Helsing comes anxiously forward - stops at pillar and looks off - a look of relief lightens his face as he sees --

CUT TO

H-57   INT. MED. CLOSE SHOT
       MINA AND HARKER

> He has just taken her into his arms and she is sobbing upon his shoulder. Both are almost hysterical with relief and joy.

HARKER

> You're safe - Mina - you're safe - you're safe!

MINA

> That face - that horrible face - when he saw the sunlight!

Van Helsing enters scene - Mina looks up from the safety of Harker's shoulder, Van Helsing smiles tiredly and says:

VAN HELSING

> There is nothing more to fear. Dracula is dead - forever.

Mina draws a quivering sign of relief - turns again to Harker. They start to go - then Harker, seeing that Van Helsing makes no move to do, says,

HARKER

> Aren't you coming?

VAN HELSING

> I shall remain - and fulfill my promise to Renfield.

(CONTINUED)

RS

H-57   (CONTINUED)

    Harker looks at him for a moment - then, his arm around Mina's shoulder, half-supporting her, he turns and they exit from scene. Van Helsing stands watching them go for a moment in thoughtful silence, a little smile hovering about his lips - then turns back towards Dracula's box.

    CAMERA PANS AROUND FOLLOWING HIM INTO MED. SHOT as he crosses back to where box lies and pauses beside an arch, back to camera. As he stands there, looking down at the box, we hold the picture for a moment - Van Helsing, fore., in Silhouette, crossing himself - Dracula's box, with a shaft of morning sunlight bathing it in a golden glow - dust particles glinting in the rays.

H-58   INT. LOWER CRYPT - VERY LONG SHOT

    Shooting from fore., up the winding stairs, to where Harker and Mina are walking slowly up towards the top of flight - through the breaks in the walls, the morning sunlight streams - they pass from the shadows of the dim old stairway into a broad beam of light and continue on up, as we

                          FADE SLOWLY OUT

                          (ON FADE, THE SOUND OF ORGAN MUSIC STARTS TO ACCOMPANY FOR FINAL ROUNDING OFF OF FADE. THEN IT IS SUDDENLY CUT OFF AS we hear a voice command)

                          VOICE

                          Wait!

RS

H-59   FADE INTO:

INT. MED. SHOT STAGE

Corner of proscenium
arch, with motion picture
screen in background.

Van Helsing steps quickly
up to fore., holding up his
hand in a gesture of command -
calls peremptorily:

> VAN HELSING
>
> Please! One Moment!
>
> (looks out into
> audience and says,
> with a smile)
>
> Just a word before you go.
> We hope the memories of
> Dracula won't give you bad
> dreams - so just a word of
> reassurance! When you get
> home tonight and lights
> have been turned out and
> you're afraid to look be-
> hind the curtains - and
> you dread to see a face
> appear at the window - why,
> just pull yourselves to-
> gether and remember -
>
> (Pause)
>
> - that, after all, <u>there
> are such things!</u>

<u>QUICK FADE.</u>

<u>THE END</u>

On the following pages we present the original Pressbook which was distributed to theater owners for publicity purposes.

THE BOOK IS ONE OF THE WORLD'S GREATEST SELLERS -- TIE IT UP TO THE PICTURE! REACH THAT READY-MADE AUDIENCE!

OVER ½ MILLION COPIES SOLD

CO-OPERATE WITH BOOKSELLERS!
NEW POPULAR-PRICE EDITION PERMITS EXTENSIVE EXPLOITATION

See that local book stores, drug stores, stationery stores, cigar stores, newsstands and circulation libraries feature the new 75c edition of "Dracula" in advance and during the engagement of the picture. Have _____ put his stock of the _____ this window and arrange _____ a suggested copy for the tie-up card. _____ have read "Dracula," you will thrill to it on the sc_____. If you have seen it on the screen, you will want to _____ the book—on sale here. "DRACULA" is showing _____ (dates) at the Roxy Theatre.

Should your local dealer not stock the books, have him communicate with the publishers.

Published by
GROSSET & DUNLAP
1140 Broadway :: New York City

EMBODY BOOK JACKET IN YOUR LOBBY DISPLAY

"Dracula" has been read by hundreds of thousands of people. You will find it worth your while to play up the book. One way of doing it is to make a reproduction of the book in enlarged size by using the 1-sheet poster for the jacket and then painting in pages or building a compo-board representation of the book's thickness. Set this up in your lobby with the eyes of the "shadow" cut-out to permit the light of two green electric light bulbs to shine through. Insert a regulation button flashers in the sockets before inserting the globes so that the eyes seem to blink. Use this giant book either in the lobby or on each end of your marquee or in vacant store windows.

STUNT FOR 3-SHEET EASEL

Get a copy of the Grosset and Dunlap edition of "Dracula" and look through it. Find what pages in the story are illustrated by your set of production stills. Tear out these pages and mount on a 3-sheet easel, together with the proper stills. Have arrows pointing from the pages to the pictures.

READ IT OVER THE AIR

Arrange for someone familiar with the book "Dracula" to broadcast daily readings of the story. The announcer can synopsize the events leading up to a certain passage and from then on, the reader can give thrilling excerpts of the action picked for the purpose. The station will probably welcome the stunt as something new and if someone with a good dramatic voice does the reading, it will be a popular feature with listeners-in. At the end of the program, a plug for the picture and your theatre can be announced.

Note: Any eerie sound effects that you can put on with this stunt will add to its effectiveness. A wind effect, flapping of wings, strangled screams—these are just a few suggestions for starting off the program with a thrill!

OFFER BOOKS AS PRIZES

Buy about five books from your local bookstore and donate them to his circulating library to be loaned free to regular readers. Do this several weeks in advance of the picture's engagement. Also buy the same number of books to be used as prizes. Offer a copy to the first person in line at the matinee performance. Turn a few over to _____ newspaper as prizes for the contests described in detail _____ on pages of this press sheet.

BOOK BALLYHOO

Build a compo-board replica of the book so that a few pages can be turned and place this on a truck to be driven around town. When the pages are turned, posters advertising the picture should come into view.

Or build the book hollow so that the cover, when thrown back, reveals your ballyhoo man in "Dracula" costume. The character, after coming to life, can go through a little pantomime with clutching hands, then step back into the book.

HERE IS YOUR BOOK MARK

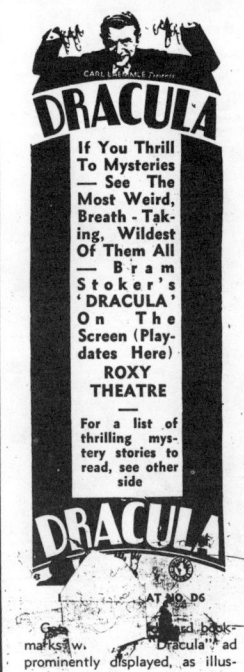

AT NO. D6

Ge_____ard book-marks _____ "Dracula" ad prominently displayed, as illustrated above. A mat of the necessary cut for this bookmark is available at your local Exchange. The type can be set by your local printer. On the other side of the bookmark, your bookseller can put his imprint and other matter.

---

8 SPECIAL TIE-UP STILLS -- 75c
At The Exchange

UNIVERSAL'S NEW STYLE TIE-UP STILLS

These stills are just what showmen have been waiting for—neat, interesting, practical, complete with tie-up line and picture credits! Sets like these issued on previous productions have proven a sensation. Get a trial set on "Dracula" if you haven't used them before—you will find it makes difficult windows easy to land. Local dealers are glad of the opportunity to exhibit these stills which sell specific commodities as well as your attraction.

For Smith Brothers' or Luden's Cough Drops

For General Tie-Ups | Gold Dust, Old Dutch Cleanser, Etc. | Perfumes | Cosmetics | Clothing | Lucky Strikes | Ostermoor Mattress

---

TWO HIGH—POWERED SLIDES

SLIDE "A"

Choice of two highly colored slides — order from your Exchange. Price 15c each

SLIDE "B"

2 TRAILERS! 1 TALKING 1 SILENT!
THRILL TRAILERS THAT PACK THE PUNCH OF THE PICTURE!

Write or wire to National Screen Service, Inc., 126 W. 46th St., N. Y. C.; 810 S. Wabash Ave., Chicago, Ill., or 1922 So. Vermont Ave., Los Angeles, Calif.

REAL SHOWMEN'S SMASH IN THESE SEAT-SELLING ACCESSORIES! 2 HERALDS -- A FLASH HANGER

FOUR-COLOR OFF-SET HERALD

AMPLE IMPRINT SPACE ON BACK PAGE.

SIZE 5½" x 7"

PRICE $3.50 PER THOUSAND.

A herald that in color, cuts and copy suggests the creepy thrills of "Dracula". Every selling point that ought to be played up is properly exploited in this choice accessory. A striking, seat-selling piece of advertising that every showman will want. Order in large quantities. Test out the reaction on your box-office of a greater herald distribution. Try it with "Dracula"!

ORDER AT YOUR UNIVERSAL EXCHANGE

USE-- MORE HANGERS
For A Flashy Front
FRONT   SIDE

Here is the greatest colored hanger ever conceived for a mystery thriller. Designed to help give your theatre front a spooky atmosphere, it shows to good advantage also as a hanging sign. Big block letters proclaim "DRACULA". Cut-out, printed on two sides, on good quality stock. From every angle a necessary and indispensable accessory for your big "Dracula" campaign. SIZE 21" HIGH.

ORDER FROM YOUR EXCHANGE.

PRICE: 15c EACH
(in lots of 25 or over)
20c EACH for 10 to 25
25c APIECE, SINGLY

RICH TWO—COLOR ROTOGRAVURE
Back Page Blank For Theatre Imprint And Local Ads :: :: :: Size Flat 10½ x 16¼

You will find many special uses for this beautiful, impressive roto herald printed in a soft brown and mystery blue. Illustrates many spectacular moments in the picture. Compelling captions and forceful sales copy clinch the readers' attention. Your imprint on back provides the tie-up that sends them into the theatre.

Order plenty of these heralds. Arrange with your local newsdealers to slip them into every paper sold. Use them as a special supplement to your own house organ. Distribute them in hotels, big stores and transit centres.

AT YOUR EXCHANGE
PRICE $5.00 PER THOUSAND IN THOUSAND LOTS :: :: :: $7.00 IN BROKEN LOTS

REVERSE SIDE   NOTE IMPRINT SPACE

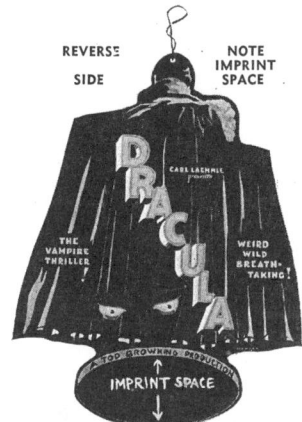

EASEL-BACK CARD
Just the thing for window and counter displays! The front side only of the hanger above, reproduced exact size, and provided with an easel-back.

PRICE: Same as Hanger.

ORDER EXTRA QUANTITIES -- TO-DAY!

THE STORY OF THE STRANGEST P[ICTURE]

SHOWMANSHIP!
THE BIG ONES DESERVE BIG CAMPAIGNS! GO THE LIMIT ON "DRACULA"

"DRAC[ULA]"

WILD—WEIRD—BREATH TAKING—DRAMAT[IC]

PROMOTE THIS "ART" STUNT FOR BIG SPACE FROM LOCAL PRESS

Art contests, conducted in conjunction with a newspaper, always are good exploitation stunts for a picture, and here's one that is particularly appropriate because of the mystery element in the production.

Tie up with the best newspaper in your town, ordering the service cut illustrated here (available in 1 or 2 col. size) far enough in advance so that the contest can be run for a week or two before the opening of "Dracula" at your theatre.

Get the newspaper to give it a good break as far as space and position are concerned. Offer various prizes, consisting of cash, drawing sets and passes, for the finished drawings mostly closely resembling the actual features of "Dracula" as he appears in the picture.

Divide the contest into two sections—one for amateur artists and for students in art schools. State

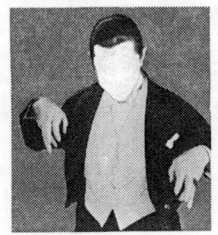

FILL IN THE FACE OF "DRACULA"

(Exp. Service Mat, No. D1)

Submitted by.....................
Address........................

in your publicity that, in fairness to all, no picture of "Dracula" will be printed in advance and that the sketches must be based on the contestants' imaginative conception of a mysterious vampire.

The daily publication of the sketch should be accompanied by your playdate announcement in order to capitalize on the publicity.

The contest should end on the day before the opening, in order to allow you to display the winning contributions and others in your lobby. They should also be reproduced in the newspaper co-operating and a number of them can be displayed in the window of an art dealer, who can be promoted into supplying drawing sets as prizes.

Induce two or three local artists to act as judges of the contest and publicize it thoroughly in your newspaper ads and programs.

24-SHEET CUT-O[UT] and CANOPY for MARQ[UEE]

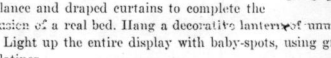

DRESSING UP THE THEATRE FRO[NT]

The cut-out from the 24-sheet showing Dracula bending over the sleeping girl can be used on your marquee and will attract extra attention if you utilize the stunt suggested by the sketches shown here. Place two practical bedposts on either side of the cut-out to represent bedposts and extend a canopy across, with valance and draped curtains to complete the illusion of a real bed. Hang a decorative lantern over it. Light up the entire display with baby-spots, using green gelatines.

You can use this idea effectively for some advance teaser by putting up the display several days ahead of your playdate, having the curtain closed covering the cut-out. On the curtain, a conspicuous question-mark. When your engagement of "Dracula" [begins] the curtain can be opened revealing the 24-sheet.

Also illustrated above is an idea for giving the title extra [punch]. Suspend cut-outs of the book from the marquee, and have each one letter of the title "D-R-A-C-U-L-A." This accessory. See page 7.

Jumbo Cut-Out Letters

The title "Dracula" is so short that you should take advantage of it by making giant compo-board cut-outs of each letter and [placing them] across your theatre building. Make these letters ten feet, twelve as high as your front permits. It will be a great flash.

MASK YOUR USHERS

As an advance teaser stunt, provide domino masks for your ushers and doorman, as illustrated here. These can be cut out of heavy satin and painted by your house signpainter. Make a little higher than ordinary to provide room for the lettering. Use a week ahead of your engagement.

 **CUT-OUTS** from the 3-sheet and the 6-sheet

ADVANCE COPY ON LOBBY MIRR[OR]

According to the story of "Dracula," a vampire has no reflection in a mirror. This offers a basis for the stunt illustrated here. Cover one or more of your lobby mirrors with lamp-black, in a jagged pattern so as to resemble a broken fragment (see drawing). In the center of this black spot, leave enough of the mirror to show through to reflect a face. Over the face, use the following copy: If You Cannot See Your Reflection In This Mirror, You Are A Vampire Like "DRACULA." Arrows pointing to this stunt to attract extra attention. Borrow a mirror from local furniture store if your lobby is not provided with one.

TRY A "WHISPERING" CAMPAIG[N]

A week or ten days in advance of your "Dracula" playdates, attaches, doorman, cashier, ushers, etc. to whisper to every patron of the theatre, these three words: "Dracula" is coming! It is important voice be kept down to a whisper and a finger be held to the lips, in order announcement mysterious.

SEE PAGE 2 FOR BOOK TIE-UPS

DRACULA CLOAK FOR BALLYHOO

Dress your ballyhoo man like "Dracula"—in cutaway, top-hat and opera-cloak. Powder his face a dead white or green. On the outside of his opera-cloak, have a large conspicuous question-mark. This can be cut out of some brightly colored cloth and lightly stitched to the cloak. The same thing can be done for the advertising message inside the cloak: "DRACULA" It's Terrific! Your theatre name and playdates can be painted on the white shirt-front, as shown. Have this man walk around the streets with the cloak closed until sufficient curiosity is aroused. Then let him open the cloak to its full width and reveal your ad.

Portable Direction Signpost

The ballyhoo man, instead of carrying the usual type of sign, can attract attention by carrying about a portable direction signpost with the usual red arrow on top. On this arrow is painted—"Dracula"—the thrill sensation!—at Gem Theatre. At intervals, the ballyhoo man sets down the signpost as if to rest, taking care that the signpost is pointed in the right direction (toward the theatre). Persons approaching are handed advertising material.

For Tack Cards or Teaser Ad

The copy suggested here can be used for a tack card to be distributed around town or for a teaser newspaper ad. Instruct the printer to set this up in big black type for the best effect.

BEWARE!
Be on guard for One who roams the night!
Lock and bolt the doors and windows!
Investigate all strange noises!
Be on guard against the woman in white!
Wolfbane will make you immune from danger!
Get set for **"Dracula,"** the vampire mystery thriller!

WHAT TO PLAY UP

1. The Title: "Dracula" has become known to the reading public through the wide sale of the book, to theatre-goers through the tremendous success of the play which broke attendance records in every [large] city on the way, and to movie-fans by reason of Universal's great national advertising and publicity campaign.

* * *

2. The Cast: Great acting talent! Among the stage celebrities are Bela Lugosi who created the original role of Count Dracula in the stage hit and Dwight Frye and Edward Van Sloan who were with him in the play. David Manners, new juvenile find, and Helen Chandler of screen fame are both well known and popular. Bill every one of these players and bill them big. See credit box for proper order of importance.

* * *

3. The Director: Tod Browning, whose name is associated with the many successful Lon Chaney pictures, put everything on the ball when he worked on "Dracula" which will be a new triumph for him.

* * *

4. The Theme: Based on an old-world legend which still has many believers, this story is the creepiest, shiveriest, most bizarre entertainment seen in years! Simply terrific in its strange, sensational plot!

YOUR IDEAS, PLEASE!

Universal is eager to hear from exhibitors as to how their campaigns go over. If you try out any new stunts or have any suggestions that will help your brother exhibitors, tell us about them so that we can spread the word to other enterprising showmen. Send your ideas and your campaign on this picture to

Joe Weil

DIRECTOR OF EXPLOITATION
730 Fifth Avenue   New York, N. Y.

STORE WINDOW OR LOBBY STUNT

Get a cedar chest that will look as much as possible like the one used by "Dracula" in the picture (see production stills). Copper-studded leather straps around the chest will help get the effect.

On the box, place seven tall candles of assorted colors. At their base, have cards spelling out the title as shown in the illustration. Have these candles lit and invite passerby to guess which candle will burn longest—and just how long it will burn. Supply blanks in two sections upon which guesses can be recorded. One part, which the person retains, can carry an ad for "Dracula." The other part, which is the name and address blank, can be used for building up your theatre mailing list.

Teaser Treasure Chest

The chest mentioned above can be used as a teaser stunt also: Simply exhibit the box with a sign saying: *This chest holds the secret of "Dracula." It will be opened on (Date).* When opened, a selection of stills and cut-out of "Dracula" can be revealed.

Which candle will burn the longest? How close can you come to guessing when it will go out? A Pass to see "Dracula" for the most accurate guess!

ION THE WORLD HAS EVER KNOWN!

"LA" featuring BELA LUGOSI, DAVID MANNERS, HELEN CHANDLER, DWIGHT FRYE, EDWARD VAN SLOAN -- A TOD BROWNING PRODUCTION

ENSATION—TERRIFIC VAMPIRE THRILLER

ongue-Tangler Contest

at this "Tongue-Tangler Con-
in your local newspaper, using
t shown at right. The copy ac-
nying the illustration should be
ows:

YOU WRITE A TONGUE-
LER FOR "DRACULA?"

sets of guest tickets to the Star
e await those who write the
t tongue-tanglers describing the
sal production "Dracula" which
to our local playhouse this
ay. Here are the rules:

ongue-tangler must not be over
ds long. (But more than one
e may be used.)

tangler must contain the name
la" and describe the picture,
story of that title.

y word must begin with "D."
mple: "Dracula"—dark, deep,
e, distinctly, different, drama!

our tongue-tangler all thought
d then print it in the space
d above in the picture of
la" posed by Bela Lugosi. Sign
me and address below the pic-
nd submit it to the Tongue-
r Editor.

Write A Tangler

Available in 1 or 2 Col. Size
(Exp. Service Mat, No. D2)

Submitted by......................
Address...........................

TONGUE-TANGLER ACROSTIC "AD"

u can use the Tongue-Tangler Contest described above with an extra twist, if you
Make your newspaper announcement this way:

TONGUE-TANGLER ACROSTIC CONTEST

re is your chance to get a bigger price than the foremost fiction writers for
erary work! Words fail the Management of the Roxy Theatre in attempting to
e the Universal production "Dracula" which will play there (dates). Can
ate an advertisement for the picture in the form of a Tongue-Tangler Acrostic?
rd will be paid for the best ad! Read the book and you will get a good idea of
e picture is like. Then, all that is necessary is to write an ad like the sample
using four words to each letter in the title Dracula, that is, four words with D,
ith R, four with A and so on. For example:

Distinctly	Different,	Daring	Drama,
Really	Remarkable,	Rare	Romance,
Astonishing,	Astounding,	Absolutely	Absorbing,
Captivating,	Chilling,	Completely	Convincing,
Unusual,	Unparalleled,	Unbelievable,	Unique,
Long-lauded,	Luring,	Love	Legend,
Audiences	Applaud,	Ask	Anyone!

RRENT STUNT: WOLFBANE IN ENVELOPES

any stunts have been created to bring patrons into the theatre; the stunt to
em talk after they go out has evidently been overlooked. Here is one to start
rolling:

tribute to your first-night audiences, *as they go out*, small envelopes contain-
....
olfbane," the herb which is mentioned in "Dracula" as a sure safeguard
the vampire. Of course, the "wolfbane" can actually be ferns or tea-leaves
ing similar. Imprint the envelope as follows:

Here Is Your Wolfbane! Put It Under Your Pillow To-Night and then
Need Not Fear "Dracula" Who Will Remain Safely On The Screen
The Gem Theatre Until (Final Day of Engagement). P. S. Do Not
ulge The Plot of the Picture To Your Friends. Permit Them To Enjoy
Its Surprises Just As You Did!

LETTER TO LOCAL DOCTORS

following letter can be sent to doctors, surgeons, local hospital heads, etc.:
r Sir:

vampires really exist?

ask you this question because an unusual screen production entitled
la" advances the premise that they do exist! In this Universal picture which
our theatre (dates) you will find the following situation:

irl who is under doctor's care continues to lose weight consistently regardless
act that she is in excellent health and upon a careful diet. Is it possible that
circumstances such as these that some inhuman vampire is sucking the blood
e veins of the girl? Could Bram Stoker's fantastic character of "Dracula"
real life? Is it possible that a victim of a vampire can be affected with the
ge and in turn become a vampire?

would appreciate your professional opinion and take this opportunity of
you to see the picture "Dracula" as a guest of the management. We are
that you will be particularly interested and entertained by this type of
ion.

Yours very truly, THE MANAGEMENT.

ou get any written replies to this letter, be certain to get the consent of the
efore reproducing.

DISPLAY LINES

Weird! Wild! Breath-taking!

* * *

The story of the strangest passion the world has
ever known!

* * *

TERRIFIC in its startling drama! AMAZING
in its daring theme!

* * *

Gripping! Exciting! Shivery! Eerie thriller of
One who roamed the night!

* * *

Its daring will ASTOUND you! Its suspense will
chain you to your seat! You'll never forget
"Dracula!"

* * *

He lived on the kisses of youth! "Dracula"—
the undead—the world's greatest vampire!

* * *

Everyone who has read Bram Stoker's gripping
book—all who have seen the stage shocker—will
want to see it. All others must see it for the entertainment surprise of a life-time.

* * *

Do vampires really exist? Dracula answers with
a thousand thrills!

* * *

Dracula—he walks at night—and walks alone!

* * *

Dracula will get you if you don't watch out!

* * *

He will haunt you—chill you—thrill you—BUT
you will love "Dracula."

* * *

Out of the cobwebby darkness of an age-old
castle—heavy with the dust of centuries, comes
DRACULA to roam the night in his weird, wild,
breath-taking adventures.

* * *

DRACULA! He of the fiery fingers, flaming
lips and crimson kisses!

CREDITS! IMPORTANT!

CARL LAEMMLE .... (20%)
presents
"DRACULA" .... (100%)
with
BELA LUGOSI .... (20%)
DAVID MANNERS .... (20%)
HELEN CHANDLER .... (20%)
DWIGHT FRYE .... (20%)
EDWARD VAN SLOAN .... (20%)
A TOD BROWNING .... (15%)
Production
(75% of stars)
From Bram Stoker's play .... (5%)
Produced by Carl Laemmle, Jr. ..... (10%)
A Universal Picture .... (20%)

ASK 'EM THIS QUESTION:

WHAT IS A "DRACULA" KISS?

(Exploitation Service Mat, No. D3)

FOR LOCAL NEWSPAPER OR THROWAWAY

The sketch above is available in the form of an Exploitation Mat (2 column size)
at your local Exchange. Plant it in your local newspaper or print it on a hand-bill
along with the following copy:

CAN YOU DESCRIBE A DRACULA KISS?

The most unusual and dangerous kiss that a human being can receive! A
mother's kiss is sweet, a baby's kiss brings joy, a friendly kiss is welcome, a sweetheart's kiss makes for happiness—but the "Dracula" kiss ... feared, despised, hated!
Why? Write a 50-word description of "Dracula" kiss and if yours is the best
contribution on the subject, you will see "Dracula"—Universal's startling screen
version of the famous book and play—at the Blank Theatre, as a guest of the management, when the picture plays there (dates).

ESSAYS ON "DO VAMPIRES REALLY EXIST?"

Another possibility for a newspaper contest exists in the question "Do
Vampires Really Exist? This question, incidentally, is mentioned and answered
in the picture. Ask readers of the paper to submit their opinions, quoting
from first-hand experiences, if possible. Prize essays and other interesting contributions can be exhibited in the lobby as well as printed in the local paper.

NEWSPAPER DRAWING CONTEST

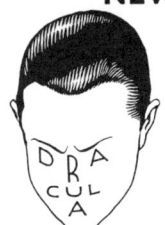

Here's a drawing contest to give to the editor of the magazine page on your local newspaper. It
is a contest that sells your picture title. An idea of this sort proved very popular in connection with
another Universal release. Try it with "Dracula." The prizes mentioned in the suggested contest copy
given below can be promoted from the local art supply store.

"Dracula" Drawing Contest

Prizes of the book "Dracula" or passes to
see the screen play for the Ten Best Faces
Drawn With Letters In Picture Title.

The face sketched at the right represents
"Dracula," the mysterious vampire in the
Universal production of that title, which will
show at the Strand next week. Notice how the
artist has sketched the face, using the letters
that spell D-R-A-C-U-L-A. Can you do the
same? Shift your letters around, of course, and
change the angle of the face. Prizes will be
awarded for originality, neatness and talent
shown by the drawing. Anyone can enter.
Address the "Dracula" Drawing Contest
Editor, in care of this paper.

The cut shown here is available in 1 or 2 col. size in the form of an Exploitation Service Mat, No. D4.

WRITE YOUR OWN ENDING FOR "DRACULA" AND WIN A PRIZE!

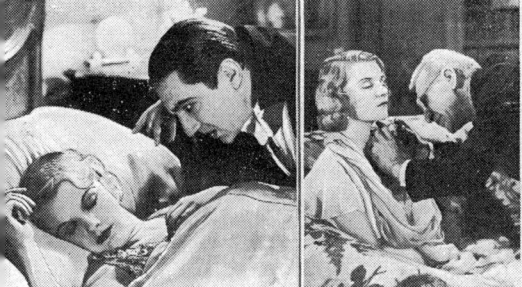
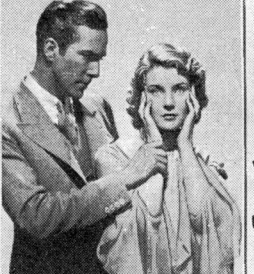

WHERE THE PLAY ENDS PUBLICITY BEGINS!

The ending of "Dracula" is
difficult to guess and provides a
surprise twist to the picture.
Which offers you an opportunity
to plant the panel strip shown
here in your local newspaper and
invite readers to submit their
ideas of a proper ending to the
action shown in the photos. Ask
for a 50-word suggestion for an
ending scene and offer a copy of
the book, "Dracula," or a pass
to see this exciting, thrilling
Universal production. The
size strip is 3½" x 10" (exact
size illustrated) and will fit a
tabloid page perfectly as well as
being suitable for regular-size
newspapers. Ask your Universal
exchange man for Exploitation
Mat, No. D5.

1. "Dracula," one who roams the night, retly visits one of his victims in the angest mystery story ever filmed. 2. Of all the medical experts, Dr. Van Helsing alone scents a mystery in the tiny fang-like marks he discovers on Mina's neck. 3. Mina's fiancee, John Harker, threatens to avenge himself on the sinister force that is stealing his sweetheart from him. Can Dracula be defied? Will the girl be saved? How will it end? What should the last panel of the strip above show?

ELECTRIFYING LOBBY DISPLAYS--A LINE OF ACCESSORIES THAT COMPEL ATTENTION

INSERT CARD

EXCITING! SIZE 14 x 36!

Here's A Great Cobweb Stunt for Your Lobby -- Just What You Want!

Cobwebs sell mystery! You can make a cobweb like that which appears on the 22x28 shown below. Take ordinary black netting and have your sign painter reproduce the cobweb with silver flitter. Cut out the head of "Dracula" which appears on the 1-sheet and place it behind the cobweb which should be mounted in a corner of your lobby where it will look realistic. If you flash a green spot on this display, the black net will be invisible but the silver cobweb will show up in a very effective way and the face peering through will "stop" everyone. Cut out letters below the cobweb should read: "DRACULA" COMING SOON!

14x17's IN FULL COLOR SET OF 8

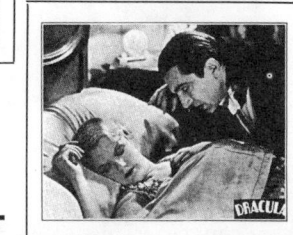

FOUR UPRIGHTS
FOUR "FLATS"

Finished in Spooky Tones of Purple and Green with Yellow Highlights—Varnished To Look Like Real Paintings.

JUST THE THING FOR DE LUXE LOBBIES!

ORDER EARLY AT YOUR EXCHANGE!

$1.50 PER SET

EIGHT 11x14's WITH A BIG SOCK IN EVERY SCENE! NO ONE CAN RESIST THE LURE OF THESE THRILLING PICTURES!

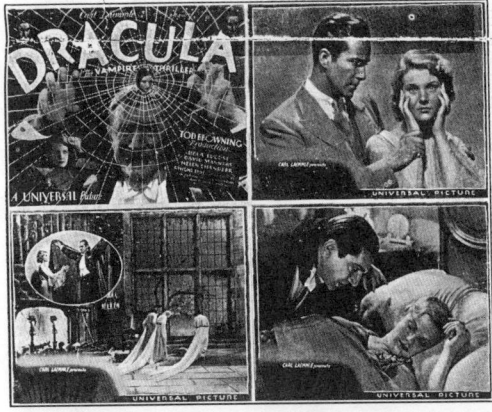

A WEIRD COLOR SCHEME CARRIES OUT THE SPOOKY EFFECT OF THIS SEAT-SELLING SET OF 11 x 14's

THESE ARE YOUR TWO EXCEPTIONALLY ATTRACTIVE 22 x 28's
Great for Window Displays As Well As Lobbies!

THESE ACCESSORIES ON "DRACULA" TOP THE BEST EVER PUT OUT!

THEY SMACK OF REAL SHOWMANSHIP!

Order Early From Your Local Universal Exchange

FOR SLIDES, TRAILERS, TIE-UP STILLS, ETC.--SEE PAGE TWO!

ANOTHER 1-SHEET AND 2 GREAT WINDOW-CARDS!

COLORFUL! **STRIKING!**

ONE SHEET "F"

WINDOW CARD, STYLE "G"

WINDOW CARD, STYLE "H"

LOBBY STREAMER OF HUGE, DIE-CUT LETTERS

A GREAT CUT-OUT SIGN FOR ANY LOBBY — SIZE OF LETTERS 22 x 28" EACH
PRICE $2.50 COMPLETE — AT YOUR EXCHANGE

A BLOCK 3-SHEET

3-SHEET BLOCK

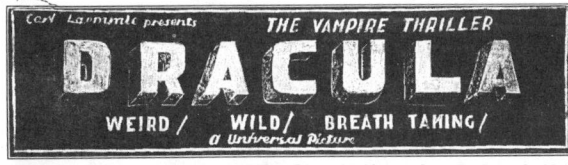

BANNER! GLINTING, METALLIC CUT-OUT LETTERS ON FELT BACKING. 3 COLORS: PURPLE, SILVER AND GREEN.

SIZE 3 x 10 FEET. PRICE $10. EACH

Order Direct from METALLITE SIGN CO., 385 Halsey Street, Newark, N. J.

15 MINUTE RADIO RECORD FOR BROADCAST

Here is something new! A 15 minute radio program on a 16 inch 33 R.P.M. record. "Dracula," all ready to turn over to your radio station. Recorded on Western Electric equipment. All you have to do is to have the station announcer introduce the subject as a Universal Picture Program. After the record plays for 14 minutes the local station anncuncer cuts in and says: "Dracula" will be shown at your theatre, etc. The program on the record consists of tabloid sketches of the picture interspersed with music. You can make a deal with the local radio station to put it on gratis for you and in turn give them free screen publicity or you can let a local merchant put it on for you in return for screen publicity. This record is available on a rental basis.

Made by Famous Artists of the Air, Inc., and available through National Screen Service. Communicate with your local agency. Rates on Application.

WEEK BY WEEK
...BUILDING GOOD-WILL FOR YOU... THESE ADS IN THE "SATURDAY EVENING POST" ARE REACHING 10 MILLION PEOPLE!

DOORKNOB HANGER
PRINT UP YOUR OWN

A clever little novelty is the doorknob hanger, the front side of which is illustrated above. The reverse side carries a cobweb design and the title and allows a generous space for your theatre imprint. This is not available as an Exchange Accessory but Exploitation Service Mats are provided for both sides and you can have this doorknob hanger printed up locally at very little expense. The mats are 4" wide each, giving you a good-size hanger of the right proportions for stringing up around town.

ASK FOR EXPLOITATION SERVICE MAT NO. D7 AT YOUR EXCHANGE

Publicity "DRACULA" Scene Cuts

...gosi, "Dracula" Star, Fled for Life to America

a Price on His Head After Political Revolution, Famous Actor Found Haven Here; Has Had Remarkable Career.

(During the Run)

...e made a hit in a colorful role on the stage—but most of the time ...didn't know what he was saying! ...e of the most remarkable feats ...e annals of theatricals was accomp...ed some years ago by Bela Lugosi, ...amous Hungarian actor, shortly ...e he came to the United States ...is political activities had forced ...o flee from his native country ...a price on his head.

...pearing as the star of a traveling ...pany presenting plays in the Hun...n language, Lugosi had failed to ...English, but his performance in ...of the plays in his repertoire led ...y Baron, a New York theatrical ...ger, to approach him "with an ...er to play a role in 'The Red ...'," which he was to produce in ...lowing fall.

...tunately, Baron could talk Ger...and in this language Lugosi con...d his inability either to under...d or speak a word of English. ...ut give me a chance!" he sug...l. "Give me a tutor, take his sal...y out of my future earnings, and by ...me you are ready to start rehears...will know my part."

...ough he was at first filled with ...isition, Baron finally agreed to the ...osition, and Lugosi immediately ...ed upon an intensive course of .... At such short notice he made no ...tempt to learn the English lan...e, but under the coaching of his ...e he learned his entire role phone...y, as one might learn the music ...song. He simply memorized and ...ered the foreign made by the ...ters...

...months later the "company ...together" for the first rehearsal. ...other members of the cast, type...ches or stumbled through them in ...ing fashion. But Lugosi was let...perfect, and gave such a convinc...portrayal of his role that the other ...bers of the company gathered ...d him and began to offer their ...atulations...

...e embarrassed Hungarian smiled ...and shook his head. He did not ...ow what they were saying. But when ...play opened he played his part ...h such consummate artistry that ...le, the frankly vitriolic critic, ...med him "the greatest actor ever ...e to America."

...ring the run of "The Red ...' in New York, Lugosi entered ...olumbia University and took a ...e in English, and in 1927, when ...acula" was first produced as a ...play he was engaged to play the ...e of Count Dracula...

...making his two years in the stage ...say he is now to be seen in the ...e role in Universal's screen pro...ction of Bram Stoker's weird vam...story, now at the ....tre.

...her important parts in "Dracu...are enacted by Helen Chandler, ...d Manners, Edward Van Sloan, ...ht Frye, Herbert Bunston, Joan ...nding and Charles Gerrard. Tod ...wning, famous as a director of mo...pictures with unusual back...nds, played an important part in ...ucing of "Dracula" that is said to ...e of the most powerful produc...s in the history of the screen.

Weird Scenes in "Dracula" Vampire Drama

(Advance Story)

FASTNACHT—the night of evil; swirling fog, and wolves howling in the mountain passes; a solitary traveler waiting at the crossroads; the clatter of approaching hoofs, and a coachman with feverish eyes glowing above his great muffler.

The traveler enters the coach, which continues on its headlong flight; but as soon as it is again under way, the driver disappears, and his place is taken by a giant bat which flaps over the heads of the galloping horses. Silence settles over the misty landscape. The mysterious coach is swallowed up by the dense fog, and makes its way to the crumbling castle of the terrible Count Dracula, vampire!

This is one of the opening scenes of "Dracula", Universal's strange motion picture drama which was adapted from the stage success of the same name, and which comes to the .... Theatre on ....

The cast is headed by Bela Lugosi, who created the title role of "Dracula" on the stage, and other players appearing in prominent roles are Helen Chandler, David Manners, Edward Van Sloan, Frances Dade, Dwight Frye and Herbert Bunston. Tod Browning directed.

"DRACULA" STRANGE DRAMA OF "UNDEAD"

Ancient Superstition Basis of Thrilling Picture, with Great All-Star Cast, Coming Here Soon

(Advance Story)

AN ancient superstition, which claims that "undead" persons, hovering strangely between life and death, leave their graves on a certain night of each year, forms the basis of "Dracula", the hair-raising Universal drama which comes to the .... Theatre on ....

"I never want to know," says Van Sloan, "exactly how the playwright visualized a character which I am to play. In all my years on the stage I have studiously avoided reading what he has to say on this subject, caring little whether he described him as a man with his hair cut pompadour, with or without glasses, or a moustache, or any of those little details which really mean nothing in arriving at a characterization. The actor has his own physical and temperamental limitations, and must be guided, it seems to me, by his own qualifications.

"Similarly, I have never read the book from which was made the stage adaptation of any play in which I have appeared. I did not want to be bound down by someone else's conception of a character which might conflict with my own, and thus perhaps be the means of developing a character which was neither one thing nor the other.

"Count Dracula is the strange vampire of this startling story, and a trail of terror and death results from his horrible influence. The picture, it is said, has been produced with such sincerity and such artistry that the spectator is apt to forget for the moment that the story is what might be described as a glorified fairy tale, and to be completely carried away by the strange atmosphere of the play."

Bela Lugosi plays the title role of "Dracula" while other members of the cast are Helen Chandler, David Manners, Edward Van Sloan, Frances Dade, Dwight Frye and Herbert Bunston. Tod Browning directed.

CURRENT NOTES

"DRACULA," Bram Stoker's novel on which is based Universal's weird screen story of vampires and their terrifying life after death, is one of the most popular books in the realm of fiction. Though originally published many years ago, the yearly sales of this fascinating volume average 40,000 copies. "Dracula," with Bela Lugosi in the title role, opens an engagement at .... at the .... Theatre.

THE play, "Dracula," enjoyed unusual success on the stage, running continuously in England for five years and in the United States for three years. Universal's photoplay of the same name, which is also based, as was the play, on Bram Stoker's strange novel of human vampires, is now playing an engagement at the .... Theatre, with the famous Bela Lugosi in the role of Count Dracula, which he created when the stage play was first presented in America.

DWIGHT FRYE, who is appearing at the .... Theatre in one of the leading roles of Universal's strange production, "Dracula," is one of the most versatile young actors of the American stage, having appeared in the New York in roles ranging all the way from low comedy to high tragedy, in such plays as "A Man's Man," "The Love Habit," "Rita Coventry" and "Goat Song." In "Dracula," he is seen as the Madman, Renfield.

—Drawn by the Noted Artist, John Rogers

Helen Chandler in "Dracula", Universal Super-Production

Scene Cut "W"

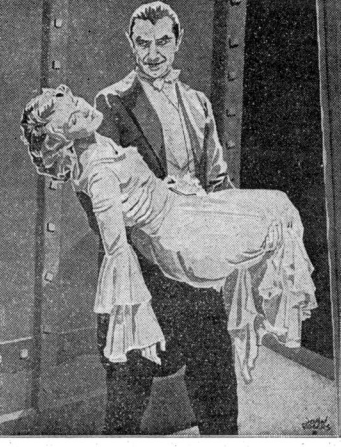

—Drawn by the Noted Artist, John Rogers

Bela Lugosi and Helen Chandler in 'Dracula', Universal Super-Production

Scene Cut "X"

Actor Should Create His Own Conception of Role

(Advance Story)

LET the actor form his own conception of the character he is to play!

This is the creed of Edward Van Sloan, the noted stage actor who makes his screen debut in "Dracula", Universal's strange drama which comes to the .... Theatre on ....

"On the stage I created the role of Dr. Van Helsing, and played the part for more than two years—but I have never read the book. Since I appeared in the play for almost a thousand performances, I, of course, became thoroughly acquainted with every move and inflection of the stage version, and I have now become almost as well acquainted with the screen play. But I must confess that there are many incidents about which I have only heard vaguely—incidents which appear in neither the stage or screen versions of this remarkable story."

In addition to Van Sloan, the cast of "Dracula" includes Bela Lugosi, Helen Chandler, David Manners, Dwight Frye, Frances Dade, Herbert Bunston, Joan Standing and Charles Gerrard. Tod Browning directed.

Though Bram Stoker's weird novel, "Dracula," was written many years before Bela Lugosi first went on the stage, the title role is one which seems to have been written to order for the actor. Lugosi was born in almost the exact spot in Hungary where the earlier scenes of the story are laid, and thus his slight Hungarian accent in Universal's screen production of this strange book is exactly "in character."

"Dracula" Is Crowning Effort Of Director Browning's Career

(During the Run)

TOD BROWNING has carved a niche for himself as the motion picture industry's leading director of weird and fantastic crook stories.

It has been suggested that the dynamic Tod first obtained his ideas of black magic, crooks and illusion in the carnival company with which he began his theatrical career, and in which he is said to have cut quite a figure as a contortionist. This was in 1918, when he was one of the principal attractions with Willard & King's Great Traveling Shows.

Later Browning did a vaudeville act in blackface, after which he spent two years as principal comedian with a burlesque company known by the euphonious title of "The Whirl of Mirth".

He made his screen debut in 1912, when he appeared as a slapstick comedian in a split-reel Biograph comedy directed by D. W. Griffith. This was followed by various roles of gradually ascending importance, and in 1918 Browning became a full-fledged director, wielding the megaphone on "Which Woman?", a drama produced by Universal.

Among his important productions in the following years were such outstanding successes as "The Virgin of Stamboul", "Under Two Flags", "Outside the Law" and "The Thirteenth Chair", as well as many of Lon Chaney's most successful pictures, such as "The Unholy Three", "The Blackbird", "The Unknown" and "The Road to Mandalay". Browning's preference is for crook stories with a definite heart interest, and an example of his work along these lines is "Outside the Law", which he wrote, as well as directed.

Quite in line with his tendency toward mystery in many of his stories, Browning's favorite author is Conan Doyle, and he is an inveterate reader of the adventures of Sherlock Holmes. And still further along the line of this liking for mystery, the director is an enthusiastic amateur magician, and is one of the most adept prestidigitators in an industry which boasts many devotees of the art of magic.

What is said to be Browning's crowning effort in the directorial field is "Dracula", the weird screen drama adapted from Bram Stoker's strange novel of the same name, and now at the .... Theatre with a cast headed by Bela Lugosi, the original Count Dracula of the stage play.

A miniature theatre, constructed by David Manners when a child, indicated the intense interest in the stage that had already been acquired by the future actor, who comes to the .... Theatre on .... in one of the leading roles of "Dracula," Universal's strange drama of human vampires.

Manners was born in Halifax, Nova Scotia, on April 30, 1902, and completed his early education in his native city. Then, thinking thus to overcome his growing interest in the theatre, his parents sent him to the University of Toronto, but his four years at the college strengthened the very purpose which he had sought to defeat, for he became a leader in the university's Little Theatre movement.

CURRENT NOTES

A ship of death sails into Whitby Harbor. Literally freighted with horrors, the cargo vessel Maude lurches up to the dock, after an escape from a terrific storm at sea. The ship has been abandoned by its crew. The mate, shrieking in terror, has thrown himself into the surging waters of the Atlantic. The captain, dead, and with a look of incredible horror on his face, slumps against the wheel, his hands lashed to its spokes. A brooding silence hangs over the vessel.

This is one of the striking situations in "Dracula", Universal's weird screen production of thrills and horrors, which is now at the .... Theatre.

Eventually the awed officials of the village go aboard the ship, to find a gibbering maniac locked in a cabin, intently engaged in catching flies. The superstitious villagers are completely mystified. They do not know that during the voyage the terrible Count Dracula, arch-fiend in human form, has crept out of a box deep in the hold of the ship and created a night of horror on the swaying decks!

Bela Lugosi plays "Dracula", Helen Chandler and David Manners assume the romantic roles. Dwight Frye, brilliant young dramatic actor, is seen as Renfield.

MORNINGS were not made for work! This is the settled conviction of Helen Chandler, popular young leading woman of the stage, who comes to the .... Theatre on .... in the leading feminine role of Universal's sensational drama, "Dracula".

"Ever since I was eight years old," explains the troubled Miss Chandler, "I have been on the stage, and since I am 21 now, it will be seen that I have had a good many childhood years in which to form the habit of staying up late. On the stage, of course, this means insincerity and there also follows the necessity of the stage art at usual midnight lunch. And so, the morning has small chance of accomplishing anything before noon of the next day. Once usually spent the morning hours in sleeping."

"But when I entered motion pictures a short time ago there came frequent demands for the cast to be 'on the set, made up' at 8:30 A. M., and it was some time before I was able to adjust myself to the new conditions—for this meant arising at some such hour as six o'clock. I had often heard of people arising at this unearthly hour, and making a regular practice of it, but on the few occasions when I had done it, I had always felt as if I were participating in a great adventure. Now I have become somewhat accustomed to the new mode of living, but I must admit that it still seems very, very strange."

In addition to Miss Chandler, the cast of "Dracula" includes Bela Lugosi, David Manners, Frances Dade, Dwight Frye and Edward Van Sloan. Tod Browning directed.

"DRACULA," which is now creating a sensation at the .... Theatre, tells a story of vampires—those strange "undead" creatures who rise from their graves at night and revenge their unsuspecting victims to madness or death. It is a tale of horror and sudden death, but it is said to constitute one of the most remarkable photoplays in the annals of filmdom.

"Dracula" was adapted from the famous play of the same name, and the original novel by Bram Stoker, which still enjoys a tremendous sale each year. The screen production was directed by Tod Browning, and the cast includes Bela Lugosi, Helen Chandler, David Manners, Edward Van Sloan, Frances Dade, Dwight Frye, Herbert Bunston and Charles Gerrard.

Facsimiles of "Dracula" Drawings by Famous Artist Available At Your Exchange

Scene Cuts "S", "T", "W" and "X", shown on these two pages are drawings by the famous New York artist, John Rogers, who is recognized as the leading newspaper artist of the metropolis.

These drawings are the finest of their type, and should prove very appealing to the newspapers in your city.

Facsimiles of the originals are available at your exchange. They are exact photographic reproductions of the originals in every detail.

"THE THREE SISTERS" "DRACULA" UNIVERSAL SUPER-PRODUCTION
WITH BELA LUGOSI, DAVID MANNERS, HELEN CHANDLER, DWIGHT FRYE, EDWARD VAN SLOAN and FRANCES DADE
Scene Cut "Y"

HELEN CHANDLER and BELA LUGOSI in "DRACULA"
UNIVERSAL SUPER-PRODUCTION
Scene Cut "T"

Publicity "DRACULA" Scene Cuts

"Dracula", Startling Drama of Human Vampires, Coming Soon

Amazing Story, One of Sensations of Screen History, Played by Remarkable Cast, Including Bela Lugosi, David Manners, Helen Chandler, Dwight Frye, Edward Van Sloan and Others—Filmed on Big Scale by Producer of "All Quiet on the Western Front."

(General Advance Story)

AMONG the important pictures booked for early showing at the .... Theatre is "Dracula", Universal's strange drama of human vampires, one of the sensations of screen history, according to an announcement issued today by Manager ....

This amazing story was first produced as a stage play in New York more than three years ago, and has since created a sensation when shown in a few of the largest cities of the country. "Dracula" deals with the startling practices of human vampires, those terrible creatures of the "undead" world, who rise from their graves at night, and is said to be, in many ways the most unusual story ever brought to the talking screen.

Since the picture is filled with such uncanny mystery, the entire setting accords with the mood of the story, and there are said to be remarkable "shots" of fog-enshrouded mountain passes, with wolves howling in the darkness; a terrible storm at sea; and a mysterious, crumbling castle where much of the action occurs.

BELA LUGOSI
UNIVERSAL
Cut "B"

STAR OF "DRACULA" FLED FOR HIS LIFE

Bela Lugosi Escaped Hanging Squad During Revolution in Hungary; Resumed Theatrical Career in United States

FUGITIVE from a hanging squad, with a price on his head! This was the rather unwelcome role which a few years ago was forced on Bela Lugosi, the famous Hungarian actor who is now appearing at the .... Theatre in the title role of Universal's sensational mystery drama, "Dracula," by Bram Stoker.

In the revolution in his native Hungary in 1918, Lugosi was one of the principal lieutenants of Count Karolyi, who seized the reins of government, and was given the newly-created post of Minister of the Theatre. This was not only because he had been an enthusiastic adherent to Karolyi's cause, but because he had long been the theatrical idol of the country, appearing as leading man for many years at the National Theatre in Budapest.

"Soon afterward, however," says Lugosi, in recounting his adventures during those hectic days, "the royalists regained control of the government, and whenever they could find a member of the Karolyi party, they proceeded to hang him. And so I decided to go away from that place. I had no desire to attend such a necking party. I escaped into Austria, then went to Germany, and finally proceeded to the United States, where I resumed my theatrical career in a new environment and in a new language.

"And I was finally starred in the stage play, "Dracula", in which for two years I had an opportunity to prove a constant irritant to other people's necks. For in this play, you know, Dracula is a vampire who always attacks the throat."

DAVID MANNERS and HELEN CHANDLER in "DRACULA"
UNIVERSAL SUPER-PRODUCTION
Scene Cut "A"

It is a startling subject for a screen story, but it is said to be done with such artistry and such convincing sincerity that it conveys the impression of actual reality, and exercises a powerful effect on the emotions of the audience. The picture, which was adapted from the famous novel by Bram Stoker, traces the devastating activities of Count Dracula, a vampire who has been "dead" for 500 years, but who has the power to return from the grave between sunset and sunrise, wreaking his terrible influence on a group of people in whose fate the spectator becomes breathlessly concerned.

The cast includes three players, who were seen in the original stage production, in the persons of Bela Lugosi, Edward Van Sloan and Herbert Bunston—while other important roles are played by Helen Chandler, David Manners, Dwight Frye, Frances Dade and Charles Gerrard. The screen production, "Dracula", was directed by Tod Browning, famous as the director and author of many of Lon Chaney's most successful pictures. It was produced by the Universal Studios, famous for "All Quiet on the Western Front," which won the Gold Award of the Academy of Motion Picture Arts and Sciences as the finest picture of 1930.

Cast of Characters

COUNT DRACULA	BELA LUGOSI
JOHN HARKER	DAVID MANNERS
MINA SEWARD	HELEN CHANDLER
RENFIELD	DWIGHT FRYE
DR. VAN HELSING	EDWARD VAN SLOAN
Dr. Seward	Herbert Bunston
Lucy Weston	Frances Dade
Martin	Charles Gerrard
Briggs	Joan Standing
Maid	Moon Carroll
English Nurse	Josephine Velez

"Dracula" Creates Furore Among Picture Fans

(Closing Short)

.... night marks the close of the engagement of "Dracula," Universal's uncanny mystery drama which has been creating a veritable sensation at the .... Theatre.

No other talking picture ever shown in (city) has created such a furore of comment, or has so powerfully gripped the emotions of local theatregoers. The strange subject of this startling picture—the nightly prowlings of "undead" human vampires—brings an entirely new note to the screen, and forms the basis of a story which is filled with the weird atmosphere of the supernatural.

Bela Lugosi is seen in the title role of "Dracula," which he created on the stage, while other prominent members of the cast are Helen Chandler, David Manners, Edward Van Sloan, Dwight Frye, Frances Dade and Herbert Bunston. Tod Browning is the director of this sensational Universal mystery drama.

MASSIVE SETTINGS IN "DRACULA" FILM

Weird Mystery Drama of Human Vampires Has Picturesque Scenes; Bela Lugosi Heads Great Cast

SOME of the most picturesque settings in the history of the screen are included in "Dracula," Universal's weird mystery drama, which comes to the .... Theatre on ....

Many of the earlier scenes are laid in and about the crumbling stone castle of Count Dracula, a vampire who has been unoccupied for 500 years—except by Dracula and other "undead" vampires who return nightly from the grave, and make of the castle a veritable house of horrors. Some of the most massive sets in the history of Hollywood were reproduced for this picture, showing various chambers in an advanced state of disorder, with stone balustrades and pillars fallen into disordered ruins, and the entire interior festooned with cobwebs.

There are hair-raising scenes in a graveyard, with a female vampire, risen from her grave, wandering disconsolately among the tombstones. Opening sequences depict a picturesque inn in the mountains of Transylvania, and a rocky mountain pass on a foggy night, with wolves howling in the darkness.

After the story is transferred to England, involving a terrible storm at sea, many scenes are laid in an ancient Abbey leased by Dracula, a location which in its ruined construction, is greatly reminiscent of the castle in Transylvania.

Amid these picturesque settings is enacted what is said to be the screen's strangest story, with the famous Bela Lugosi in the title role of Count Dracula, and a cast which also includes David Manners, Helen Chandler, Edward Van Sloan, Dwight Frye, Frances Dade and Herbert Bunston.

The ship, apparently uncontrolled, lands at Whitby, England, where Renfield's law firm has leased for Dracula an ancient dwelling known as Carfax Abbey. Next door is an insane asylum conducted by Dr. Seward, and it is here that Renfield is taken. Since Dracula can transform himself into a bat, a wolf or a cloud of mist, he easily gains the hand, and the boxes of earth are duly delivered at Carfax Abbey.

HELEN CHANDLER, BELA LUGOSI and DWIGHT FRYE in "DRACULA" UNIVERSAL SUPER-PRODUCTION
Scene Cut "D"

At A Glance

Title	"DRACULA"
Brand	Universal Picture
Cast	BELA LUGOSI, DAVID MANNERS, HELEN CHANDLER, DWIGHT FRYE, EDWARD VAN SLOAN, Herbert Bunston, Frances Dade, Charles Gerrard, Joan Standing, Moon Carroll, Josephine Velez
Produced by	Carl Laemmle, Jr.
Directed by	Tod Browning
Associate Producer	E. M. Asher
Story	From the Novel by Bram Stoker and Stage Play by Hamilton Deane and John L. Balderston
Screen Adaptation by	Tod Browning
Playscript by	Garrett Fort
Added Dialogue by	Dudley Murphy
Art Director	Danny Hall
Photographer	Karl Freund
Film Editor	Milton Carruth
Editorial Supervision	Maurice Pivar
Sound Recording	C. Roy Hunter
Versions	All-Talking and Silent
Time	The Present

Thumbnail Theme

COUNT Dracula is a vampire, who has apparently died 500 years ago, but who retains the power, since he is buried in his own home soil, to rise from the grave each night and to assume several forms. He is one of the terrifying "undead."

Dracula secretly visits Lucy, a relative of Dr. Seward's daughter Mina, and finally changes her into a vampire. Dracula then transfers his horrible attentions to Mina. Van Helsing, a noted scientist, who is called in John Harker, Mina's fiancee, discovers that Dracula is a vampire, and does his best to counteract his influence. He is constantly baffled, however, through the fact that Mina is now almost completely in Dracula's power and the fact that Dracula is also assisted in his designs by the mad Renfield. So desperate is the situation that Mina even endangers Harker's safety.

Finally Dracula kidnaps Mina and carries her to Carfax Abbey. Following the escaped Renfield, Van Helsing and Harker discover the fugitives, and Dracula, thinking he has been betrayed by Renfield, strangles him to death before their eyes. As the sun rises, Dracula, powerless in the day, reclines in one of the boxes and sinks into insensibility. Here his pursuers add him and send him to permanent death.

Mina is released from further bondage, and she and Harker, now that her troubles at an end, go up out of the crypt.

For Your Program

THE next attraction at the .... Theatre is a motion picture which is absolutely in a class by itself.

It is "Dracula," a sensationally different, weird and startling story of life after death, and the strange human vampires who rise from their graves at night and bring terror to the hours of darkness.

The central character of this hair-raising story is Count Dracula, apparently a polished gentleman, but in reality a blood-thirsty vampire whose horrible attacks reduce his victims to madness or death. At length he centres his attentions on a beautiful young girl, and a famous scientist is brought from a foreign country in an effort to prevent her being forced into the strange Legion of the Undead.

Bela Lugosi and Edward Van Sloan, who appeared in the original stage production of "Dracula", were engaged by Universal to play the roles which they created, and other important parts are enacted by Helen Chandler, David Manners, Dwight Frye, Herbert Bunston, Frances Dade and Charles Gerrard. Tod Browning, who achieved fame through his long association with Lon Chaney, directed the picture.

Do not fail to see "Dracula". Everyone will soon be talking about this exotic, fantastic drama, which is creating a new milestone in the history of the talking screen.

The engagement opens on .... Theatre on ....

BELA LUGOSI in "DRACULA" UNIVERSAL SUPER-PRODUCTION
Scene Cut "C"

Who's Who in the Picture

IT is a singular fact that Bela Lugosi, who plays the title role in "Dracula", Universal's uncanny mystery drama scheduled to open an engagement at the .... Theatre on .... was born in the very neighborhood where the opening scenes of this weird story are laid. Lugosi is a native of Lugos, Hungary, a city which was originally named after his family.

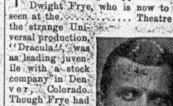

BELA LUGOSI
UNIVERSAL
Cut "E"

Making his stage debut at the age of 20 as "Romeo" in a Hungarian production of "Romeo and Juliet," Lugosi subsequently appeared in a repertoire of Shakespearean and other classics, finally becoming leading man at the Royal National Theatre in Budapest. Here he attained such popularity that he remained at the head of the company for ten years.

Coming to America at the close of the war, Lugosi organized a traveling Hungarian dramatic company, serving for four years as producer, director and star. His first appearance in English was in "The Red Poppy", and this was followed by a number of other plays. Finally, in 1927, he created the role of Count Dracula in "Dracula", and was starred in the play for more than two years.

His motion picture debut followed, and he appeared in important roles in such screen plays as "Prisoners", "The Thirteenth Chair", "Such Men Are Dangerous" and "Renegades." Then he was engaged by Universal for his original role in "Dracula".

DWIGHT FRYE
UNIVERSAL
Cut "H"

THE first stage appearance of Dwight Frye, who is now to be seen at the .... Theatre in the strange Universal production, "Dracula," as leading juvenile with a stock company in Denver, Colorado. Though Frye had frequently been offered small parts by O. D. Woodward, the manager, he was averse to appearing in "bits" in his home town, so he bided his time until he was offered the position on which he had set his mind. With this auspicious beginning, he remained with the Woodward company for more than two years.

He became one of the most versatile young actors of the American stage, having appeared in New York in roles ranging all the way from low comedy to high tragedy, in such plays as "A Man's Man", "The Love Habit", "Rita Coventry" and "Goat Song." In "Dracula" he is seen as the madman, Renfield.

EDWARD VAN SLOAN, who plays the role of Dr. Van Helsing in Universal's hair-raising drama of horrors, "Dracula," which comes to the .... Theatre on ...., was born in San Francisco, Cal., on November 1, 1885, and completed his education at the University of California at Berkeley. While still a college student he appeared weekly at San Francisco in plays given in German, under the direction of the professor of German dramatic literature at the University.

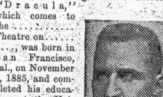

EDWARD VAN SLOAN
Cut "I"

Van Sloan's first professional appearance was in "Under the Greenwood Tree," and this was followed by a number of years of stock work in Montreal, Boston, Newark and other cities. Other plays in which he later played prominent roles were "Polly Preferred," "Maximilian and Juarez," "Morals," and "Schweiger." Van Sloan's role in the latter production they really held the attention for his appearance in the stage play, "Dracula", in which he created the role in which he is seen on the stage. Van Sloan appeared in the original New York production with Bela Lugosi, who is also seen in the screen version of this weird drama of horrors. "Dracula" is Van Sloan's first motion picture.

A MINIATURE theatre, constructed by David Manners when a child, indicated the intense interest in the stage that had already been acquired by the future actor, who comes to the .... Theatre on ...., as one of the leading roles of "Dracula", Universal's strange drama of human vampires. Manners was born in Halifax, Nova Scotia, on April 30, 1902, and completed his early education in his native city.

DAVID MANNERS
UNIVERSAL
Cut "F"

Then, thinking that to overcome his growing interest in the theatre, his parents sent him to the University of Toronto, but his four years at the college strengthened the very purpose which his parents had sought to defeat, for he became a leader in the university's Little Theatre movement.

Though he had graduated with the degree of bachelor of science in forestry, he went to New York and almost immediately secured a role in "Dancing Mothers", at the Maxine Elliott Theatre. Later he appeared with the Guild Theatre, but finally yielded to the wishes of his parents and entered business.

Happening to be in Hollywood in 1929, however, he was cast for a prominent role in "Journey's End", and found himself definitely committed to a motion picture career. Since then he has played important parts in "Kismet", "Mothers Cry", "The Right to Love" and other screen plays.

IF they hadn't passed drastic laws against race track gambling back in 1917, Helen Chandler might never have gone on the stage. For, though she was born in New York City, her parents took her in early babyhood to the Southern part of the United States, where her father, a breeder and racer of horses, was campaigning at all the Southern tracks. But when the anti-gambling laws were passed her father decided to go into another business, and the family moved to New York.

HELEN CHANDLER
Cut "G"

Here, at the age of eight, Helen began to play child roles on the stage, first appearing in five successive plays for Arthur Hopkins, and later supporting Marie Doro. Then she was with John Barrymore in "Richard III" and with Lionel Barrymore in "Macbeth", later creating the leading girl's role in Booth Tarkington's "Penrod". Among her roles after she had grown into young womanhood were Hedwig in "The Wild Duck," Ophelia in the modern-dress "Hamlet" and "Marguerite in Faust", while other plays in which she played important roles were "The Constant Nymph", "The Silver Cord", "Mr. Pim Passes By", and "The Marriage Bed".

Miss Chandler made her screen debut in 1926, appearing in "The Music Master", while among her subsequent talking pictures are "Salute", "Rough Romance", "Outward Bound" and "Mother's Cry." Now Miss Chandler is to be seen in the principal feminine role of "Dracula", Universal's sensational mystery drama which comes to the .... Theatre on ....

FRANCES DADE, born in Philadelphia on February 14, 1910, made her stage debut in 1926, when she was given an important role in a road company playing "Gentlemen Prefer Blondes". During an engagement in Los Angeles the young actress was seen by a prominent film director, and was promptly engaged for a part in "Grain Snatchers", which was then about to go into production. But while on her way to the studio Miss Dade was injured in an automobile accident, and when she was discharged from the hospital many weeks later the picture had been completed.

Returning East, Miss Dade played leading ingenue roles in stock companies in Toronto and in Ann Arbor, Michigan, and at the opening of the 1930 season was playing leading parts with a stock company at Birmingham, Alabama.

While in New York on her Christmas vacation, she was engaged for the leading feminine role in "Raffles", opposite Ronald Colman, and has also played prominent parts in "Grumpy" and "He Knew Women." Now Miss Dade is to be seen at the .... Theatre in one of the principal feminine roles in "Dracula", Universal's strange drama.

HERBERT BUNSTON, who plays the role of Dr. Seward in "Dracula", Universal's astounding mystery drama, now at the .... Theatre, was born in Dorsetshire, England, on October 21, 1870, and began his theatrical career in 1896, remaining on the stage in his native country until 1922, excepting only six months which he spent in the United States as a juvenile lead in "Drink".

Coming to America in 1922 to remain permanently, he has been seen in many prominent stage roles, including "Dracula", creating the role of Seward in the first production of the play in 1927.

Bunston made his screen debut in "The Last of Mrs. Cheyney". Other talking pictures in which he has been seen are "The Lady of Scandal", and "Old English".

Publicity "DRACULA" Scene Cuts

Lugosi At High Emotional Pitch in "Dracula" Role

Famous Actor Tells of Terrific Strain on Nervous System When He Played Vampire On Stage, Night After Night, For Years.

(Advance Story)

BELA LUGOSI never did learn to play "Dracula" mechanically. The famous Hungarian actor was starred in this strange play for more than two years, and during all that time he was worked up to a high pitch of emotional intensity which actually had a devastating effect on his health.

"After I had been in the play for a month," said Lugosi recently, "I began to 'take stock of myself', and I realized that for my own well-being I should make some attempt to conserve my mental and physical strength—to throw myself with less fervor into the depiction of the role. By that time I knew every inflection, every movement, every expression required of the character, and I decided that if I could go through the play somewhat mechanically—somewhat more placidly within myself—there would be no lessening of the effect of my performance on the audience, but a decided lessening of the effect on my own nervous system.

BELA LUGOSI in "DRACULA"
UNIVERSAL SUPER-PRODUCTION

Scene Cut "Q"

"But I could not do it. The role seemed to demand that I keep myself worked up to a fever pitch, and so I sat in my dressing room and took on, as nearly as possible, the actual attributes of the horrible vampire, Dracula. And during all those two years I did not speak a word to any person behind the scenes during the progress of the play. And, since everyone knew the strain I was laboring under, no one spoke to me. When I came off the stage after a scene I went silently to my dressing room, and did not emerge until it was again time for me to go on the stage. I was under a veritable spell which I dared not break. If I stepped out of my character for even a moment, the seething menace of the terrible Count Dracula was gone from the characterization, and my hold on the audience lost its force."

Lugosi recently spent many weeks at Universal Studios in California, where "Dracula" was made into a motion picture, including all the startling scenes which could only be talked about on the stage. This weird screen mystery opens an engagement at the .... Theatre on ...., with a cast which includes, in addition to Lugosi, Helen Chandler, David Manners, Edward Van Sloan, Dwight Frye, Frances Dade, Herbert Bunston, Joan Standing and Charles Gerrard. Tod Browning directed the filming of the picture.

"Dracula" Causes Sensation Among Picturegoers

(Closing Date Story)

THE entire city is gasping over "Dracula", Universal's strange drama which closes its run at the .... Theatre on .... night, and which has created a veritable sensation among local theatre-goers.

Never before, it is said, has the screen presented a story which exercises such a powerful effect on the emotions of the audience dealing as it does with the terrible depredations of a human vampire and his steadily mounting influence over the very lives of a group of people, combatted by the apparently hopeless efforts of a scientific physician.

Bela Lugosi, the famous Hungarian actor, is seen in the title role, and the cast also includes Edward Van Sloan and Herbert Bunston, who appeared with Lugosi in the original stage production of the play. "Dracula" was directed by Tod Browning.

"MIKE" PERFECTED FOR TALKING FILMS

Recording of Scenes for Big Pictures Like "Dracula" Now Achieved with Maximum of Efficiency

(Advance Story)

THE microphone as perfected for the making of talking pictures is one of the most sensitive and most delicately attuned mechanical instruments ever invented.

Though this is not generally recognized by the layman, the fact is becoming increasingly apparent to studio workers, even though they have become more or less familiar with the apparatus. The constant improvement of the "mike", and the consequent widening of its range, continually astounds even those who are best acquainted with its workings. It is no longer necessary for the actor to stand directly underneath the microphone, since "lines" spoken in an ordinary conversational tone many feet from the instrument are perfectly "picked up" and reproduced.

It is this fact, indeed, which has added immeasurably to the flexibility of the talking picture, and has entirely done away with the stiltedness of which many critics complained in the early days of the talkies.

There have been many stories of airplane exhausts and frog croaks interfering with the proper recording of scenes, but nothing better illustrates this sensitiveness of the microphone than an incident which happened during the filming of "Dracula", Universal's strange drama which comes to the .... Theatre on ....

Even though there were no "mikes" within many feet of a fireplace used in certain scenes of the picture, the very slight roar of the blaze was "picked up" by the instruments to such an extent that it was necessary to postpone the filming of the scenes until the fire had died down.

Bela Lugosi, the original Dracula of the stage production, plays the title role in this startling picture, and Edward Van Sloan, the original Dr. Van Helsing of the stage, also repeats his role on the screen. Other players appearing in important roles are Helen Chandler, David Manners, Dwight Frye, Herbert Bunston, Frances Dade and Charles Gerrard. "Dracula" was directed by Tod Browning, famous as the director of many of Lon Chaney's weird stories.

—Drawn by the Noted Artist, John Rogers

Bela Lugosi in "Dracula", Universal Super-Production

Scene Cut "S"

—Drawn by the Noted Artist, John Rogers

Bela Lugosi in "Dracula", Universal Super-Production

Scene Cut "T"

"Dracula", Greatest Film Made By Director of Chaney Pictures

(Advance Story)

TOD BROWNING is Hollywood's leading collector of skeletons. As the motion picture's leading director of weird, fantastic stories — morbid tales of strange lands and stranger happenings—there is not merely a skeleton in Browning's closet, as the saying is. There are many.

For many years he has directed, as well as written, most of the screen stories in which the late Lon Chaney has appeared, and he has become famous throughout the industry as the creator of some of the weirdest characters in the fiction of filmdom. "The Unholy Three", that strange story of thieves, is one of them; "The Unknown", dealing with the adventures of an armless man in a traveling gypsy circus, is another; still another is "London After Midnight", in which members of a vaudeville act are engaged to impersonate human vampires, and bring to the story an atmosphere of intense creepiness. Another of Browning's productions, though one in which Chaney did not appear, was "The Thirteenth Chair", involving a "spooky" seance, with dead men in the circle.

But now the director has just completed the filming of "Dracula", which far exceeds the others in the strangeness of its story.

"The character of Count Dracula", says Browning, "is by all odds the weirdest character in fiction. To the screen is brought a strange 'undead' creature—a man neither living nor dead, and bringing death and madness to his victims. Alive and active during the hours of darkness, the coming of daylight returns Dracula until sunset to a temporary death from which he can only rise if he has lain in a casket filled with his own native earth.

"It is a terrifying story, and it is presented with such sincerity and with such an assumption of truth that it exercises a most powerful effect on the emotions of the spectator. The audience watches it frozen with horror, but so fascinated that even those who faint insist on returning to the auditorium to see the conclusion of the picture.

"'Dracula', in short, among all the motion pictures which have been shown since the inception of the industry, is absolutely in a class by itself, since it is the only picture dealing seriously with this strange subject of vampires. In fantastic horror it far exceeds anything that Chaney ever did during his lifetime, and takes its place at once as the most unusual production in the history of the screen.

"The original novel was written by Bram Stoker, an Englishman, and the stage play based on the story was given its first presentation in New York City in 1927. And now the screen presents this hair-raising tale with a wealth of detail and a dramatic intensity which makes of 'Dracula' one of the outstanding productions of the year."

Local theatregoers will have an opportunity to see this strangest of all motion pictures when "Dracula" opens an engagement at the.......... Theatre on........, with a cast which includes three members of the original stage company—Bela Lugosi, as Count Dracula; Edward Van Sloan, as Dr. Van Helsing; and Herbert Bunston, as Dr. Seward. Other members of the screen cast are Helen Chandler, Dwight Frye, David Manners, Joan Standing, Frances Dade, Charles Gerrard and Moon Carroll.

EXACTLY one year after the day on which he did his first motion picture work, David Manners was engaged by Universal on "Dracula", the strange mystery drama which is now the attraction at the .... Theatre.

Manners made his screen debut in "Journey's End" in 1929, and has since appeared in a number of important productions, including "Kismet", "Mothers Cry" and "The Right to Love."

For a short time Manners appeared on the stage, but abandoned it four years ago to take up a business career.

The cast of "Dracula", which includes Bela Lugosi, Helen Chandler, David Manners, Edward Van Sloan, Dwight Frye, Herbert Bunston, Frances Dade, Charles Gerrard and Joan Standing.

CURRENT NOTES

A NEW noise has arisen to assail the sensitive ears of the microphone. Frogs, airplanes and various other noise makers of greater or less degree have at times interfered with the production of sound pictures, but no one ever expected that a grate fire would be added to the list until Director Tod Browning was on the point of making a scene at Universal Studios during the filming of "Dracula", the strange mystery drama which opened an engagement at the .... Theatre on ....

A log fire blazed merrily in a gigantic fireplace which formed a part of a set representing an enormous room in a crumbling stone castle, and though the microphones were hung at a considerable distance away, the sound technician promptly brought work to a standstill. "Too much roar in that fire," he said.

And so Bela Lugosi and Dwight Frye, who were to appear in the scene, sat around on the stage for a while, waiting for the fire to die down.

HELEN CHANDLER simply refuses to grow up! Since the little blonde actress went to Hollywood three years ago, the entire film colony has united in assuring her that she still seemed like a little girl. But since Helen has reached the ripe old age of 21, and had spent 13 years as an actress, she was inclined to consider herself a grown-up lady.

But when she recently arrived at the Universal "lot" to begin filming of "Dracula", in which she plays the leading feminine role, she had an experience which convinced her that perhaps she did not look so grown up, after all. Montagu Love, who was just completing his role in "The Cat Creeps", accosted her as she walked across the lot. "Aren't you the little girl", he asked, "who worked in a picture with me at the Fort Lee Studio 12 years ago?"

And she was! The picture was "The Cross Bearer", directed by Ralph Ince, and at that time Helen was nine years old!

Miss Chandler plays the leading feminine role in "Dracula", Universal's weird vampire drama which is now at the .... Theatre on ...., with a cast which also includes Bela Lugosi, Edward Van Sloan, Dwight Frye, Frances Dade, Herbert Bunston and Joan Standing. Tod Browning directed this unusual picture, which is based on the famous novel of the same name by Bram Stoker.

A MOTION picture director — speechless! Such a condition presents a strange picture to the mind, because directors have always been regarded as somewhat loquacious individuals, who kept up a running fire of suggestions and instructions to the actors during the progress of a scene. But the advent of the talking picture has accomplished the impossible—it has placed the seal of silence on the director.

For while a scene in a sound picture is actually being filmed, there must be absolutely no sounds except those which may properly be heard when the picture is exhibited in a theatre. During the progress of a scene, if it is necessary for the director to indicate the proper time for any particular speech or action, he must do so by motions or by flashing a tiny red light placed well out of sight of the cameras. And so, except for the speech of the cameras, the sound stage is as hushed and silent as the grave.

The latest talking picture, and one that is said to be one of the most remarkable productions in the annals of the screen, is "Dracula", the strange mystery drama which has just been completed by Universal, and which is playing at the .... Theatre on ...., with a cast ncluding Bela Lugosi, Helen Chandler, David Manners, Dwight Frye, Edward Van Sloan and Frances Dade. Tod Browning directed.

They Always Gasp When They Meet Bela Lugosi, Star of "Dracula"

(Advance Story)

THEY always gasp when they meet Bela Lugosi! For years Lugosi played on the stage a sinister vampire, Count Dracula, in the stage play of "Dracula," and the character was maintained at such a high pitch of dramatic intensity that he came to be looked upon by theatregoers as really a strange being of the most horrible description. This reputation clung to him outside the theatre, since the artistry of his performance created an effect on the audience that was not dissipated at the close of the performance.

And so when the actor was presented socially to some person, either male or female, there always came that little catch in the throat, and some such exclamation as, "Oh! You're Dracula."

The polished, kindly gentleman, smiling his shy, warm smile, has ceased to be surprised at such a reception, but he is inclined to regret it a tiny bit.

"Always they gasp!" he says with his slight Hungarian accent. "For a few moments they fear me a little, I think, but soon I think, too, that they begin to like me. I want them to, because, really, I am only bad when I have my makeup on."

Lugosi comes to the .... Theatre on .... in the title role of "Dracula," produced by Universal, and boasting a cast which includes Helen Chandler, David Manners, Dwight Frye, Frances Dade and Edward Van Sloan. Tod Browning Directed.

HELEN CHANDLER, EDWARD VAN SLOAN and DAVID MANNERS in "DRACULA" UNIVERSAL SUPER-PRODUCTION

Scene Cut "R"

HELEN CHANDLER and BELA LUGOSI in "DRACULA"
UNIVERSAL SUPER-PRODUCTION

Scene Cut "U"

Talking Pictures More Natural Than "Silents", Says Director

(Advance Story)

SCREEN actors have again become natural. This is the declaration of Tod Browning, one of the industry's most successful directors of strange and unusual motion pictures.

"Up to two or three years ago," said Browning recently, "film actors were entirely natural, and perfectly at home in the environment. They had thoroughly mastered screen technique—which, by the way, differs very materially from the technique of the stage. Even though the actor must always go through his action with the location and limitations of the camera in mind, there was nothing to indicate that he even realized its existence.

"Then came the talking picture, introducing a new feature which must be kept constantly in mind—the microphone. On account of the mechanical limitations of the earlier instruments, and the limited field of their reception, the actor could only speak his "lines" at some particular point or points on the "stage", or "set", instead of being allowed the latitude that had always been possible in the silent picture. As a result there came a certain restraint on the part of the film player, and there was even a tendency to glance upward, to make sure that he was standing in the proper place.

"But now, through growing familiarity with the new medium, as well as the perfection of the microphone, with the heightening of its sensitiveness and the consequent widening of its field, the actor is again moving about naturally. Relieved of the necessity of literally toeing a mark, he is free to give his entire thought to the playing of his role, and this fact has brought a vast change in the quality of acting on the talking screen. The talking picture now displays a smoothness and an unconscious precision which were never exceeded in any silent picture ever made."

Tod Browning was the director of "Dracula," Universal's startling drama of human vampires and their strange life after death which comes to the .... Theatre on........, with a cast which includes, Bela Lugosi, Helen Chandler, David Manners, Edward Van Sloan, Dwight Frye, Frances Dade, Herbert Bunston, Joan Standing and Charles Gerrard.

Famous Scientist in "Dracula" Besieged with Strange Queries

(Advance Story)

"HOW long does the soul live after death? What is the secret of the apparently genuine visitations from my sister, who has been dead for more than 40 years?"

This is the sort of question that has been continually asked of Edward Van Sloan during the past three years, and all because he has been playing the *role of the scientific Dr. Van Helsing* in the weird stage play, "Dracula," which has just been made into a motion picture by Universal, and which comes to the .... Theatre on .... Depicted thus as a learned scientist, he has been bombarded with a constant stream of letters which give him credit for the deepest occult knowledge of those things about which human beings really know nothing, and he has been at considerable pains to acquit himself according to the ideas of those who know him in his fictitious character of Van Helsing, and not in his true person of Van Sloan.

"I appreciate the confidence of those who have written to me in the past three years," says Van Sloan. "Surely one could do no less. But the reason that I have not attempted to offer any solutions of the many problems which have been presented to me is simply this: I just did not know! I have been merely an actor playing a part, and while I have gone somewhat deeply into the subject of *my role, I have been groping, as have many members of my audience, in an* attempt to find a solution of many of life's strange and perplexing problems.

"And now that I am appearing as the same scientific doctor in the screen version of 'Dracula', I suppose that my particular type of fan mail will show a great—and rather disconcerting—increase."

In addition to Van Sloan, the cast of "Dracula" includes Bela Lugosi, Helen Chandler, David Manners, Dwight Frye, Frances Dade, Herbert Bunston, Joan Standing and Charles Gerrard. Tod Browning, famous director of unusual screen stories, wielded the megaphone.

Bela Lugosi Haunted By Role He Made Famous in "Dracula"

(Advance Story)

ONE of the most famous of all actors on stage or screen would like to forget the character that made him famous! Audiences on Broadway were thrilled for more than two years by his artistry; millions of picture fans throughout the country are being fascinated by the startling impersonation he gives on the screen. But the character haunts him, and he never wants to play it again.

The actor is Bela Lugosi, and the character is Count Dracula in the most startling of all plays or pictures—"Dracula". Bram Stoker, the famous English novelist, wrote it first as a novel—this terrifying narration of an "undead" being who rises from his grave at night and through his horrible influence brings death and suffering to his victims.

For more than a thousand nights, Lugosi played it in the theatre. Then when the Universal Studios decided to produce the great story as a picture, Lugosi was the natural choice for the role he had made so famous on the stage.

At first, it was difficult to prevail upon him to appear on the screen. He had lived with the horrible vampire character so long on the stage that he wanted to forget, and how could he forget if he played it again on the screen?

But he finally consented, and for weeks at the Universal City studios while the picture was in production, he lived again the startling, fantastic role of Count Dracula. Those who have seen both play and picture assert that his impersonation for the films is even greater than his stage work.

But, now that the picture is finished and shortly to be shown at the .... Theatre, Lugosi says he will never play the role again.

And Lugosi's determination is in itself a great tribute to his ability as an actor. If he had been able to act the part mechanically — had not thrown himself heart and soul into the role—it would not have the terrors that it now has. But a great artist does not play mechanically, and Lugosi is a great artist. Thus, each night in the theatre and for many days at the picture studios, his nervous system has been subjected to a terrible strain.

"Dracula" brought him fame and fortune, but Lugosi wants, more than anything else, to escape from Count Dracula.

It is well, however, that he did not reach this decision before the making of the picture—well for the millions of fans who will be fascinated by his great work on the screen.

When "Dracula" is shown at the .... Theatre, local theatregoers will see one of the most remarkable casts ever assembled. Besides Lugosi, two other players of the original stage cast appear—Edward Van Sloan and Herbert Bunston. In addition, there are many other favorites, including David Manners, Helen Chandler, Dwight Frye, Frances Dade, Charles Gerrard and Joan Standing. Tod Browning, creator of weird and unusual films, directed the picture.

BELA LUGOSI in "DRACULA"
UNIVERSAL SUPER-PRODUCTION

Scene Cut "V"

...ighty "DRACUL...

"Dracula", Supreme Film Mystery Scores Sensation At Premiere Here

Audiences Enthralled at Unfolding of Weird Events on Talking Screen—Production, Dealing with Human Vampires, Absolutely Unique— Famous Novel and Play Put Into Pictures.

GREAT CAST INTERPRETS POWERFUL STORY

(Review)

A STRANGE, weird motion picture that outdoes all previous mysteries of the screen is "Dracula", the startling Universal production which opened an engagement at the................ Theatre yesterday, and scored a sensational success.

It may safely be said that this story is distinctly in a class by itself, and that its subject matter is absolutely unique among film productions. For "Dracula", which was adapted from Bram Stoker's famous novel of the same name, deals with human vampires, which ancient superstition describes as horrible "undead" creatures who rise from their graves at night.

Whether or not you believe in this major premise of the story, you will be enthralled by its presentation on the screen. The entire picture is done with such artistry and such compelling sincerity that while the story is unfolding on the screen one can hardly fail to regard its incidents as true representations of actual occurrences. It is as powerful in its effect on the emotions of the audience as any picture we can recall.

Great is the power of illusion. This was never better illustrated than in "Dracula".

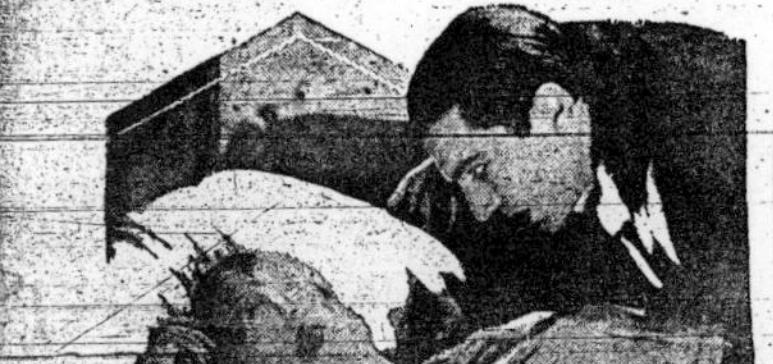

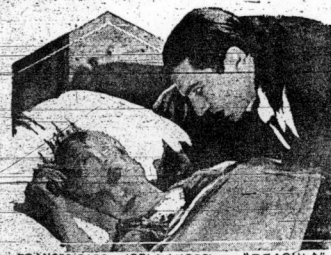

FRANCES DADE and BELA LUGOSI in "DRACULA"
UNIVERSAL SUPER-PRODUCTION

Scene Cut "K"

On leaving the theatre the audience knows that it cannot be true, and yet while the story is unfolding on the screen the spectators sit enthralled by its gruesome horrors. Their belief, temporary though it may be, is indicated by the powerful manner in which the picture affects them. Indeed, it is stated that no other motion picture ever made equals this in its hold on the emotions of the audience—which, perhaps, is a compliment to the artistry with which the film was produced.

Scenically, "Dracula" is magnificent, and its settings fully preserve the thrillingly uncanny atmosphere of the story.

The title role of Count Dracula is played with remarkable effect by Bela Lugosi, who created the same part in the stage play, and who delivers an arresting performance as the sinister vampire who is the central character of the story. Helen Chandler is altogether charming and capable in the principal feminine part, and David Manners, as her fiancé, does the type of work which has made him one of the most popular of leading men. Other members of the cast who contribute outstanding characterizations are Edward Van Sloan, Dwight Frye, Frances Dade and Herbert Bunston. Van Sloan and Bunston, by the way, are seen in roles which they created in the stage play, when they appeared in company with Lugosi.

Great credit is due Tod Browning, director of "Dracula", and for many years director, as well as author, of many of Lon Chaney's most successful productions. Browning has maintained a sinister atmosphere to a remarkable degree and has turned out by long odds the best picture he ever made. Browning and Garret Fort prepared the screen play and dialogue.

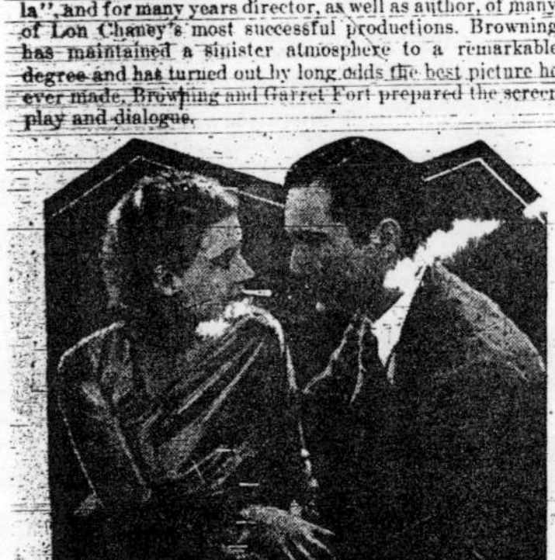

HELEN CHANDLER and DAVID MANNERS in "DRACULA"
UNIVERSAL SUPER-PRODUCTION

Scene Cut "L"

50 Enormous Bats In New Mystery Film

FIFTY enormous bats, those strange flapping creatures of the night, were recently taken to Universal City for use in a number of scenes of "Dracula," the amazing drama which comes to the ________ Theatre on ________, with a cast which includes the famous Bela Lugosi, the original Dracula of the stage play.

The bats were captured in a great cave in Nevada by three residents of Las Vegas, who made an expedition into the nearby hill region when an emissary of Universal arrived in town with the strangest order ever delivered into the desert country.

It is interesting to note that for two months Universal City qualified as the only place in the world where a large number of giant bats were being maintained in captivity.

In addition to Lugosi, the cast of "Dracula" includes Helen Chandler, David Manners, Edward Van Sloan, Dwight Frye, Frances Dade and Herbert Bunston. Tod Browning directed this sensationally new mystery play.

CURRENT NOTES

PERHAPS no other actor in the history of the American theatre has become so associated in the minds of the public with a character he has played on the stage as Bela Lugosi, who created the title role of Count Dracula when the strange vampire play, "Dracula", was first produced in New York, and who has since been seen in the character in every important city in the United States. By most theatregoers his own personality has been entirely overlooked, and he has seemed actually to be Dracula, the most terrible vampire of Central Europe. The screen version of this hair-raising story, just completed by Universal, is now showing at the........ Theatre, with Lugosi in his original role.

ONE of the most valuable books in Hollywood is used in one of the early scenes of "Dracula", Universal's uncanny vampire drama which is now playing at the............ Theatre. This treasured volume, which was borrowed from a noted collector of the film capital, is an enormous medical book printed in Latin, and makes its appearance in a scene laid in the laboratory of Dr. Van Helsing, the scientific doctor of the story. The book was printed in the year 1652, and is in a remarkable state of preservation.

"THE Last of Mrs. Cheyney" marked one of the most successful stage appearances of Herbert Bunston, the noted English actor, and it was in the screen version of this same play that he made his motion picture debut. Bunston is now to be seen at the............ Theatre in Universal's strange vampire drama, "Dracula", in the same role which he created on the stage when "Dracula" was first produced in New York in 1927. Others who appear in this startling screen drama are Bela Lugosi and Edward Van Sloan, who also were members of the original stage cast.

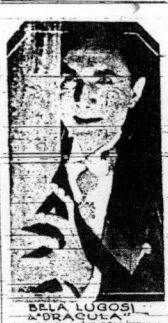

LUGOS, Hungaria, was the birthplace of Bela Lugosi, the noted actor who plays the title role in "Dracula", Universal's strange drama now playing at the............ Theatre. Lugosi's ancestors, a long line of noblemen, formerly owned many thousands of acres of farm land, where the the city now stands, and the original settlement at this point was built to accommodate the large number of servants on the estate. Gradually the hamlet grew to larger proportions, until the city of Lugos now boasts a population of more than 50,000 people.

A SEVERE concussion of the brain marked the screen debut of Frances Dade, the blonde young actress who is now to be seen at the .... Theatre, in one of the principal feminine roles of "Dracula", Universal's weird story of human vampires. On her way to a Hollywood studio to start work in her first role, in "Cradle Snatchers", Miss Dade suffered an automobile accident which sent her to a hospital for a period of eight weeks. When she was finally discharged from the institution, the picture was finished and on its way to New York.

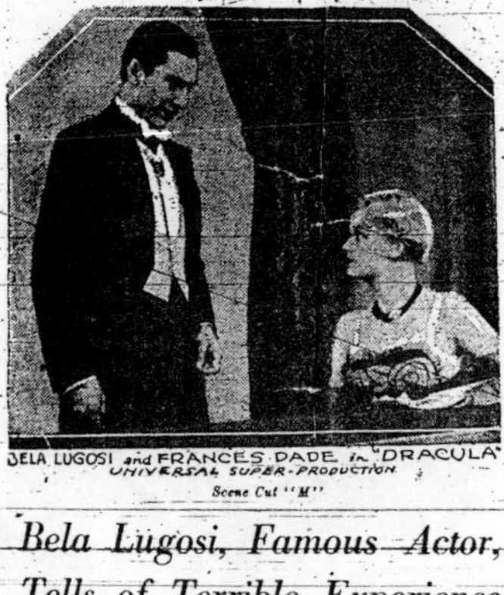

BELA LUGOSI and FRANCES DADE in "DRACULA"
UNIVERSAL SUPER-PRODUCTION

Scene Cut "M"

Bela Lugosi, Famous Actor, Tells of Terrible Experience With Actual Human Vampire

THE strangest creature in America is living today in Hollywood, surrounded by a brooding atmosphere of horror and madness. A tall, straight figure of a man, he goes among his fellows with a strange aloofness that marks him as a man apart. Unfathomable thoughts gleam behind his deep-set eyes, and on his throat he bears two tiny wounds that prove a terrible attack by a human vampire.

Bela Lugosi is the name of this strangest of men, a Hungarian born amid the black, mysterious mountains where vampires take a heavy toll among the natives, and the whole countryside lives in terror of the night. For it is only after sunset that these strange undead creatures rise from their graves.

Lugosi is loath to discuss his terrifying experience in his native land. "It is all a terrible nightmare which I am destined never to forget," he says, "until a certain woman in Hungary shall go to a peaceful and lasting death. She is an actress with no more than usual amount of feminine charm, but many men are her abject slaves, because within her smoulders the burning flame of the vampires.

"It was her sharply pointed teeth which made these wounds in my throat, and it was her unspoken but irresistible commands which caused me to visit her again and again. At length my mother noticed that I was rapidly losing weight, and she soon divined the cause. I had fallen under the influence of a vampire. Shortly afterward, at my mother's insistence, I fled the country—and I shall probably never go back.

"But even now I dare not sleep at night. This is the time when we feel the thought impulses of the vampires, and I dare not lose consciousness during the hours of darkness. With a light burning low in my bedroom, I read and pace the floor—and think. If I rest at all, it must be during the day.

"I had been an actor in Hungary, and when I fled to New York one of the first parts offered me was the role of Count Dracula in the play, 'Dracula', which was then about to be produced for the first time. And, most strangely, this story dealt with the very subject which has caused me to leave my native country—vampires of the night, and the strange Legion of the Undead. Possibly because I was so strongly drawn to the subject, and had not been able to escape from the menace which constantly hung over me, I took the part, and appeared in the play for more than two years. Literally fascinated by the role, I lived in another world, and I actually seemed to have become Dracula himself.

"And when I learned that Tod Browning was at Universal to make 'Dracula' into a talking picture, this strange fascination drew me to the studio. I have played the role on the screen, and I often sit in dark theatres, watching, and wondering if the sinister character in the picture is Bela Lugosi—or Dracula."

The cast of "Dracula", which comes to the................ Theatre on ...., also includes Helen Chandler, David Manners, Edward Van Sloan, Dwight Frye, Frances Dade, Herbert Bunston, Joan Standing, and Charles Gerrard.

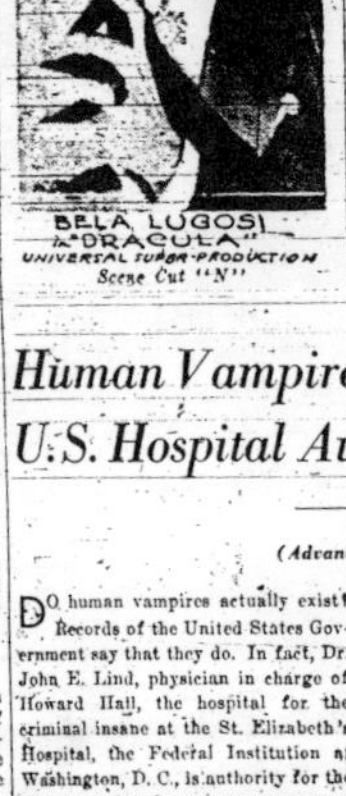

BELA LUGOSI in "DRACULA"
UNIVERSAL SUPER-PRODUCTION

Scene Cut "N"

Human Vampires Actually Exist, U.S. Hospital Authority Declares

(Advance Story)

DO human vampires actually exist? Records of the United States Government say that they do. In fact, Dr. John E. Lind, physician in charge of Howard Hall, the hospital for the criminal insane at the St. Elizabeth's Hospital, the Federal Institution at Washington, D. C., is authority for the statement that for many years a vampire has been one of the inmates—a sailor.

Thus a measure of credibility is given to "Dracula" Universal's strange drama based on Bram Stoker's famous novel, and scheduled to open an engagement at the .... Theatre on................ Count Dracula, the central character of the story, is a vampire, and his attacks on other persons in the story are the means of forcing them, too, into the terrible Legion of the "Undead."

Three members of the original cast of the stage play, in the persons of Bela Lugosi, Edward Van Sloan and Herbert Bunston, appear in the screen version, while other important roles are played by Helen Chandler, David Manners, Frances Dade, Dwight Frye and Joan Standing. Tod Browning directed "Dracula", the screen adaptation of which was written by Garrett Fort, and Mr. Browning with added dialogue by Dudley Murphy.

SAYS 90 [...] ARE M[...]

Tod Browning, Director of "Dracula", Supreme Mystery Film, Finds Most People Are Lured by the Fantastic.

(Advance Story)

"NINETY per cent of the people are morbid minded!" This is the sharp declaration of Tod Browning who as director of the late Lon Chaney filmed more weird, fantastic motion pictures than any other man in the industry.

"I have set an arbitrary figure at 90 per cent," says Browning, "But I am not sure that the average should not be higher. O. Henry once remarked that more people would gather to look at a dead horse in the street than would assemble to watch the finest coach pass by, and this homely observation comes very close to representing the actual fact.

"An automobile accident brings great numbers of people running to the scene, and the more horrible the accident the greater the crowd attracted. This is simply another illustration of the morbid curiosity which animates a large proportion of our population. Women rush to the scene of the accident, well knowing that they will faint if the catastrophe happens to be a particularly bloody one. It is probably a fact that more fainting spectators are carried away from automobile accidents than injured participants, but this does not deter those who are attracted to the scene simply by morbid curiosity.

"The strangest, most morbid motion picture I have ever directed is one which I have just completed, and which presents in its principal role what is undoubtedly the weirdest character in fiction. The play is 'Dracula', and the terrible being around whom the strange events of the story revolve is Count Dracula, an 'undead' creature of the night, roving in search of victims during the hours of darkness, and literally dead in his coffin from sunrise to sunset. This character is played by Bela Lugosi, the noted Hungarian actor who created the same role when the stage version of Bran Stoker's strange novel was first produced in New York in 1927."

...............(City) will have an opportunity of seeing "Dracula" on the screen when this remarkable motion picture, one of the most elaborate productions the screen has known, comes to the................. Theatre on............., with a cast which includes not only Lugosi himself, but a large number of popular players, such as Helen Chandler, Edward Van Sloan, Dwight Frye, David Manners, Frances Dade, Herbert Bunston, Joan Standing, Charles Gerrard and Moon Carroll.

GIGANTIC COBWEB BUILT FOR PICTURE

Filmy Fabric 18 Feet in Diameter Constructed by Novel Method for "Dracula", Weird Mystery-Drama.

THE world's largest spider web, a great filmy fabric 18 feet in diameter, is seen in "Dracula", Universal's strange vampire drama which comes to the............ Theatre on ....

This gigantic cobweb, entirely fills the grand stairway in the ancient stone castle of Count Dracula—a magnificent pile, hundreds of years old, which has fallen into ruin and decay. And it is through this great web that Dracula, vampire, walks at will without harming it.

The construction of this artificial cobweb is most interesting, illustrating as it does the uncanny artistry of studio technical departments. After long experimenting it was found that rubber cement, if drawn out to filmy fineness, exactly simulated cobwebs, and there remained only the necessity of finding some method of reducing the sticky material to the form of delicate threads. This finally brought about the invention of a sort of rotary gun, electrically operated, which expels the cement in such a filmy form that it is almost invisible as it comes out. The magazine having been filmed with rubber cement, then, it is only necessary for the operator to turn on the current, point the gun at the desired spot, and within a few seconds an apparently genuine cobweb begins to form.

Though this entire set in the picture is festooned with cobwebs, in only this largest one was it necessary to construct an artificial framework on which to hang the filmy threads.

The cast of "Dracula", which was directed by Tod Browning, includes Bela Lugosi, Helen Chandler, David Manners, Edward Van Sloan, Dwight Frye, Frances Dade and Herbert Bunston.

HELEN CHANDLER, who plays the leading feminine role in "Dracula", Universal's strange drama which comes to the.......... Theatre on ...., divides her spare time between reading and writing, perusing biographies and novels when she is not writing short stories and poems. At the present time she is even engaged in the writing of a full length novel, which she hopes to complete within a few months.

TOD BROWNING, director of "Dracula," Universal's weird drama which comes to the.......... Theatre on............, has long specialized in writing and directing strange stories for the screen, usually with Lon Chaney as the star. Among Browning's productions during the past few years have been "The Unholy Three", and recently Universal's "Outside the Law" with Mary Nolan. But "Dracula" is said to excel them all in the amazing strangeness of its story.

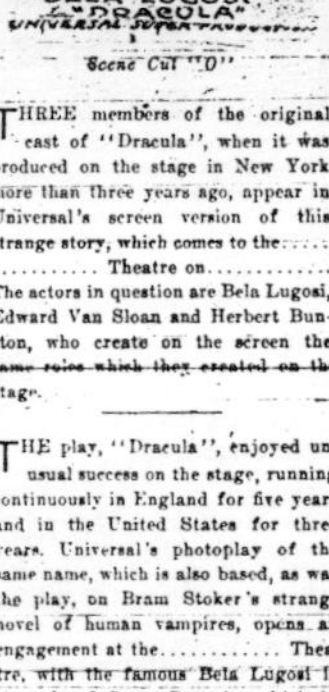

BELA LUGOSI in "DRACULA"
UNIVERSAL SUPER-PRODUCTION

Scene Cut "O"

THREE members of the original cast of "Dracula", when it was produced on the stage in New York more than three years ago, appear in Universal's screen version of this strange story, which comes to the........... Theatre on.............. The actors in question are Bela Lugosi, Edward Van Sloan and Herbert Bunston, who create on the screen the same roles which they created on the stage.

THE play, "Dracula", enjoyed unusual success on the stage, running continuously in England for five years and in the United States for three years. Universal's photoplay of the same name, which is also based, as was the play, on Bram Stoker's strange novel of human vampires, opens an engagement at the............ Theatre, with the famous Bela Lugosi in the role of Count Dracula, which he created when the stage play was first presented in America.

EDWARD VAN SLOAN, who plays the role of Dr. Van Helsing in "Dracula", Universal's weird vampire screen play which comes to the .... theatre on............, is never happier than when engaged in some intricate bit of cabinet making. Van Sloan comes by his ability naturally, since his mother—(strange as it may seem)—is an accomplished cabinet maker, and mother and son often engage in arguments over the respective merits of this or that type of mortise. Completing the chain, Mrs. Van Sloan's father was a carpenter by trade.

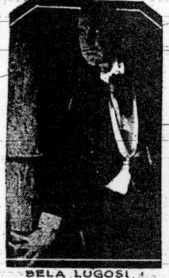

HERBERT BUNSTON, the Engli[sh] actor who is seen as Dr. Seward [in] the Universal screen production "Dracula", the strange tale of va[m]pires which comes to the.......... Theatre on..............., was bo[rn] in Dorsetshire on Trafalgar D[ay] (October 21), one of the historic En[g]lish holidays and almost the equiv[a]lent of the Fourth of July in t[he] United States. And so each year [on] Bunston's birthday, the entire Briti[sh] Empire is decorated with Union Jac[ks] and bunting, and the actor is greet[ed] on every hand by vociferous cheeri[ng] and salutes of big guns.

TWO years ago David Manners, w[ho] comes to the .... Theat[re] on........... in Universal's stran[ge] drama, "Dracula", contracted [a] severe case of pneumonia, and on [his] recovery went to Arizona to convalesc[e]. There he became a guide on a "du[de] ranch", and spent several months pointing out "the sights" to parti[es] of enthusiastic tourists. Manners ma[r]ried in Arizona, and he and his bri[de] started for Honolulu on their hone[y]moon. Stopping off in Los Angele[s] Manners was given a role in his fir[st] motion picture—and he has been in t[he] studios ever since. The honeymoon [is] still in the future.

THOUGH Bram Stoker's weird nov[el], "Dracula", was written man[y] years before Bela Lugosi first we[nt] on the stage, the title role is one whic[h] seems to have been written to orde[r] for the actor. Lugosi was born in a[l]most the exact spot in Hungary wher[e] the earlier scenes of the story are lai[d] and thus his slight Hungarian accen[t] in Universal's screen production o[f] this strange book is exactly "in char[]acter". "Dracula" comes to the... ....Theatre on ...., wit[h] Lugosi in the same fascinating rol[e] which he created on the stage.

"DRACULA", Bram Stoker's nov[el] on which is based Universal['s] weird screen story of vampires an[d] their terrifying life after death, [is] one of the most popular books in th[e] realm of fiction. Though originall[y] published many years ago, the yearl[y] sales of this fascinating volume ave[]rage 40,000 copies. "Dracula", wit[h] Bela Lugosi in the title role, opens a[n] engagement on.............. at th[e] .... Theatre.

DAVID MANNERS, who will soo[n] appear at the .... Theatre in the strange Universal pic[]ture, "Dracula", evinced an intens[e] interest in the stage when he was [a] young boy, and built a miniature thea[]tre, with many changes of scenery, an[d] puppets to represent the players [in] various stage productions he had seen. In addition to dramatic plays, he ha[d] settings and puppets for several com[]plete operas.

THOUGH born in San Francisco, th[e] first stage experience of Edwa[rd] Van Sloan, noted actor, was in Ge[r]man, and he appeared for three yea[rs] as an amateur in German plays pro[]duced weekly in his native city, unde[r] the direction of the professor of Ge[r]man dramatic literature at the Un[i]versity of California. Appearing [in] his first motion picture, Van Sloan [is] now to be seen as Dr. Van Helsin[g] in "Dracula", Universal's strang[e] play of horror's which is coming [to] the .... Theatr[e]

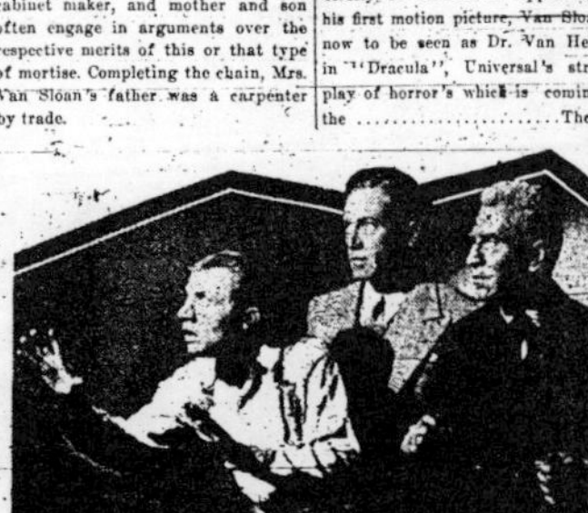

DWIGHT FRYE, DAVID MANNERS and EDWARD VAN SLOAN in "DRACULA" UNIVERSAL SUPER-PRODUCTION

Scene Cut "P"

The LAST WORD

DRACULA

● DIRECTED by Tod Browning for Universal Pictures Corporation.

The kind of a picture it is and how it should be sold .. a synopsis of the story and exploitation angles that should be avoided.

● FOR its entertainment this picture depends upon thrills and "horror" situations. Very little stress is placed on the love story .. the whole hinging on Dracula .. who, though dead for five hundred years .. comes back every night after sun-down .. seeking human blood.

A picture of creeps .. chills and all those other adjectives that have been used to designate productions of this type.

Of course, the picture has been treated in its advertising for just what it is.

We had noticed some talk in the trade press that this picture was going to be roadshowed in the east .. it is our humble opinion it has the entertainment qualities to push it over as a special .. it is not playing any of our ace spots here in Los Angeles .. while it must be admitted it is a thriller .. still there are spots where it sags and takes it out of the big class .. or even the semi top class.

There are those, however, who are going to find this mighty fine entertainment. Fortunately, the gruesome scenes where Dracula sucks the blood from the necks of his victim have been suggested .. and not actually shown.

In any event .. play it for a thriller .. a picture that will give them the chills .. that will make their spine tingle.

The play was a big success on the stage .. running for several years.

● THE exchange has prepared .. according to the list issued by the Universal company .. a line of paper in both large and smaller sizes that carries out the theme of the production .. suggesting mystery .. playing on the thrilling situations.

Undoubtedly it will be possible to make cut-outs for marquee display of the bats and vampires given on this paper .. it will also be a chance to use blue lights .. in your lobby .. around your border .. to give a ghost-like appearance to your lobby .. You will want to create an eerie atmosphere in and about the theatre.

● THIS is hardly classed as a child's picture .. we would not attempt any contest among school children .. it is a bit too nightmarish.

Your best bets are your own screen .. your lobby and the newspapers .. and of course .. your posters where they can be used to advantage.

We believe, however .. that one of the strongest mediums is your own screen .. it keeps them advised as far in advance as you wish ..

● HERE is the story .. it gives you the highlights of the picture .. it may suggest exploitation angles to you:

Count Dracula is a vampire,

● MAT shown above is actual size, two columns by nine and one half inches. It is number 558.

● THE mat in upper right is two columns by eight inches and is number 559. Mat directly at right is number 560 and is reproduced in actual size.

FEB. 14 1931

The LAST WORD

DRACULA
(Continued)

who has apparently died 500 years ago, but who retains the power, since he is buried in his own home soil, to rise from the grave each night and feast on the blood of the living.

Renfield, an English lawyer, pays a business visit to Dracula at the latter's castle in Transylvania, and they return to England together by boat, though Renfield has been driven insane by his experiences during his single night at the castle. Dracula, having arranged to take with him three great boxes of earth from his home, is smuggled lying inert in one of the boxes. Emerging at night, his terrible advances drive the entire crew to insane suicide.

The ship, apparently uncontrolled, lands at Whitby, England, where Renfield's law firm has leased for Dracula an ancient dwelling known as Carfax Abbey. Next door is an insane asylum, conducted by Dr. Seward, and it is here that Renfield is taken. Since Dracula can transform himself into a bat, a wolf or a cloud of mist, he easily gets ashore, and the boxes of earth are duly delivered at Carfax Abbey.

Dracula secretly visits Lucy, a relative of Dr. Seward's daughter, Mina, and finally brings about her death from loss of blood, which he has consumed by making two small holes in her neck with his fanglike teeth. Instead of going to a death of peace, however, Lucy has now herself become a vampire, rising from her tomb at night and feasting on the blood of children.

With the death of Lucy, Dracula transfers his terrible attentions to Mina, and begins the process of drawing out all her blood. Van Helsing, a scientist, discovers that Dracula is a vampire, and does his best to counteract the influence of the Count, who lies in a coma each day in one of his hidden boxes of earth. Bringing into play a small crucifix, and also springs of a plant called wolfbane, both deterrents to vampires, Van Helsing endeavors to save Mina. He is constantly baffled, however, through the fact that Mina is now completely in Dracula's power, and the fact that he is also assisted in his designs by the mad Renfield, who has become his abject slave.

Finally Dracula forces Mina to drink blood from an opened vein in her arm, and she is now imbued with the same appetite as the arch-fiend that she endeavors to draw the blood from the neck of her fiance, John Harker. Dracula kidnaps Mina and carries her to Carfax Abbey, where the two enter the burial crypt beneath the old house, preparatory to lying in a state of coma during the coming daylight hours in two boxes of earth which are hidden there.

Trailing the escaped Renfield, Van Helsing and Harker discover the fugitives, and Dracula, thinking that he has been betrayed by Renfield, strangles him to death. As the sun rises over the horizon, Dracula reclines in one of the boxes and sinks into insensibility, and the pursuers send him to permanent death by driving a stake through his heart.

Through the death of Dracula, Mina is released from further bondage, and she and Harker, their troubles at an end, go out of the crypt. Van Helsing remains to drive a stake through the heart of Renfield, and thus insure a peaceful and lasting death.

● HERE is a suggested trailer . . It is possible to glean from this copy for program, etc.

A Creature of the night . . Dead for more than five hundred Years . . Living from sunset to sunrise . .
(Fade)
Dracula . . the vampire . . demanding youth . . the blood of youth . . driving his victims insane . .
(Fade)
The greatest thrill story of the age . . for years the biggest success for the speaking stage.
(Fade)
The thriller . . of all thrill plays . . creepy . . mysterious . . bats fly over the heads of horses . . directing them to the castle of Dracula . .
(Fade)
Wolves howl . . and his victims understand their message . . a mist surrounds them . . it is Dracula himself . .
(Fade)
His eyes fascinate beautiful women . . and he condemns them to a living death . . instilling in them the thirst for blood . . the blood of those they love.
(Fade)
You'll thrill . . you'll shudder at DRACULA coming to this theatre—
(Fade)

● EXPLOITATION suggestion brings bats and vampires to mind . . however these undoubtedly would have to consist of cut-outs of parts of the paper. There is the part of the story where this strange creature must be buried in the ground from his home castle . . It would not be very good policy to use coffins in front of your house . . in other words . . don't go too far in gruesome exploitation . . keep it weird . . but don't suggest dead bodies.

● THESE mats literally bespeak the weirdness of "Dracula." The larger mat below also in actual size, will jump right out of the paper. It is number 561.

Cast Includes
BELA LUGOSI
HELEN CHANDLER
DAVID MANNERS
DWIGHT FRYE
EDWARD Van SLOAN

A UNIVERSAL PICTURE
DIRECTED BY
TOD BROWNING

DRACULA

. . the vampire . . the dead thing that lived only from sun to sun . . demon of the night . . companion of the evil one . . fascination lurked in his eyes . . Dracula will haunt you . . he will thrill . . and yet amuse . . of all the spine chilling eerie . . weird melodramas ever conceived . . Dracula is the master of them all!

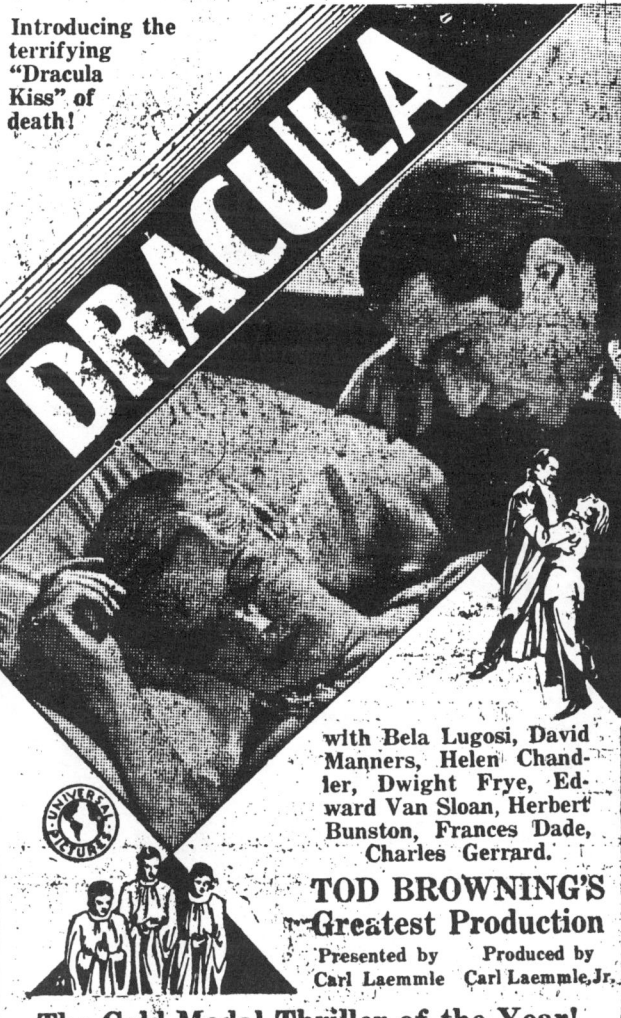

"DRACULA" A Universal Production MADE IN U.S.A.

(Above) The famous Roxy Theater where "Dracula" premiered 60 years ago

(Below) One of the ornate Roxy lobbies that greeted the audience on opening night

The New York Times
FRIDAY, FEBRUARY 13, 1931

Bram Stoker's Human Vampire

By MORDAUNT HALL.

DRACULA, with Bela Lugosi, Helen Chandler, David Manners, Dwight Frye, Edward Van Sloan, Herbert Bunston, Frances Dade, Charles Gerrard, Joan Standing, Moon Carroll and Josephine Velez, based on Bram Stoker's novel, directed by Tod Browning; overture, "Rhapsody in Blue"; Movietone news reel: "Hello, New York!" with Santry and Norton and others, including Leonide Massine and the Roxyettes. At the Roxy.

Count Dracula, Bram Stoker's human vampire, who has chilled the spines of book readers and playgoers, is now to be seen at the Roxy in a talking film directed by Tod Browning, who delights in such bloodcurdling stories. It is a production that evidently had the desired effect upon many in the audience yesterday afternoon, for there was a general outburst of applause when Dr. Van Helsing produced a little cross that caused the dreaded Dracula to fling his cloak over his head and make himself scarce.

But Dracula's evil work is not ended until Dr. Van Helsing hammers a stake through the Count's heart as he lies in his native earth in a box.

Mr. Browning is fortunate in having in the leading rôle in this eerie work, Bela Lugosi, who played the same part on the stage when it was presented here in October, 1927. What with Mr. Browning's imaginative direction and Mr. Lugosi's make-up and weird gestures, this picture succeeds to some extent in its grand guignol intentions.

As the scenes flash by there are all sorts of queer noises, such as the cries of wolves and the hooting of owls, not to say anything of the screams of Dracula's feminine victims, who are found with twin red marks on their white throats.

The Count is able to change himself into a vampire that flies in through the window and in this guise he is supposed to be able to talk to his victims, who are either driven insane or are so thoroughly terrified that they would sooner do his bidding that pay heed to those who have their welfare at heart. Martin, the keeper in the sanitarium in which an unfortunate individual named Renfield is under supervision, fires at the big bat with a shot gun, but, of course, misses.

To enhance the supernatural effect of this film there is a fog in many of the scenes. The first glimpses are of ordinary humans, but so soon as Renfield goes to the Transylvania castle of the Count, who lives on for centuries by his vampirish actions, there are bony hands protruding from boxes, rats and other animals fleeing, and corridors that are thick with cobwebs and here and there a hungry spider.

Most of the excitement takes place in Carfax Abbey and other places in England, the Count having traveled there to accomplish his blood-thirsty intentions. To start the grim work he causes all the ship's crew to go insane and commit suicide, but his subsequent activities are not as fruitful as he anticipates.

Helen Chandler gives an excellent performance as one of the girls who is attacked by the "undead" Count. David Manners contributes good work. Dwight Frye does fairly well as Renfield. Herbert Bunston is a most convincing personality. Charles Gerrard affords a few laughs as Martin.

This picture can at least boast of being the best of the many mystery films.

In 1931 the audience viewed DRACULA in full 4x5, silent aperture. The white lines represent the masking necessary to convert the frame to accommodate the sound-on-film format. The restored DRACULA on MCA Laser disc contains not only the missing 25% of the frame, but also presents the original clean soundtrack instead of the static hissing so noticeable in all previous prints (due to the condition of the sound discs at the time of conversion).

FINISHED NEGATIVE TITLES & INSERTS   PICTURE #106-1 BROWNING
                                              (SOUND)

PART TITLE   U N I V E R S A L   FEET   FRAMES
                  PART 1   8   8
                  "DRACULA"

FADE IN - PICTORIAL MAIN TITLE   File No.
              CARL LAEMMLE   Picture No. (675)
              PRESENTS
              "DRACULA"
              With
              BELA LUGOSI
        From the book by BRAM STOKER
           A TOD BROWNING PRODUCTION   103   3
        PRODUCED BY CARL LAEMMLE, JR.

    Copyright MCMXXXI by Universal Pictures Corp.
         Carl Laemmle, President
                                    ...DISSOLVES INTO

    Associate Producer   E. M. Asher
    Play Script   Garrett Fort
    Art Director   Charles D. Hall
    Recording Supervision   C. Roy Hunter
              MPPDA
    Cinematographer   Karl Freund
    Film Editor   Milton Carruth
    Supervising Film Editor - Maurice Pivar

                                    ...DISSOLVES INTO

        DIRECTED BY TOD BROWNING
                                    ...DISSOLVES INTO

            The Players
    Count Dracula   BELA LUGOSI
    Mina   HELEN CHANDLER
    John Harker   DAVID MANNERS
    Renfield   Dwight Frye
    Van Helsing   Edward Van Sloan
    J. Seward   Herbert Bunston
    Lucy   Frances Dade
    Maid   Joan Standing
    Martin   Charles Gerrard

                                    ... FADE OUT

The original titles from the copyrighted cutting continuity in 1930

Information in this volume has been compiled from the following sources:

The Academy of Motion Picture Arts and Sciences, Margaret Herrick Library
The Billy Rose Theater Collection, New York Public Library, Universal & Special Collections
U.S.C. Universal Collection
The Ackerman Archives
MagicImage Filmbooks Archives
An interview with Carl Laemmle Jr., 1973 with the author
MGM Central Files
Universal Central Files
The Estate of Lon Chaney Sr.
Los Angeles County Court documents
The personal scrapbooks of Bela Lugosi
An interview with Paul Kohner, 1972 with the author
Interviews with Lon Chaney Jr., 1971-73 with the author

(Other sources are noted in the text)

The editor gratefully acknowledges the assistance and contributions provided by the following individuals in the preparation of this series over the past 20 years:

Bud Abbott (Late)
Patty Andrews
Lew Ayres
William Bakewell
Ralph Bellamy
Stanley Bergerman
Robert Bloch
Richard Bojarski
Lincoln Bond
Ronald Borst
David Bradley
Kevin Brownlow
Ivan Butler
James Cagney (Late)
John Carradine (Late)
Ben & Anne Carre
Jeffrey Carrier
Ronald Chaney
Lon Chaney Jr. (Late)
Carlos Clarens (Late)
Mae Clarke
Franklin Coen
Ned Comstock
Mary Corliss
James Curtis
Nancy Cushing-Jones
Robert Cushman
Walter Daugherty
Gary Dorst
Todd Feiertag
Bramwell Fletcher (Late)
Robert Florey (Late)
A. Arnold Gillespie (Late)
Curtis Harrington
Patricia Hitchcock
Valerie Hobson
Bob Hope
David S. Horsley (Late)
Henry Hull (Late)
Paul Ivano (Late)
Steven Jochsberger (Late)
Zita Johann
Raymond F. Jones
Boris Karloff (Late)
John Kobal
Carl Laemmle Jr.
Carla Laemmle
Elsa Lanchester (Late)
John Landis
Janet Leigh
Celia Lovsky
Arthur Lubin
Rouben Mamoulian (Late)
Paul Mandell
Howard Mandlebaum
Gregory Mank
David Manners
Lester Matthews
John McLaughlin
Scott McQueen
Patsy Ruth Miller
Jeff Morrow
Gary Pasternak
Jim Pepper
Anthony Perkins
Mary Philbin
Armando Ponce
Vincent Price
Dr. Donald Reed
William Rosar
Margaret Ross
Hans J. Salter
Anne Schlosser
Martin Scorsese
Sherry Seeling
Wes Shank
Curt Siodmak
Robert Skotak
Joseph Stephano
James Stewart
Glenn Strange (Late)
Kenneth Strickfaden (Late)
George Turner
Edward Van Sloan (Late)
Elena Verdugo
Marc Wanamaker
Dan Woodruff
Wallace Worsley Jr.
and
FORREST J ACKERMAN, Founder of the Ackerman Archives. During the early 30s, FJA had exchanged 62 letters with Carl Laemmle Sr. As a result, Mr. Laemmle on his President's stationery, wrote a note to whom it may concern saying, in effect, "Give this young man anything he wants." As a consequence, the young Forry Ackerman acquired stills, posters, pressbooks, and the sound discs from FRANKENSTEIN, THE MUMMY, THE OLD DARK HOUSE and MURDERS IN THE RUE MORGUE. Since that date, the collection has grown to hundreds of thousands of items dealing with the classic Universal films, and items from the Science Fiction and Fantasy genre. We are indeed fortunate to have this wonderland of memorabilia as our foundation. Nearly 60 years later, almost to the word, Universal Studios has granted Philip J. Riley, one of Ackerman's former assistants, and MagicImage Filmbooks the same gift in recognition of their concern and realization of Universal's great heritage in the art of Motion Picture Production. Combined with the talents and contributions of those named above, we pledge to produce the highest quality historic works, so that future generations may benefit from firsthand knowledge of the magical city of Hollywood which created a new art form - and unknowingly protected the greatest gift of our childhood - the imagination.